BRUCE A. SHUMAN

AMERICAN LIBRARY ASSOCIATION
Chicago and London
1999

veral public and state libraries as
He has taught graduate library
a University, the University of
Oklahoma, Queens College (CUNY), Wayne State University, and the University of South Florida. He is the author of seven other books.

Cover by Tessing Design

Text design by Dianne M. Rooney

Composition by D&G Limited in Sabon and Frutiger using Quark XPress

Printed on 50-pound white offset, a pH-neutral stock, and bound in 10-point coated cover stock by McNaughton & Gunn

The paper used in this publication meets the minimum requirements of American National Standard for Information Sciences—Permanence of Paper for Printed Library Materials, ANSI Z39.48-1992. ∞

Library of Congress Cataloging-in-Publication Data

Shuman, Bruce A.

Library security and safety handbook : prevention, policies, and procedures / Bruce A. Shuman

p. cm.

Includes bibliographical references (p.) and index.

ISBN 0-8389-0714-8 (alk. paper)

1. Libraries—Security measures—United States. 2. Libraries—United States—Safety measures. I. Title.

Z679.6.S52 1999

025.8'2—dc21 99-18484

Printed in the United States of America.

03 02 01 00 99 5 4 3 2 1

Come sempre,
per miei bambini:
Bekki, Ben, e Josh . . .
ma soprattutto per Ann Cameron Shuman—
mia moglie, la mia consigliera,
e la mia migliore amica

Contents

Preface

I am a child of the movies—always have been and probably always will be. I grew up sitting—on at least a weekly basis—in large, darkened auditoriums, surrounded by dozens of other people, munching popcorn and occasionally commenting aloud on the action on the big screen. Given that biographical fact, I hope I may be forgiven for injecting one of my favorite movie scenes here to make a point about security.

The overarching topic of this book is security, and Clint Eastwood, to my mind, portrayed security in its best and purest form in his celebrated movie, *Dirty Harry* (1971). While the sequel may have contained the more memorable line, "Go ahead . . . make my day!" the bit of dialog that really got to me was in the original. What follows may not be the exact wording of that scene, but it's close enough.

In the film, Eastwood's title character, Harry Callahan, is a San Francisco police detective who has, without knowing it, blundered into an early-morning hold-up in progress at the coffee shop where he stops every day for his cup of carry-out coffee. His friend, the waitress, seems uncharacteristically nervous and distracted this morning. Harry, still sleepy, shrugs it off as he orders his coffee, pays for it, and departs. She's unable to tell him what's really going down. Two bad guys (whose guns were concealed while Harry was in the shop) now feel free to finish their robbery and promptly proceed to do so.

But the plucky waitress has cleverly figured out a way to alert Harry to the problem without speaking a word of warning. Intentionally, she has over-sugared Harry's cup of java tremendously, figuring that upon tasting it, he'd gag on the unaccustomed sweetness and return to complain. And sure enough, as she intends, once he's back out on the street, Harry takes a sip and spits it onto the pavement in disgust. Puzzled, he stands looking back in the direction of the the coffee shop, wondering how she could have so badly messed up his usual order. As he returns to discuss it with her, he happens to peer through the shop's window and discovers the real reason for his spoiled breakfast beverage: two agitated young men pointing guns at the terrified occupants of the diner and screaming commands that Harry cannot make out.

Now aware of the true situation, Harry goes around back and enters through the restaurant's kitchen. Drawing his police revolver and silently creeping up behind the felon who is holding a gun on the waitress, Harry identifies himself as a policeman and orders both men to drop their guns. A shoot-out ensues; there's a lot of gunfire, screaming, and shattered crockery. Harry dispatches the second hold-up man with a few well-placed bullets and turns his attention to the first criminal, who is still aiming his pistol at the terrified waitress. Gently sliding the barrel of his 44-Magnum into the man's sweaty ear, Harry conversationally reflects that he may well by now be out of bullets because he hasn't been counting, and asks the nervous man in a deceptively conversational way what's going to happen now. Nudging the pistol barrel a little deeper into the other man's ear, Harry reasons out their mutual situation, thus:

> Yeah, what with all the excitement and everything, I may have lost count and fired the last round in my revolver. And if I'm out of bullets, you might be able to shoot me now and get away clean. On the other hand, maybe I do have a round left in the chamber, who knows? . . .

Harry then favors the bad guy with his famous Eastwood clenched-teeth grin. "So I guess the question you have to ask yourself now," he says, reasonably, "is whether you're feelin' lucky, today." There follows a delicious pause at this point, while you can see the criminal's eyes reflect his frenzied thought processes as he weighs his chances and calculates his odds. Harry's slightly demented smile, on the other hand, has turned into the legendary cold stare of fury that made actor Eastwood a legend from the first time audiences saw it in his first spaghetti western. Giving the bad guy no more time to think about it, Harry snarls, "Well, are ya, punk?"

At this question, the perspiring perpetrator clearly reaches a wise decision, sheepishly (and doubtless gratefully) dropping his gun and surrendering, clearly preferring to live on—even in prison—than to have his head splattered all over the coffee shop. Harry disarms the man and leads him away to the delight and relief of all concerned, and justice and public safety prevail again. Whether or not Harry was, in fact, out of rounds and bluffing is beside the point. He was very persuasive and that was convincing enough.

Now consider the events just described from the standpoint of security for the lives and property of ordinary citizens in public places. Harry just happened to be in the right place at the right time (thanks to a heads-up waitress) and successfully bluffed his way to victory. Who knows what might have happened had he not? Sadly, there aren't enough Dirty Harrys walking around risking their lives, protecting us and our possessions (which may be just as well, given the propensity of some people for vigilante behavior). Yet there's a demonstrable and generally increasing need for security in public places in communities of all sizes, and libraries, as public places, have to figure out what they can do to maintain that security—without Dirty Harry around.

The professional journal *Library and Archival Security* (which I edited from 1992 to 1997) is devoted to the problems and solutions of libraries and other institutions of knowledge and preservation beset by criminals, opportunists, the socially maladjusted, and others bent on depriving them of their assets and acquisitions, and, occasionally, their lives. The point of this tale—and the entire book that follows—is to demonstrate that the need for libraries, as public buildings, to upgrade their security postures is now more critical than ever.

Why now more than ever? Security seems especially necessary in these perilous times when almost every day's news brings us stories of theft, arson, random violence, sexual assault, and murder. Libraries, as repositories (and librarians as custodians) of books, journals, computers, and other things of considerable value, need practical and sound advice on building security, both for the protection of property in their care and for the safety of all who venture into their buildings. And while all situations involving risk in libraries cannot be addressed, a mixture of empirically based advice and creative solutions may go a long way toward reducing the security problems encountered by libraries of all types every day.

To the goal of establishing or beefing up such public places' security postures, I earnestly dedicate this book. And even if you, personally, don't think that you necessarily have "the right stuff" to become a Dirty Harry—the public hero, riding in to the rescue to save the day—there are suggestions and guidelines in this book that are intended to make you a bit more willing and able to become—if and when necessary—like the waitress who had the presence of mind to summon help in time of crisis to avert disaster or loss.

CHAPTER 1

Overview: Library Security and Safety

A recent survey by the Urban Libraries Council says that public library directors feel that theft and mutilation of library materials are not only a greater concern now than in the past, but that the problem will get worse during the next five years.

—*American Libraries* (August 1996)

The objectives of this chapter are to:

- review the history of security in libraries
- introduce the various components and features of library security
- discuss common types of library crime and explain the motivations and methods of library criminals
- discuss responses and deterrence measures to library crime

Close your eyes for a minute. Now think of a library—any library. What comes to mind? Naturally, different people will imagine different things, but in general, you probably think the library is a quiet place—a safe haven from the dangers and troubles of the world outside where you can spend quiet hours in study and contemplation. When the average citizen considers using a library, what should never come to mind are any of the following: homicide, rape, sexual assault, aggravated assault, simple assault (against staff members or other patrons), robbery, larceny, burglary, grand theft, personal property theft, harassment of staff, obscene phone calls, nuisance calls, indecent exposure, pickpockets, elevator crime, or crimes committed by staff members. Understandably, as with all public places, the library has its risks. Demonstrably, library materials are constantly at risk, as are those who visit or work in library buildings. The sooner we admit this fact, the sooner we can begin to consider ways to minimize and reduce that risk.

The Library and Security

This book surveys and discusses problems associated with library security and safety. It attempts to provide suggested remedies for these problems. However, the overarching issue is really that of security, of which personal safety is but one very important aspect. The central question is how we keep our buildings, shelves, and stacks open and free without losing many items we have available or putting individuals at unacceptable risk from the malicious, avaricious, or senseless acts of others. Since such acts occur daily, we must ask why. Perhaps this problem has its roots in human nature.

The Nature of Human Nature

Americans expect and prize the right and ability to roam the stacks of libraries without supervision, surveillance, or interdiction. Free access to collections and public rooms is a hallmark of American public libraries, but such access involves risks to collections, and, even worse, to the persons who work in or come to the library to use them. Why does crime occur in such sedate and peaceful places as libraries? The answer may have its roots in human nature—the essential untrustworthiness of the breed. Perhaps, to one degree or another, we are all crooks. Like you, probably, I consider myself a decent, honorable, ethical, and truthful human being. And yet every one of us has the potential to be or become a petty crook. Upon examination, one will find that there is a recognizable vein of larceny in every human heart. Take a moment and examine your life and habits. If you are honest, you will probably confess that you have, at one time or another, committed one or more of these minor offenses:

- Sneaked into more than one theater at the local cinema without paying for a second show.
- Grabbed a handful of chocolate-covered peanuts from the bulk foods store bin and devoured all the evidence before reaching the checkout counter.
- Made personal long-distance calls or sent personal Internet messages to friends or family from work.
- Revisited the buffet table despite the posted one-visit rule or hidden food for later consumption at home.
- Appropriated pens, pencils, coffee, or sundry paper products from your office supply closet at work.
- Sneaked into the expensive seating section at the ball game despite the fact that you had a general admission ticket.
- Said nothing when the waitress in a restaurant inaccurately computed your bill, undercharging you by a few dollars.

One may ask why have a discussion of human foibles in a book concerned with security and safety in libraries? There are thousands of crimes committed in the nation's libraries every day—crimes that individually may not disrupt our social fabric or spell the end of civilization as we know it, but which collectively lead to major economic loss for the nation's libraries and eventually for taxpayers.

This discussion of human foibles brings up another regrettable aspect of human nature: an innate sense—in some individuals, at least—of anarchy. When there are rules to follow, most will obey, but some will seek and find ways to get around them simply because they hate rules. Therein lies the key to most small crimes. Most of us are honest most of the time. Still, there's a devilish side to almost everyone who likes to see what can be gotten away with.

Historical Library Security

There's an old saying that there is nothing new under the sun. Certainly, library crime and the need for library security are nothing new or recent; rather, reports of such actions date back to the beginning of library history. There is nothing new about security challenges in libraries at all, and while it may seem that such crime is on the rise based on your reading of contemporary library literature, it's probably just being reported more frequently. Libraries, for example, have always been subject to the whim of rulers; and when rulers have quarreled, wars have become the enemies of library collections. Conquerors knew that in order to truly subjugate a people, they must first destroy their literature.

> When the Persians went into Egypt and withdrew papyri from the library of Rameses II, without stopping for any formalities at the charging desk, they began a practice that has remained to torment libraries ever since. Book theft is thus as old as libraries themselves. It might almost be listed as an original and basic sin of humankind.
>
> —Ralph Munn, "The Problems of Theft and Mutilation," *Library Journal,* August 1935

Even in peacetime, library security has always been a problem, although in the past it was somewhat less problematic than it is now. In the Middle Ages, security, inventory, and bibliographic control weren't nearly as difficult as they are today, due to several factors:

- Highly motivated, zealous staff.
- Fewer materials to watch over, making those present easier to supervise.
- Smaller rooms, usually with excellent sight lines.
- Fewer people able to read. Illiterates are unlikely to value or even make use of most library materials. The ordinary citizens of European countries hundreds of years ago were, in fact, rarely caught stealing books.
- Fewer visitors to libraries, and those few were often known to the librarians by name.
- Impermissible for books and other library materials to leave the premises or go home with patrons.
- Primitive but effective security measures acted as deterrents to theft. For example, books were chained to their shelves; there were dire curses.
- Severe forms of intimidation and control (e.g., threats of beatings, excommunication, going to hell, loss of limbs, or suspension of privileges) provided incentives for potential delinquent borrowers to be honest.

Theft from libraries, however, is not merely a modern problem. It's been with us for centuries. In the Middle Ages, priests and monks, not satisfied with their attempts to keep quick-fingered thieves from stealing by chaining books, imposed even more horrible curses of doom on anyone who stole a book. Here is a particularly unpleasant warning from sixteenth-century France:

> *Qui ce livre emblera*
> *A gibet de Paris pendu sera*
> *Et, si n'est pas pendu, il noiera*
> *Et, si ne noie, il ardera*
> *Et si n'art, pire fin fera*
> (Rough translation: He who steals this book will be hanged on the gallows in Paris; and if not hanged, he'll be drowned; and if not drowned, he'll burn; if he's not burned, his end will be even worse.)

Perhaps the most effective means ever devised of keeping patrons honest was a simple but eloquent old-fashioned curse, invoking divine (or satanic) wrath, which often acted as an effective deterrent to those inclined to larcenous behavior:

> For him that stealeth, or borroweth and returneth not this book from its owner, let it change into a serpent in his hand and rend him. Let him be struck with palsy, and all his members blasted. Let him languish in pain crying aloud for mercy, and let there be no surcease to his agony till he sing in dissolution. Let bookworms gnaw his entrails in token of the Worm that dieth not, and when he at last goeth to his final punishment, let the flames of Hell consume him forever.
>
> —from the front of a medieval English library book

How eager would *you* be to test the love or patience of whichever supreme being you pray to if you read that warning message on the inside front cover of the book you had checked out? I don't know about you, but upon finding that message inscribed in a book I had borrowed, even I—who consider myself an enlightened, skeptical, nineties sort of guy—would do all I could to make sure that it was returned promptly and in good condition.

Throughout the history of civilization, people have attempted to protect their ownership of books in various ways. Some have tried blunt threats or intimidation, such as this inscription found penned into a front cover in eighteenth-century England:

> This book is one thing
> My fist is another.
> Steal not the one thing
> For fear of the other.

One respected European author, who happened to be the son of a bookseller, threw up his hands at the impossibility of trying to keep his book collection intact, and became a sort of miser:

> Never lend out books, because no one ever returns them. The only books I have in my library are books that other folk have lent me.
>
> —Anatole France (from *Bartlett's Familiar Quotations*)

Stealing library books and other materials has always cut across social lines. From available evidence, library book thieves throughout recorded history have included high-ranking officials and church elders as well as librarians themselves. More recently, some notorious book thieves ("bibliokleptomaniacs"; see chapter 2) have fed off libraries to the tune of thousands of stolen books each. Much of the literature of security in libraries deals with suggested and recommended countermeasures used to catch these systematic and resourceful felons while preventing other would-be book thieves from following in their footsteps. See figure 1.1.

- The library's central location and hours of operation attract a wide variety of visitors, as intended.
- Usually anyone may enter, and it is normally not necessary for visitors to answer questions concerning their intentions, or even to speak to anyone else.
- There is no admission fee, and most services are provided without cost.
- As a public building full of people, the library may be a good place to look for a victim to those inclined to various forms of criminal activity.

FIGURE 1.1
Factors Contributing to Library Theft, Violence, and Other Crime

- There are no metal detectors to pass through or sniffing dogs to pass upon entering.
- Many library buildings are large structures with secluded areas, private study carrels, and quiet corners.
- Open stack policies make it possible for people to go more or less where they wish without challenge.
- Libraries are open for long hours, including after dark, evening hours.
- Light levels vary in different areas.
- As public buildings, libraries feature public rest rooms.
- There aren't always staff members or other library personnel working on every floor or in more isolated areas.
- Low budgets or the desire to make the library an open, inviting place result in few if any security guards or other surveillance personnel.
- Surveillance, even where present, is uneven.
- Overworked staff members have so much to deal with in performing their primary duties that they have little time for monitoring public behavior.

The Ongoing Problem of Library Security

Why does crime—both crime against people and crime against property—continue to fester in libraries across the country? There would seem to be a number of reasons, which singly or in combination may influence the rate of crime:

- Direct access to the stacks. "Three hundred thousand of the Library of Congress's twenty million books cannot be accounted for," said Librarian of Congress James Billington in 1992, yet his decision to close the stacks was widely criticized. But look at it from his side: Securing materials makes the library a safe place for patrons. If your patrons don't feel comfortable using your facility and they are afraid to come, to linger, to send their children, then isn't the community that you serve being denied access to the library, and thus its materials?
- Placement of high-risk materials such as rare and valuable books either in vulnerable places or in low-visibility areas.

- Allowing too many staff members access to rare and valuable materials.
- Having too many keys to the building or to locked cases in circulation among staff.
- Apathy or indifference about library crime.

A few words about the last point: Library crime is often not taken seriously by the general public, perhaps because it is seen as unimportant or perhaps because it tends to be seen as victimless crime. The public is too tolerant of misbehavior and property damage in the public sector. People think it's naughty but not morally wrong, and frequently steal books not out of criminal mentality, but because it costs too much to copy, the photocopier was not working, they didn't have change, or the line was too long. In short, it seems so much easier just to take what you need. An interesting idea—with its own cost, of course—would be free photocopying (up to a specified number), which could deter the casual or lazy thief, but also might create too much cost for the library.

Librarians have had to be concerned with theft since libraries first came into existence, thousands of years ago. The medieval chains dangling from handwritten codices and incunabula at the Bodleian Library of Oxford University, England, and elsewhere, while keeping books on their shelves, attest silently to this simple truth. Monastic and civil librarians have always attempted to foil crooks. Only today's methods differ from those of centuries ago; their aim has not changed at all. Wherever there have been collections of important books or other materials—things worth holding onto—there have also been book thieves and mutilators of library materials.

Economic Aspects of Library Security

How much does library security (or more accurately, the lack of library security) cost America's libraries each year? Statistics are hard to come by, and reliable statistics seem an impossibility. One thorny aspect of the economics of library security is computing—or even estimating—the price of vandalism and theft. The main problem is that until a book is requested or needed, there is no indication that it is missing. For example, at a large midwestern university, it was recently discovered that almost the entire circulating collection of books on Hmong culture was missing. Although the books were reordered, no one knew exactly how long they had been missing. Circulation statistics contain their checkout dates as well as a wealth of other information. Unfortunately, such item record data is irrelevant when the computer shows that the entire section (or even a particular book) is available but the corresponding shelf space is empty. Interestingly, in several research studies of college students, about half (after being reassured of the anonymity of their responses) admitted having torn out pages from library books or magazines at one time or another, while a somewhat smaller yet significant percentage confessed that they had stolen something. A few even admitted that they had done both. If this set of findings is representative of library users in general (and it is possible that it isn't; survey results are often skewed), then approximately one out of every eight users is a potential thief or vandal!

How much do libraries spend on security? In 1994, the St. Louis Public Library claimed that it spent nearly $280,000 to hire five full-time security guards and twenty-five or thirty part-time, off-duty police officers to help protect libraries. In that year, seventy-five persons were told to leave the building. Additionally, there were four incidents of indecent exposure, five calls to the police, and several incidents of weapons on library premises.

Also to be factored in are such cost considerations as those shown in figure 1.2, many of them renewable annually.

Electronic "bugs" (security tags) at $.25 each × 100,000 new items annually	= $25,000
Exit security system: estimated cost = $20,000 per year plus $3,000 per year for maintenance	= $23,000
Intrusion, perimeter, and sonic alarms, estimated to cost $20,000 per year, plus $2,000 maintenance	= $22,000
The additional cost of monitoring of silent alarms and maintenance	= $ 8,000
Lockdown devices for equipment (one-time charge)	= $ 5,000
Television surveillance cameras, closed circuit	= $ 1,000
Encryption coding in computers and networks	= $20,000
Staff training, guard training, annually	= $ 5,000

FIGURE 1.2
Additional Annual Security Costs

Summing up, it would take at least $100,000 annually (clearly a significant percentage of most libraries' total annual budget) just to have some minimal measure of adequate security and security-related measures in a typical large library building. Such daunting numbers must account for the fact that many libraries have no security staff whatsoever and only minimal theft-detection devices in place. Inflation—though modest in recent years—also eats away at the budget, but we'll leave that factor out of our calculations due to the uncertainty of the rate from year to year. Still, and just for the exercise, if we multiply our mean figure of $100,000 by the number of public libraries in the United States (according to the *Statistical Abstract of the United States, 1994,* there were 8,946), the total annual cost of public library security would become an impressive figure, indeed: very close to a billion dollars a year. And keep in mind, this figure is just for public libraries and is exclusive of the salaries and benefits paid to security guards. Adding the cost of academic and school library security, and corresponding figures for those special libraries in the public sector, the cost becomes far greater.

This rough aggregate estimate is offered as further proof that library security is a significant expense. It also may increase your understanding of why security is lacking in many libraries. It's just too expensive—prohibitively expensive for some—so they do without. One library administrator in a large city claims that her library doesn't need a security force because everyone on staff performs security as a part of his or her job description. However, the truth is that libraries probably think it's a lot less expensive to let people take what they like than to make much of an effort to prevent or stop them.

Even the staggering financial projections above do nothing to refute the notion that libraries, as public places, present risks to those who enter them, and that library users have a right—and even an expectation—that they may use such buildings in safety and security.

Users' Expectations

Users expect libraries to be safe places to study, read, browse, acquire information, or attend meetings, workshops, and classes—places out of harm's way, neutral zones, and safe havens for children. Most people, thankfully, do not equate libraries with muggers, thieves, perverts, and other dangerous people. Yet libraries are open to the public, and by their very publicness, often serve as magnets for such predators as well as for legitimate patrons. In the language of librarianship, we refer to those who break the rules as "problem patrons," a blanket term that covers everyone from mild nuisances to extremely violent people (see chapter 3). Library literature provides examples of the endless variety of problem library patrons, including rule breakers of various types, sociopaths, disgruntled spouses, the depressed, the mentally disturbed, the suddenly irate, the paranoid, the eccentric, and even, sometimes, the certifiably insane.

Those who work in library buildings expect library patrons to behave in certain ways consistent with their own notions and expectations of proper behavior. But are patron expectations of the library and the librarians too old-fashioned for today's reality? Today, people expect much more in the way of service and services from libraries than before, and they want it faster or immediately. This attitude can make them aggressive, demanding, and problematical. Additionally, our rules or procedures may cause problems. Patrons who are used to automatic teller machines (ATMs), fast-food restaurants, and drive-throughs may not like waiting patiently in a line to check out, renew, or return materials or ask reference questions. They may be impatient or argumentative once they reach the clerk who is "taking so long" to process materials. They may, on the other hand, be having a particularly bad day, and therefore be unable to prevent their bad mood from leaking into their dealings with other people.

Perhaps part of the problem of irate patrons is the "image" problem of our profession. To impatient people, libraries (and those who work in them) are often perceived as being antiquated and slow moving. Even though we now use computers, we are perceived, even in today's media, as having to do things a certain way, deeply committed to procedures and routines to be followed. Regardless of objective reality, many members of the public still think that the library is a musty, dusty place, and those who work there are musty, dusty, boring people well suited to those tasks. In most cases, however, expectations of libraries are at odds with our services and capabilities.

People want to feel safe and secure wherever they are, whatever they are doing. Most adult patrons want relative quiet and good, efficient service, with their personal safety assumed. If the public feels that the library cannot provide these things together with a safe environment, they will, if they can, go elsewhere to satisfy their information and recreational goals. They will either buy books and information from those who sell such things, or they will go to libraries that can provide better service and freedom from trouble.

Security Preparedness

Given the range of potential threats to building security and public safety, how can the library ready itself to counteract them? The answer is simple: by being prepared. Preparedness involves careful planning and a continual state of vigilance in libraries because they are public buildings. The definition of public places themselves is not always easy to pin down. Alan Lincoln spends over a page and a half in *Crime in the Library: A Study of Patterns, Impact and Security* (New York: Bowker, 1984) trying to provide a workable legal definition of a public place, and discovers that "the term public place is not as simple to define as it appears." He uses two criteria: (1) ownership of the location and (2) whether access by the public is encouraged or discouraged. *Ballentine's Law Dictionary* defines a public library as being "a general library for the use of inhabitants of a city, village, or political subdivision." It defines a public institution as "one which is created and exists by law or public authority, such as an asylum, charity, college, university, hospital, schoolhouse, etc."

Lincoln says that the term "library" may be used to refer to a locale either privately or publicly owned. On the public side, we find one group of settings such as municipal parks, museums, and libraries, and a second group consisting of police departments, fire stations, city hospitals, and so on. Although all these places may share the trait of public ownership, they differ in the way they treat the public. People visiting the second group of facilities are normally not free to enter as they choose and go where they like.

Libraries, mass transit facilities, parks, and museums depend on—and even encourage—access by the public. Their very existence usually is dependent upon public use and support. Police departments, fire stations, and government agencies, by contrast, are publicly owned, but the public is generally not particularly welcome unless they have business within. Actually, such institutions function more efficiently when access to the public is limited. So for libraries of all types that allow public access, the question becomes how we maintain open access without being forced to move toward limited access to protect the people and property within. Specifically, questions such as "How can we control public behavior?" and "How can we determine what is acceptable use of public libraries?" are serious issues for library administrators and their staff members who actually deal with the public on a daily, one-to-one basis.

As the only public buildings normally open evenings and weekends, libraries attract the homeless and other people who have no place else to go. And while staff are empowered to evict (or seek the eviction of) persons not following established rules and laws, staff members also have to deal with patrons leaving the library after closing time, fearing that these people may be waiting for them outside.

In a perfect world there would be no need for library security policies, police, or security guards in the library. In our imperfect world, unfortunately, security problems exist in profusion for a variety of reasons. Of course, one way to cut down severely on security threats in libraries would be for libraries to be places where only those with high-level clearance or permission are permitted access. But erecting barriers to free access would be contrary to most of the reasons that libraries exist in a free society, and the more a library resembles a fortress or a prison, the less free people will feel, once inside.

For libraries that do allow public access—or even limited access—the central question becomes how to maintain open access without being forced to move toward undesirable or undue restrictions on who may enter or what they may do, once inside. More specifically, how we determine what is acceptable use of libraries and how we control the public behavior of persons inside our buildings are serious issues for library administrators and staff members.

What Constitutes Crime in Libraries?

Crimes and misdemeanors of various sorts occur in library buildings all the time. While most library crime is of the small-time chump-change variety, it is crime, nevertheless, and indirectly costs taxpayers money. And people are constantly committing crimes in libraries: stealing books, mutilating periodicals, misusing computers, abusing staff verbally, assaulting one another, or otherwise preying upon or harassing other people.

Before we can truly discuss crime and other unacceptable behaviors in libraries, however, we must first take a stab at trying to define—or at least describe—what is acceptable (and thus legal) use of libraries. And though libraries may seem "safer" places than other public buildings in your town, those who work in them must constantly consider several security-related issues on an ongoing basis. The courthouse building in my hometown, for example, now has a metal detector you must pass through in order to enter, as does the Empire State Building's observatory attraction since a shooting incident. However, curiously, just about anybody may enter the public library in most cities with anything they like in their hands, such as briefcases, or notebooks secreted on their persons.

This raises a set of security considerations that every library must address, or at least consider seriously if it hopes to safeguard its collections. Among these:

- Building security (planning, alternatives, implementation)
- Equipment security (protecting computers, terminals, and other property)
- Materials security (trying to hold onto books and other materials as community property)
- Personal safety (freedom from dangers of various kinds)
- Personal comfort (freedom from nuisances and avoidable distractions)
- Financial liability (cost factors of security, safety)
- Legal issues (specifically what local, state, or federal law provides or bans)
- Problem patrons (rights in conflict)
- Ethical issues (attitudes: right vs. wrong)
- Electronic security (protecting and safeguarding information, records, and personal privacy from unwarranted electronic intrusion)

Common Library Crimes and Misdemeanors

The following list includes only a handful of the countless examples of the types of petty crime in libraries that take place every day. Note that the perpetrators vary from juveniles to respected senior members of the university community and cut across all social strata. If you look hard, you may even find yourself on the list. What the items on this list of crimes have in common is that they are generally nonthreatening; more about property than people. (Crimes against people are covered in chapter 3.) Ask yourself, as you read them, how you would attempt to handle each problem, remembering that you have a wide range of options ranging from ignoring the problem behavior to calling the cops immediately:

An elderly woman is reading a book a little bit at a time every afternoon in the public library but lives outside the library's jurisdiction and does not wish to (or cannot) pay for borrowing privileges. Upon leaving the building at 5 P.M. each day, she hides the book in a place where only she will find it.

A compulsive kleptomaniac, who has been made uncomfortably aware that stealing merchandise from department stores is too risky and that repeat infractions could lead to jail time, indulges himself by stealing library books because security is normally quite lax, penalties for getting caught are not severe, and besides, everyone knows that libraries never press charges.

A lifelong book lover, appalled at finding out that several of the library's rarest and most treasured books have been reported missing, stolen, or mutilated, decides that it is up to him to rescue them. Whenever the opportunity arises, he appropriates them because no one else can be trusted to treasure and protect them as well as he can.

A patron borrows a video and, upon receipt of an overdue notice, discovers that he seems to have misplaced it. He takes the notice to the library and argues vociferously that he did, indeed, return the video on time, that the library is mistaken to think otherwise, and that he will sue unless the library stops harassing him.

A clever and observant teenager figures out how the library's tattletape book security system works and proceeds to steal books from the library on a regular basis, just because he can.

A distinguished and senior university professor who has been given a study carrel in the university library building takes a number of books and journal volumes—one or two at a time—to his carrel and keeps them there indefinitely for his consultation and convenience. The library, unable to account for the whereabouts of the missing items, eventually deletes their records from the shelflist database, depriving the entire university community (except one faculty member) of their use.

A woman figures out a way to open one of the library's sealed windows and, when unobserved, throws several books out the window and into the dirt under the bushes outside. Upon leaving the building, she goes around to the side of the building, collects her items, and departs.

A man runs up a considerable fine at the public library for an overdue book and refuses to pay his bill, preferring to accept loss of borrowing privileges than to settle his account. Advised that he must pay a fine for the overdue materials, he refuses, saying he'll just wait for the next amnesty day.

An impatient businessman, finding that all the library's photocopiers are either in use or out of service and faced with the unpleasantness of copying extensive information from a page of a large commercial directory, looks left, then right, and tears out the page, folds it, puts it in his pocket, and walks away.

An undergraduate student, learning that a professor grades on the curve, appropriates library materials on the class reading list for the purpose of depriving his classmates of their use by slipping them into his book bag and carrying them past the inattentive security staff. At the end of the term, he unobtrusively drops the "borrowed" materials into the library's after-hours book drop, and salves his conscience by reasoning that he didn't really steal them.

A man spends a month going around to libraries in his metropolitan community and stealing one volume of an encyclopedia from each one until he owns a complete set.

A malicious patron deliberately infects each of the library's public access computers by unobtrusively introducing a computer virus which wipes out each terminal's memory.

A group of teenagers, in hopes of getting money for drugs, breaks into the library after hours by jimmying a window. Once inside, after finding and taking a few dollars in petty cash from the circulation desk drawers, they vandalize the building in their anger over finding so little cash.

A disgruntled former library staff computer programmer, who feels that she was unjustly fired, hacks into the library's database. She inserts obscene words into public records and then enters the employee staff records program and maliciously alters the personnel file of her former superior.

A library staff member working in technical services covets a new library acquisition and takes it home that night. The next day, after destroying the purchase record and claiming the title as paid for but not received from the wholesaler in its scheduled shipment, she has committed the perfect crime.

Some of the situations listed above could conceivably be prosecuted as crimes, particularly the break-in and the intentional introduction of a computer virus. While a few others are misdemeanors as petty theft, the rest of these acts are most likely to be viewed as day-to-day nuisances and just a part of doing business with the public. The last two examples are inside jobs, which are the hardest types of infractions to detect and deal with.

Sadly, people both inside and outside of libraries are stealing or mutilating books and other library materials in significant numbers every day. Precisely how many of our books and other materials disappear is difficult to assess because librarians don't often have a convenient way of noticing such shrinkage, short of a troublesome and time-consuming full-scale inventory, which no one enjoys performing. Perhaps more to the point, librarians don't really like to talk about this vexing and embarrassing problem, which may be one of the reasons why there are no reliable statistics.

Note that in talking about the vast majority of library thieves, we're not referring to hardened criminals, sociopaths, or bibliokleptomaniacal felons. No, we're talking about those average folks like you and me who are responsible for the sort of minor wrongdoing that will almost never show up on a police report, but that costs the nation's libraries and taxpayers untold millions of dollars in losses every year. These small-time criminals are everywhere, working their mischief on all types of libraries. Often the motive isn't larceny but just plain laziness—it is, after all, easier (and certainly cheaper) to tear out the page one wants than it is to copy it, whether the person copies it laboriously by hand or electromechanically by using a coin-operated copy machine. Motive notwithstanding, the result is the same. When a page is removed from a work to satisfy one patron's needs, all other users are deprived of the information on that page.

Is taking things from (or mutilating things in) libraries a crime? And, if so, how does it differ from robbing a bank or driving off in someone else's car? On the face of it, you'd probably say that theft is theft, whatever the stolen commodity or its free-market value, but it's not really all that simple. What is the legal definition of crime? In simple words it is doing anything against the law, or anything that is officially forbidden, or taking that which does not belong to you. What you do may be officially classed as a misdemeanor or a felony, depending on the local jurisdiction, but it is still a form of crime, by definition. Thus, stealing or destroying library materials is, by all measures, not just morally and ethically wrong, but against the law and therefore a crime.

How can a library fulfill its mission and maximize access to its collections and services while protecting staff and patrons from danger? The answer seems to be a trade-off: As free access rises, personal security and safety drops. Conversely, whenever personal security is maximized, there is a corresponding diminution of personal liberty. Some people resent this intrusion into their freedom. No one enjoys being searched, interrogated, or denied admission, especially to a tax-supported free library, but some restriction on the use of libraries is inevitable.

Two Kinds of Library Crime

Broadly speaking, there are two kinds of library crime: crime against property and crime against people. Regardless of motive, most library crimes are opportunistic in nature and occur when the risk of getting caught is low and the likelihood for success is high. In any case, the typical punishment for getting caught is a nominal fine—the whole situation is usually considered by administration and staff as well as the discovered perpetrator as more embarrassing than serious. Libraries become easy targets for opportunistic crime because of their policies, their architecture, the lack of vigilance on the part of their employees, and a pervasive view on the part of perpetrators that there is little or no danger of being caught—and even if they are, their punishment will be minimal.

The most common criminal activity occurring in libraries is theft or damage to the collections, which are forms of vandalism usually classed as misdemeanors rather than crimes. Estimates vary, and statistics are notoriously unreliable, but a typical library loses between 5 and 10 percent of its collection annually (and some much higher) to theft and mutilation, despite all efforts to deter and prevent such crimes. Other crimes of opportunity, including the theft of personal property (e.g., wallets, purses, briefcases) or library equipment, occur with depressing frequency.

Not as common, but still significant, are acts of sexual activity or perversion, especially voyeurism and exhibitionism. Even more frightening is that the fact that, in the past few years, verbal and physical abuse of library staff members has been increasing, possibly on the rise because of new addictive drugs that cause their users to become more aggressive while under their influence. Although most incidents of this nature do not entail actual assault or violence, they are, nevertheless, distressing and disturbing. They are especially problematic since most library staff receive little or no training in how to cope with such abuse, and too many of them work alone or in secluded areas of the building.

The overall effect of the security countermeasures described in succeeding chapters of this book is intended to be an across-the-board bolstering of the library's security posture, which will result in enhanced physical and psychological security for all. But the risk of overconfidence is always with us. For one thing, when anyone may walk into a library, there is always the risk of assault. There is always the risk of inside jobs—crimes committed by persons who have been entrusted with the keys or combinations to restricted areas or collections. In general, Robert Frost had it right when he said that good fences make good neighbors. But even having the best locks money can buy is not always a guarantee of being able to stop theft or violence from occurring, despite the best efforts of all staff members to deter or defeat the perpetrators. The good news is that no security problem is so intractable that it cannot be combated. The bad news is that new security problems crop up all the time. It must also be borne in mind that money is a serious constraint to good security—effective security is always costly, no argument there. But in many respects, what it really takes to improve library security is some deep thinking about the problem . . . and the will to defend its possessions, and, where necessary, to fight.

Deterrence Measures

Now that the problem has been defined, or at least described in some detail, we turn to comprehensive and logical methodologies for effectively dealing with it. The two-pronged object of all efforts toward library security is that of deterring crime and keeping loss of library property to minimal levels. Demonstrably, the best way to deal with crime in a library is to prevent it from happening at all. As Winn Schwartau in *Information Warfare* (New York: Thunder's Mouth Pr., 1996) points out eloquently, "The best defense against the damage caused by any type of bombs is to prevent their delivery in the first place." Another way of putting the same thought is the old saying that an ounce of prevention is worth a pound of cure. Keeping any library collection totally intact—despite your most strenuous attempts to do so—may well be an impossible task. But to throw up your hands and concede defeat risks much more than a few books: It is gambling with both the library's reason for being and our collective cultural heritage. To repeat, in slightly altered form, the central question of this book: Is it possible to be an open, full-service institution and still maintain building and personal security at acceptable levels? Yes, but what is needed is careful planning and commonsense advice so that we can meet the whole spectrum of challenges to library security with effective solutions, or—better yet—with prevention. Since we are unlikely to change the behavior of those who threaten our security, let's at least find and use better means of deterrence, detection, interdiction, apprehension, prosecution, and possibly rehabilitation of those who look upon libraries as prime targets for crime.

How can libraries deal with crime and make their institutions safe for their patrons, staff, and collections? One immediate way is to control access to and egress from the building. Years ago, larger library buildings offered several entrances and exits for the convenience of the public. Now the more safety-conscious libraries have a single public entrance/exit, and the ones who can afford it post uniformed security guards just inside the doors not only to keep an eye on people entering the building but to make them aware that they are being watched. But the mere presence of guards at the exits isn't sufficient to deter crime. Patrolling the library and checking out all public areas is equally important, especially during the evening hours.

Good security, however, as previously stated, is prohibitively expensive, given typical library budgets. The result is that a number of municipal libraries, and most smaller libraries, cannot afford the simple requirement of at least one security staffer in the building during all hours that the library is open. These libraries, forced to make a choice between good, visible security and more money to spend on materials and public services, usually opt for the latter.

The presence of uniformed municipal or campus police, just to remind people that someone trained and equipped to handle problems is on duty for their protection, might be a desirable countermeasure to theft and personal crimes. Again, such personnel aren't cheap. In the absence of police, unarmed security staff wearing uniforms resembling those worn by police (for example, dark pants, a white or blue shirt, and perhaps a military-looking cap and a tie) can sometimes create at least the illusion of enhanced security and potentially serve both as warning to would-be criminals and reassurance to the rest of us.

Another issue is punishment as a deterrent. However, the punishment for getting caught in various infractions of the law is not terribly severe for most of the crimes against property in libraries. In cases of crimes against people, law enforcement usually takes a stricter approach to punishment. In the case of crimes against property, however —such as the theft of a single book or two—few libraries are willing to go to the trouble of pressing charges, and most library administrations profess themselves to be happy just to have their books returned. But in the United States, where personal freedoms are prized above just about anything else, there are limits to punishment that most people would deem appropriate. Massachusetts recently passed a law providing for fines of up to $25,000 and five years in jail for stealing from libraries, which, if enforced, may prove to be an effective deterrent to crime.

Looking elsewhere—at Nigeria, for example—Steve Ezennia, a university library employee, writing for the journal *Library & Archival Security,* notes that in his country, conviction of theft of library property (even of a single library book) can lead, if a magistrate sees fit, to up to seven years in prison for the offense. This may seem a bit severe, but the threat of such a penalty is bound to serve as a real deterrent if you post a notification of such punishment in a prominent place in the building where those entering can read it.

Here at home, however, the whole issue seems to be about scale. In the minds of both the perpetrators of crime and the library's guardians, taking a library book by clandestine means isn't like swiping a car or robbing a bank and certainly—in many people's minds—not really worthy of prosecution. Besides, petty library crime goes on all the time, as people may occasionally:

- Take books home because they are unable or unwilling to buy them.
- "Borrow" books just for a while without going through the tiresome and time-consuming formalities of checkout.
- Keep materials beyond their loan period, out of laziness or being too busy to get to the library and return them.
- Beat or defeat the library's security system, just to see if they can.
- Photocopy material outside the "fair use" provision, even when they know (or may suspect) that what they're doing is illegal.
- Make unauthorized copies of right-protected computer programs, despite having read (or acknowledged by removing the shrink-wrap plastic covering) that this is illegal.
- Download electronic files in ignorance of or violation of copyright.
- As staff members, see to it that they get first crack at a hot new book and take it home before members of the public who are waiting for it even know that it's arrived.

And these infractions are only about the illegal removal of property. While safekeeping of a library's collection is of great importance, personal safety is far more important, because human lives may be at stake. After all, books, videos, and even computers can be repaired or replaced, but such is not the case with people.

The primary objective of all security precautions in libraries is to discourage crime and misdemeanors, whether the infraction in question concerns the illegal removal of books from the collection, the filching of wallets from unattended purses, or a range of violent acts. It would be wonderful to report that any library could effect 100 percent interdiction of crime due to an adroit mix of mechanical/electrical surveillance devices and alert human surveillance, but such perfection is impossible. The best way to prevent crime before it happens, however, is to assess the risks in and around the library and take measures to correct or eliminate them.

Physical features and arrangement of the building are a significant variable. Most library buildings are, by their nature, places where all are free to enter, which unfortunately puts everyone at risk. And some buildings, due to surrounding neighborhood, design faults, layout, or lighting, are more conducive to violent incidents than others. Too many nooks and crannies in the stacks mean security personnel and other staff must patrol these places frequently. Some library staff work in isolated sections of a large building, which presents an additional problem for security. While these circumstances cannot always be avoided, paying extra attention to these areas through monitors or security phones is one approach. And there is no excuse for poor lighting in any remote area of the library.

Besides sharp-eyed staff and security personnel, however, there are a variety of weapons available in the library's arsenal against crime, all of which will be discussed in more detail later. Among these are

- Closed-circuit television cameras
- Electronically accessed entryways
- Alarms on exit doors
- Access authorization cards
- Sign-in sheets
- Placing facilities and equipment in high-visibility areas

These and other high- and low-tech solutions to crime are considerably effective in preventing crime in libraries, although they vary widely in their affordability and thus ultimately, their feasibility. Maybe the problem can be resolved by changing the behaviors of the people who visit libraries by the thousands every day. Can problem patron behavior be modified? Not entirely. Surveillance cameras, staff communication systems, card key systems, metal detectors, and the like, however, may be useful just to help keep them honest. A few public libraries now require patrons to show a library card to gain admittance. This seemingly harsh measure followed repeated incidents in which pages had been ripped from magazines and reference books, materials stolen, rest rooms "misused," and staff members verbally abused. The thinking is that if all visitors know that they are identified and known to staff, fewer of them will be rash or foolish enough to risk being caught committing a crime or misdemeanor. What is done in such libraries about a would-be borrower who lacks a card? He or she can apply for a card on the spot. Staff members report that they feel safer now that such procedures are in place, but how long will it be before someone challenges the constitutionality, legality, or "fairness" of such a rule?

To reiterate, a big part of the problem in most, if not all, issues connected with library security may be that the general public tends to think of people ripping off libraries as no big deal, nothing to get all upset about, anyway. When it comes to personal safety, however, people sit up and take notice, especially in the wake of some crime involving the personal injury of a library patron or staff member. This book's main task is to publicize some problems of protecting libraries, and to present practical ideas and effective security methods. Library employees, and their security staffs, are the first line of defense.

The issues connected to library security—collection and equipment preservation and personal and public security—are intertwined, but for purposes of clarity will be treated separately in subsequent chapters of this book. And if many of the recommendations in this book seem more like advice than fact-based knowledge, so be it. Library security, while as old as the hills, is still evolving, and those charged with preserving both materials and public safety are always experimenting with new things to see what works.

There is one obvious solution to library crime, but one that many libraries are disinclined to use—prosecute those caught committing misdeeds. Get tough and get serious about security. Commitment to the goal of getting tough with those who commit offenses against library materials or property would help a lot. Mutilating library materials is a crime under state and municipal statutes in almost all communities, although librarians are characteristically disinclined to follow through and press charges. Sometimes, however, lack of time to follow through is as serious a disincentive to getting serious with criminals as is lack of will.

What's the best means of security for library buildings, property, and occupants? (Warning: You may not like the answer!) Trust no one, or be extremely careful about those you do. This seems to be the lesson we can absorb from observing the human condition. That means upgrading and updating security throughout the library. In most libraries, security precautions are in dire and obvious need of embellishment. Therefore, in the next two chapters, we will discuss library security and library safety, with the understanding that they are really parts of the same concern.

CHAPTER 2

Protecting Materials in Libraries

Despite valiant, ordinary, and innovative approaches to securing the general collection, 73 percent of the chief librarians of 255 public libraries rated book theft as their number one problem.

—Study by the Burns Security Institute, 1973

The objectives of this chapter are to:

- show how extensive and pervasive the problem of library theft is
- highlight the personalities, motivations, and methods of some of the more notorious perpetrators of library crime
- review current research on methods of deterring library theft
- recommend programs for theft deterrence and discuss how to react when thefts occur and the need to have better theft avoidance techniques

An important distinction must be made at the outset. This chapter deals with *property* security issues as opposed to issues of personal physical safety, even though they are often the same, or at least halves of a common problem. The distinction is that security issues concern loss or defacement of library property without threat to the lives or safety of persons present in the building, while personal safety issues (see chapter 3) deal with threats to human safety, and primarily concern the welfare and bodily security of the people inside the building, employees and patrons alike.

This chapter is intended to prepare library staff members to deal effectively with the potential for threats to the security of the library's property, including all materials, equipment, and structure. Unplanned emergencies, involving either personal safety or the integrity of the collection of materials and equipment, are integral to both chapters.

Why Do People Steal from Libraries?

In this highly cynical and largely secular age, the destruction of libraries and books is perhaps one of the last acts still almost universally greeted with a shudder, as sacrilege once was. As librarians, mindful of our role as the keepers of memory, we not only recoil but also take it personally when someone attacks or tries to steal items from the collections in our care. Stealing is not only against the law, but it is also condemned as wrong by virtually all societies. The stealing of another's property was specifically condemned in the Ten Commandments millennia ago, and is still universally proscribed in both civil and common law.

Steal a single book from a retail bookstore and you risk being arrested and made to pay the penalty for larceny. Yet the theft of library books is not generally considered to be a serious crime, perhaps because owning books (and the acquisition of books) is seen by many people as worthy and intrinsically good, and perhaps because stealing books is sometimes explained as a form of "borrowing." And borrowing is acceptable behavior at libraries, a hefty component of their collective raison d'être.

Book theft from libraries has often been taken lightly or even lampooned by the media and accepted as "ok" by society in general. After all, as long as people are stealing our books, they're showing us how much they value our principal products and services, so it's acceptable if not precisely condoned. Book theft is seen as distinct from such major crimes as stealing cars or computers, despite the fact that a single rare book that a skilled thief may take from a library may be worth more individually (to the extent that an actual dollar amount can be assigned to it) than a new luxury automobile.

Does the motive for stealing books make a difference? Books may be stolen to help the thief achieve economic goals or to further political aims, to "rescue" the book from abuse at the hands of its uncaring custodians, or just for the sheer joy of possession of something desired. In some cases, people steal books only to prove that a resourceful thief can defeat the library's pathetic attempts at security. But the end result of all such crime is the same: The book is missing, and no one may any longer consult it or use it. Therefore, all library crime should be taken as equally seriously as shoplifting in commercial establishments, and every person found guilty of library crime should be prosecuted. Successful prosecutions given adroit publicity will not only punish those who attempt to diminish libraries by misappropriating our property, but may serve as a possible deterrent to the next little person with big ideas who sees the library as an opportune cash cow for exploitation.

True, some may see a rough economic justification for committing such crimes as library book theft. By stealing the books they want or need, they may save hundreds or even thousands of dollars in purchase prices over a year's time. However, that's not the usual reason people do it. Sometimes the library thief is just a person who has suffered real or perceived injustice at the hands of society, the community, or city hall. In such cases, the thief may just feel that he's merely looking for a little payback and "getting even." So he grabs a book and walks out, or maybe just defaces one inside the building. That'll show 'em!

Additionally, there are still professors in academia who grade on the curve, meaning that for every A given out, someone else will receive an F. This creates a highly adversarial relationship among students: If you want a better grade, it's in your best interest to see to it that all the other students in your class receive worse ones. Your possession of one particularly important book deprives others of its information and may thus make a difference between your getting that coveted A and someone else getting it. This provides a definite incentive, at least for highly competitive and unscrupulous students, to hide, steal, or mutilate books, because if they can appropriate the information first, no one else will have it, and that carries its own reward. There isn't much guilt attached to such an act in the minds of many students, either, especially in academic library settings. The university, the thieves think in self-justification, has created and maintained a dog-eat-dog world, and they certainly don't want to be one of those who don't survive the obstacle course of studies. So by any means necessary, they'll do what they have to do to avoid ending up becoming flunked out, unemployed, or otherwise head down from the hook. In today's job market, it's a case of "me or them," a simple matter of survival.

But what about the rules? There *are* rules written down somewhere, aren't there? Those printed—and sometimes even prominently posted—prohibitions against doing whatever you want such as theft or mutilation of library materials? People can rationalize the rules, too. A book thief will sometimes think, "This is a stupid rule. Why should I follow it?" Why, indeed? Normally, the swiping of a coveted book is so easy! The odds of complete success and getting away with the crime are heavily in favor of the would-be thief. In truth, few miscreants are ever brought to justice for such infractions, and fewer still get punished.

Many commit their acts of pilferage not because they're selfish or because they seek vengeance but because they're lazy and it's the easy way out. It's just too hard and bothersome—too much hassle—to play by the rules. So you either flout them, or you play "cafeteria," picking and choosing, deciding which rules you will follow and which you will not. Some library users even make up their own rules, based upon their perception of self-interest.

In truth, there are so many worse crimes committed today that book theft hardly seems criminal behavior to most of us because it pales in comparison with such acts as drive-by murders, serial killings, or rapes. It's just a game for some people, with its own set of low risks and high rewards. Or maybe there is something anarchistic in human nature that relishes the excitement of ripping off the system. But there is always the risk that this excitement can get out of hand. An initial small crime might go so well that the criminal might decide to take it one step further. Taking a stapler or a pack of Post-its home from work or a book out of the library without going through procedures doesn't necessarily lead down the slippery slope that results in holding up the corner bank or embezzling funds from a company's holdings. But suppose you steal one book, just to see if you can. Maybe you call it an experiment or an intellectual exercise. That doesn't make it a real crime, does it? Then you take another, because it was so easy the first time, and then you get into the habit of doing it, until you find it difficult to stop. It's called kleptomania, if you have to put a name to it, but many people so afflicted are deep into denial and don't call it anything of the kind. Committing a small crime may be a one-shot event, but for some people, it can actually become addictive and can lead to a destructive major behavior pattern. Countless case study profiles, thumbnailing criminal careers in libraries, demonstrate the chronicles of people who started small and then gradually became . . . well, more ambitious after initial successes.

Who Steals What from Libraries?

Library theft, much of it petty, goes on all the time. But big-time operators are also at work in libraries, using their considerable intelligence and resources to make off with our most cherished treasures. Consider, by way of evidence for that assertion, some recent history, taken from library literature:

- 1995: A former student worker at the UCLA library is found guilty of the theft of books and manuscripts valued at more than $1 million from the university library.
- 1995: A Florida man is caught removing maps from eighteenth-century books from Baltimore's Johns Hopkins University library, among other academic institution libraries.
- 1995: An art history professor of Ohio State University approaches a rare books dealer, attempting to peddle purloined hand-illustrated pages cut from a medieval book.
- 1996: A man is caught stealing historic letters signed by Abraham Lincoln and Jefferson Davis from the rare book and manuscript collection of the University of Bridgeport (Connecticut).
- 1996: A man is arrested for theft of manuscripts on Civil War guerrillas and presidential letters from university libraries in Kansas and Arkansas.

Just who steals library materials, and what types of materials do they steal? For the sake of classification and convenience, library thieves may be divided into six basic classes, based on their principal motivation for committing theft. Such people, however, do not necessarily fit the stereotype of what you may think of as a criminal. Library thieves, in fact, frequently turn out to be dean's-list students, distinguished professors, elected public officials, librarians themselves, or just about anybody else, and any of them may fall into two or more of the following classifications, which are anything but mutually exclusive:

1. *Bibliokleptomaniacs* who cannot keep themselves from stealing books. They take books out of a compulsion to do so, and are in need of psychiatric assistance. Such people will usually take good care of the books, and a few will even surreptitiously bring them back at a later time. The reason for their misdeeds is usually the theft itself rather than possession of the book.

2. *Thieves who steal for their own personal use,* either for the secret pride of possession or to have the materials conveniently handy for consultation. They may feel they have the "right" to have the books because they pay taxes, tuition, and so on. Most of the time they will take good care of the book because they think of it as "theirs." Many such people are actually ardent lovers of books. Some thieves in this category steal because they are concerned about the way books are being treated by other library users, and feel that only they are capable of treating books with the veneration the books deserve.

3. *Thieves who steal in anger or for revenge,* harboring a real or imagined grievance against the library or someone in a management position, possibly for having been fired. These thieves do what they do because they're looking for payback. Unfortunately, thieves in this class may destroy or deface the materials they have stolen in order to punish the library.

4. *Casual thieves,* who may steal a book because it's just too time-consuming and bothersome to go through checkout or because they do not have borrowing privileges at the library and are unwilling or unable to arrange for them. In an academic library setting, casual thieves may be students driven by academic pressure or competition to "borrow" books they need. In all types of libraries, embarrassment may lead a person to purloin materials about such delicate subjects as impotence, AIDS, abortion, or sexually transmitted diseases. In many cases, these books turn up again, someday, once the felon is finished with them.

5. *Freelance censors,* who remove books to keep them out of the hands of others, whether because of disapproval of their contents or fear of the consequences of their being accessed by susceptible readers. Such people may be motivated by the desire to protect innocent persons and the fear that, while they personally can handle strange ideas on sex, politics, religion, or lifestyles without being either depraved or corrupted, others cannot. Therefore, they tend to think of themselves

as altruistic watchdogs and benevolent protectors, and of what they are doing as a public service.

6. *Thieves who steal for profit* may be staff members or outsiders who will subsequently attempt to sell the books, and thus can be caught if booksellers are ethical and alert. But the more careful book thieves are meticulous, clever, and unlikely to make mistakes.

This last class, the major and most serious predators of library materials, do what they do for a living. Often such criminals live as transients, living out of vehicles and preying on libraries and bookstores to support themselves or just to keep in practice, as they wend their way around their region or across the country. Concern has been expressed among law enforcement agents that some crooks may know one another and sometimes work together or otherwise cooperate and/or exchange favors and spoils. These distressing facts and developments have not gone unnoticed in the library world. In 1982, the Rare Books and Manuscripts Section (RBMS) of the Association of College and Research Libraries (ACRL) created a Security Committee "with the charge to develop and disseminate appropriate guidelines to secure library collections, and to serve as a resource for libraries who have experienced theft, to serve as a liaison with other organizations . . . whose interests are deterring the theft of library materials and vigorously promoting the proper prosecution of library thieves." The committee subsequently published "Guidelines Regarding Thefts in Libraries," which called for the appointment of Library Security Officers (LSOs), persons with principal responsibility for security on the part of the library, among other things.

How Do Thieves Succeed?

How does a skillful library criminal gain his or her objectives? There is no invariable pattern of criminal behavior in libraries, but successful thieves have several attributes and behaviors in common:

- Surveillance. They study people, systems, and physical layouts.
- One or more trial runs. Many thieves caught have later confessed to having walked through the projected crime area several times prior to the actual event, to troubleshoot any potential difficulties and to assess the library's defenses.
- Careful observation. They look for the weaknesses in the library's defenses.

Would-be criminals attempt to find a path of least resistance. As an example, possession of a purloined key is much easier and works better than dynamite or drilling through locks. It is also much simpler to have the key and the code than to try to defeat an alarm system. Key control, therefore, is paramount to a secure library operation. The key thief usually assumes that even if he or she is caught, the worst-case scenario would be being found guilty of a minor infraction of existing laws or rules with little or no punishment. Another assumption made by felons and would-be felons—all too often correct—is that libraries don't communicate with one another about the problem of theft, meaning that each library the thief visits is a fresh start, with staff unaware of both who and what he is.

A skillful thief, in fact, can do untold damage to a single library or, like a serial killer, go from place to place committing crimes. It is small wonder that some libraries have become cynical about protecting their books:

> We welcome sleepers here. A sleeping reader is less of a menace to the books than a waking one.
>
> —Posted sign in Cambridge University Libraries

A variety of methods can be and have been used to gain access to libraries' special collections and steal their books. Stolen keys and picked locks can allow the thief to elude after-hours security systems. Obliteration of property markings, if properly and carefully done, will not only conceal the provenance of a book, but will make the task of figuring out its rightful owner all the harder. To show the extent to which a resourceful thief will go to obliterate the markings of book ownership, book thieves eventually caught have confessed to having done the following:

- used fictitious library stamps
- carried blank, perforated, gummed spine labels, which they affixed to book spines after removing the library's labels and on which they created fictitious call numbers
- carried bookplates, book pockets, and date due slips, and pasted them into books to create false identity or to cover up ownership marks
- sandpapered library names off spines and edges of books and removed bookplates

- cut out or blackened library names in books
- befriended and became personally familiar with library staff members, causing them to relax their vigilance and view the thief as a "regular"
- disguised themselves—dressing as everything from disheveled "street people" to college professors—when attempting to fence their stolen materials to antiques dealers
- scaled library walls using mountain-climbing equipment, or in some cases, only fingertips and toeholds in the brick facing
- obtained schematics of the libraries' alarm systems and/or floor plans
- tracked down articles about valuable collections throughout the United States to assist them in selecting targets
- taken note of newspaper articles about severe police shortages in certain cities or on certain campuses as a clue to finding the targets that are the least well defended

One has to admire—however grudgingly—such straight-ahead determination to achieve one's goals. But there is a lesson to be learned from all this. While theft, vandalism, and damage are all inevitable in libraries and other public repositories of documents, determined and clever thieves are always going to find new and better ways to make off with their books and other property. Assuming that that is true, guardians of both the public and private trust must take all necessary measures to ensure that such threats and dangers to their collections, since they can't be eliminated, are at least minimized or made much more difficult to pull off.

What Do They Steal?

On the subject of book theft and disappearance in libraries, one can't do better than to read an entertaining article entitled, "Is There a Klepto in the Stacks?" by noted author and freelance journalist John Maxwell Hamilton. Hamilton's article appeared first in the *New York Times Book Review* (November 18, 1990) and then was reprinted, with the gracious permission of the author and the *Times*, in *Library & Archival Security* (12:1, 1994). Hamilton, seemingly in the spirit of one of Dave Letterman's "Ten Best" lists, has compiled his own list of the books and other materials that are stolen more than any others, based on interviews and observations in the New York Public Library and elsewhere. The question Hamilton asked of librarians was simple —deceptively so, because it proved quite difficult for him to get a full and straight answer to it. "Which books are most frequently missing —you know, disappear from bookshelves or never seem to be returned?" he asked, innocently. Or, to put it more bluntly, "Which books do people steal most often?" Librarians, he reports, are troubled by this question. They really don't like to think about it, or about what answers they might find. All guardians of books, in fact, including bookstore proprietors, the attendants in Christian Science Reading Rooms, and people who lend their dearest books to their dearest friends, knowing but not admitting that the volumes are gone forever, dread such a question. Yet, for all the angst the question causes, it is still worth asking.

Hamilton's most-stolen list tells us which kinds of books people really want—want so much that borrowing them for a week or two is not enough. For these books, people are willing to risk arrest, or at least public humiliation. And don't dismiss book theft as the work of a few ordinary crooks, he adds. Everybody does it. "People who steal books are some of the best people in the world," says a public librarian. Journalists, seminarians, lawyers, doctors, teachers, and especially librarians steal books, "which shouldn't come as any surprise—they use them and value them," says another.

Book theft is an integral part of the lifestyles of the rich and famous. In California a few years ago, Gustav Hasford, a novelist and Academy Award-nominated screenwriter, was convicted for the theft of almost 800 library books. The Waldorf-Astoria Hotel, whose $3,500 rate for a night in the presidential suite would cover some people's annual mortgage payments, buys about 200 used books a year, according to its manager. The hotel puts these in the rooms so wealthy guests can steal them. The Hilton hotel chain, in fact, stocks guest rooms with Conrad Hilton's autobiography, *Be My Guest,* expecting that many will be "borrowed" by their guests. When the book appeared in 1957, *Library Journal* said it was "well recommended, but may have a limited appeal." Hilton executives, however, proudly report thefts of 50,000 copies a year, with another 20,000 to 30,000 tossed out because coffee is spilled on them "or whatever."

And then Hamilton drops his biggest bombshell of all concerning the epidemic of book theft: "The only thing that apparently keeps *you* from stealing books," he says, "is that it hasn't occurred to you yet."

His implication is clear: Never mind the Ten Commandments or religious preachings telling us that stealing is wrong. Everybody steals, so libraries shouldn't be surprised to discover that the book collection (and other collections) are reduced to the tune of more than 10 to 15 percent a year. Yet this staggering and pervasive crime wave is not all that frequently mentioned in print. "I have to tell you I don't enjoy talking about this subject," said one librarian in a typical statement to Hamilton. "I don't want to give people ideas."

Why, then, do they do it, when most of them know that stealing is wrong? Hamilton has a ready answer: It seems to be a matter of degree. "This primordial urge to pilfer books stems from a different part of the brain than, say, the inclination to swipe a car. Librarians admit as much when they refrain from words like 'stolen' and talk about long-overdue books not having been 'returned yet.' They obviously would not be so charitable about the kid who hot-wired their car last night and drove off. The difference between books and cars (aside from cost) is that books deal in ideas, and ideas are supposed to be free." A Washington, D.C., bookseller finds a common attitude among "customers," many wearing three-piece suits, who try to bypass the cashier: "Oh damn, I have to go through the inconvenience of paying for these!"

The problem with attempting to come up with a most-stolen list, Hamilton acknowledges, is lack of statistics. The whole idea of theft is to avoid detection, and, as previously mentioned, librarians are reluctant to discuss an embarrassing lack of security, for several reasons. Sometimes, a "missing" book turns out to be merely misplaced or temporarily stuck in limbo. "It's not always easy to distinguish between what is overdue, what is lost in the system, or what is stolen," says one librarian. Even with imperfect statistics and the reticence of some to talk about the subject, it is still possible to piece together a plausible most-stolen list in somewhat the same way police artists sketch a criminal's face from fragmentary recollections (see figure 2.1).

Following up on that last point, many people have axes to grind on controversial subjects, and will exercise their own brand of censorship by stealing books they think may misinform, deprave, or corrupt other readers. On occasion, they may even seek to replace the "bad" books they've stolen (on politics, sex, or the occult, for instance) with volumes that take more acceptable (to them) positions on controversial issues. There are plenty of recent examples of groups removing

The Bible. Surprising, but evidently true. Hamilton says that the Bible is clearly the most stolen book, an all-time favorite that people can't resist lifting. His figure includes Bibles stolen from hotels and motels, in which the Gideon Society reports losing a total of 29 million copies in 147 countries in a recent fiscal year.

Practice for the Armed Forces Test and various other how-to-prepare books are ripped off with frightening frequency. This category includes such often-stolen works as *Practice for Civil Service Promotion to Supervisory and Administration Positions* and various manuals for college entrance exams.

The Joy of Sex and similar titles. Hamilton guesses that sex-book thieves have a special motive—embarrassment. It is not just sex books that go; libraries also report routinely losing the swimsuit issue of *Sports Illustrated.*

Curses, Hexes, and Spells. This title, and others dealing with the occult, witchcraft, white and black magic, and devil worship disappear from libraries frequently, sparing curious readers the potentially embarrassing moment of having to present them at a counter for checkout.

Steal This Book. Antiestablishment books like Abbie Hoffman's *Steal This Book* invite theft. (Why not? The title tells you what to do, right?) Much black literature that is stolen also seems to fall into this category, for instance, the autobiographies of Malcolm X and Angela Davis.

Standard Federal Tax Reporter, especially at risk in law school libraries. This may be because law school students are so competitive and their professors grade on the curve; so theft of certain materials may be viewed in some distorted sense as an act of self-preservation.

Encyclopedias. Some people steal entire encyclopedias along with other expensive reference books, while a few prefer going from library to library, picking up a volume here and one there until a complete set is assembled.

The Red Pony by John Steinbeck. This novel, running just more than 100 small pages, is the shortest common work of popular fiction. Hamilton theorizes that therefore it is a perennial favorite of students who must read and review a novel but don't want to spend too much time on the assignment. Fortunately, these books often have a way of reappearing on the shelves when the assignment's due date has passed or at the end of the term.

FIGURE 2.1
Hamilton's List of Most Stolen Library Books

The Birds of America by John James Audubon, a huge, unwieldy book of color plates that would seem to defy theft. "It stands four or four and a half feet off the ground," says Maxwell, incredulously. But it is still one of the most frequently stolen of rare volumes. This book has great monetary value. Money, though, is not always the motive. Some people steal certain books because they want to own and protect them, and do not trust others (even librarians) to take good care of them.

The China Lobby in American Politics and other examples of political factional disputes spilling over into library collections. Commonly, such books are removed because the thief believes that they are dangerous if read and disastrous if acted upon.

books that challenge or do not reflect what they are pleased to call "family values" and leaving behind religious literature that better reflects their personal views.

A Rogue's Gallery of Thieves

A better understanding of how major library thefts have occurred and who has committed such crimes and why may help us to figure out what we can do to deter the stealing of our cultural history. Perhaps we can establish a working profile of the serious library thief based on a few selected case histories. In discussing such felons, we're not talking about petty sneak thieves who walk out with a novel under their coats or in their briefcases. We're more interested in examining the pasts and criminal behaviors of a few of those convicted of major and massive library theft, so that we can better understand how to deter such crime in the future.

There must be more attention paid to knowing who steals our valuable holdings, what motivates them, and how they steal, so we can thwart future crimes or at least make them more difficult to commit. Why do some people steal hundreds or thousands of valuable materials from our libraries? As might be expected, motives vary; some of those accused of major thefts even plead compulsion or insanity at their trials. Other felons claim indignantly that they did their deeds to preserve and protect materials that the city, the county, or the university was doing a poor job of protecting, leaving books and manuscripts vulnerable and requiring "rescue" by an enlightened savior.

Does this mean such people are crazy? You decide. Usually, in a legal context, the issue is whether the defendant, who might be suffering from a mental disability or illness, knows right from wrong. When defendants attempt to destroy records of their past actions, do they know right from wrong? Imagine yourself on a jury and conclude how you might decide the fate of the following noted book thieves who have been brought before the bar of justice.

Murphy

> In 1964, Elizabeth and Robert Bradford Murphy were arrested by FBI agents in Detroit and charged with theft of government property and interstate transportation of stolen property. Documents from the National Archives, valued at over $500,000, were found in six suitcases in their possession. These included letters of Presidents Monroe, Jackson, Lincoln, Cleveland, Wilson, Franklin Roosevelt, Eisenhower, and Kennedy. Following their apprehension (after eluding authorities for over a year), the National Archives instituted stricter approaches to eliminating theft.
>
> Murphy had started visiting the National Archives, stating that he was a historical researcher living in Evanston, Illinois (an address that was later found to be fictitious). He was a regular in the Central Research Room, eying materials other scholars were using. He often was reprimanded for his loud behavior and cigar smoking on library premises. By that time, Murphy was an experienced thief—he had a long record of warrants and arrests for theft of materials from professional collectors. In fact, he was observed by FBI agents in 1961 at the Georgia Department of Archives and History after archivists grew suspicious of this self-proclaimed historical consultant to the Library of Congress. At that time, no theft occurred, although many missing items were recovered later following his arrest.
>
> In 1962, posing as a journalist and using another fictitious name, Murphy stole a number of valuable letters from the Indiana State Library. With all this experience under his belt, Murphy decided it was time to tackle the National Archives. Under several aliases, he and his wife purloined and sold countless documents to collectors all over the United States. Once these thefts were identified, the FBI intervened. But despite the magnitude of the theft, the National Archives neither publicized it nor notified other archivists and dealers. Why not? The Archives and the FBI

believed that such disclosure might cause thieves to destroy precious documents. In fact, the loss was kept a secret from all but a few of the archives staff.

Found guilty of wholesale theft from multiple institutions, the Murphys were each sentenced to ten years in prison. At his court trial, Murphy was sentenced to six months additional imprisonment for contempt of court due to his continued behavior of insulting and baiting witnesses. Murphy served only four years due to good behavior in prison. However, Elizabeth served the full ten years. Some good came of all this. After the Murphys stole 210 documents from the National Archives, authorities there suggested many changes in policy because "the physical security of the Archives must always come first." New staff members were added; guard responsibilities were increased; and identification and personal possessions were to be scrutinized. Nevertheless, no great reforms took hold. In the end, individual researcher rights, though somewhat diluted, had won over much stricter security precautions.

Cheshire

Library thief Gervase Donald Cheshire used a simple stratagem to make off with thousands of materials. He simply turned on the charm and gained the confidence of library staff in various locations. In so doing, he managed to steal 15,000 books, scores, and art reproductions, right from under the noses of librarians and security staff. The cost to the victimized academic and public libraries was estimated to be $400,000 and may well have run much higher because of the previously discussed problem of nonreporting losses. The magnitude of this type of loss has been severely underestimated, and the actions of Cheshire and others led to controversial new policies concerning access to information. Because thieves mutilated its books, and missing rare prints, drawings, and photographs were not discovered for years, the Library of Congress decided on a radical solution. In 1992, it closed its stacks. As a result, the public is no longer allowed to browse —a loss to us all.

Mount

Scholar, painter, author, historian, perfect English gentleman, bon vivant—these are some descriptions of the public persona of the man who came to be known to some rare book librarians as Charles Merrill Mount. Mount, dressed in the most expensive clothes (which he purchased in thrift shops) and faking a charming English accent, fooled everyone into thinking he was a distinguished and law-abiding citizen. His talent as a successful portrait artist led him to publish biographies of Claude Monet, John Singer Sargent, and Gilbert Stuart. Mount donated all his research material to the Library of Congress. Ironically, it was because of this donation that locked doors were opened for him at the Library, facilitating his thefts. He was provided with an assigned work space for two years, during which he observed that LC employees didn't know much about the materials they possessed. In 1975, he claimed to be an FBI consultant on art forgeries. Apparently, he fooled many smart people. He got himself listed both in *Contemporary Authors* and *Who's Who in American Art* and claimed to have once had a Guggenheim fellowship. With such credentials, LC curators and librarians came to trust him. Why wouldn't he have been trusted?

In August 1987, Mount was arrested by FBI agents in Boston for attempting to sell rare letters of Winston Churchill, Abraham Lincoln, and Henry James to a bookseller. Agents summoned by the alert bookman discovered additional materials in Mount's shabby boardinghouse room in Washington, D.C., and in a bank safety deposit box. There were more than two hundred historical documents, many from the National Archives and the Library of Congress. The estimated value was more than $150,000. Several additional safety deposit boxes, registered under fictitious names, contained Civil War documents, $18,000 cash, a loaded handgun, and a large quantity of tranquilizers—presumably to be used to subdue suspicious persons should they catch him in the act of his thievery.

Mount was indicted for receiving stolen property, mail fraud, possession of a controlled substance, and illegal possession of a firearm. He faced up to 235 years in jail and a fine of $500,000. His response was, "All this is just hysteria. The whole thing has been blown out of proportion." In 1988, he was found guilty of transporting stolen documents from the National Archives and the Library of Congress. He was sentenced in federal court to three years in prison and to pay $20,000 to a Boston bookstore owner who had purchased some of the documents, only to have to surrender them to their rightful owners. In 1989, Mount was also sentenced to five years in prison for mail fraud and possession of government property. His terms ran consecutively with his prior sentence. Even at his sentencing, Mount continued to maintain that the materials had belonged to him for many years, having been purchased legitimately from dealers in Europe and the United States. At his sentencing, the presiding U.S. District Court judge said, "Never in my experience have I met a more arrogant man with your intellect. What a miserable waste of a life. . . . You're never going to change."

Witherell

Driving around the United States in his pickup truck, stealing books, manuscripts, and art while being supported by his parents, William March Witherell of San Gabriel, California, was arrested due to the alert action of an attentive librarian. Under the alias Greg Williams, Witherell tore out several pages of a valuable Ben Franklin book from the Free Library of Philadelphia. Eventually his luck ran out and his belief in the ignorance of those he dealt with proved to be unwarranted. The head of the library's rare book collection alertly recalled that the suspect in a previous nearby theft had used a similar street address, substituting New York for San Gabriel. She thereupon demanded to examine the papers Witherell had with him, discovered the torn pages, and quickly summoned the local police. He was charged with theft, receiving stolen property, and institutional vandalism.

Witherell then became a suspect in a theft from the University of Pennsylvania library. Several rare books discovered to be missing had most recently been examined by a patron residing at the New York address he had given. Once Witherell was apprehended at the Free Library of Philadelphia, police suspected him of the other theft. But Witherell was freed without bail, pending a court appearance. In the meantime, FBI agents visited his parents' home in California and found cartons of rare items he had mailed to himself from across North America. His parents cooperated with authorities, noting that their son had suffered childhood brain damage. Interestingly, years earlier, Witherell had been arrested for stealing items from a California mission church, but had been found not guilty by reason of insanity and ordered to undergo psychiatric care. Prosecutors later learned that Witherell stole rare materials from at least twenty libraries. Valued at close to $200,000, the boxes he mailed home had never been opened by his parents. Many books inside those boxes were mutilated but repairable, while a few were so badly damaged as to be unusable. Following a non-jury trial, he was sentenced to one year and one day for stealing books from various libraries. One of the stolen books was worth $50,000.

Paroled after serving less than a year in prison, Witherell went right back to his old routine. He was stopped at the Canadian border in possession of several University of Alaska special collection books. Detained by Canadian authorities, he violated his parole and jumped bail. After Witherell was also sighted in Delaware and New Jersey, the security head of the Free Library of Philadelphia issued a nationwide warning to librarians via a message on the EXLIBRIS electronic bulletin board. Police authorities eventually apprehended him in Arizona for a traffic violation and learned of the warrant. For his new crimes and misdemeanors, he was sentenced to eight additional months in prison.

Witherell obviously appreciated books. The stolen rare books in his apartment had been categorized by subject. It took over forty librarians to make a preliminary catalog of this collection. Eventually, OCLC organized a database entitled "The Book Return" to enable librarians to identify missing items. As a result of the massive body of evidence against him, Witherell was finally found guilty, sentenced to nearly six years in prison, and fined $200,000.

Blumberg

In 1990, perhaps the world's single most active book thief of the twentieth century—Stephen Carrie Blumberg—was arrested, tried, and convicted for federal crimes relating to the theft of nearly 25,000 titles over a twenty-year period from more than three hundred U.S. libraries, coast to coast. But even Blumberg's luck eventually ran out. He walked into the kitchen of his two-story house in Ottumwa, Iowa, where he was greeted by a team of Federal Bureau of Investigation agents, warrants in hand, acting on a tip from a paid informant. What the FBI found in that house was astonishing. The house was crammed floor-to-ceiling with enough stolen rare books to fill two forty-foot tractor trailers.

Blumberg's contrived insanity plea was dismissed. He was tried and convicted of four counts of possession and transportation of stolen goods. He was sentenced to five years and eleven months of prison, and the judge slapped him with a $200,000 fine. In 1987, about the time that libraries were beginning to discover books missing due to his unauthorized visits, the ACRL Rare Books and Manuscripts Section Security Committee began to gather in a single listing published reports of library thefts. The committee called this document "Incidents of Theft." A committee member volunteered to keep it up-to-date and to issue a revised version just before every ALA annual meeting. Originally no more than one page in length, this document reached twenty-two pages by 1995. This provides dramatic evidence of the extent and continuance of the problem and the increasing willingness of librarians to talk about it and exchange information. After the FBI captured Blumberg, OCLC volunteers compiled a 16,000-record inventory of the stolen materials found in his possession, searchable on the EPIC service, and urged libraries who might have been victims to access this database.

Blumberg was shown to have been stealing rare books for years. FBI records show a 1974 arrest for possession of stolen books from universities in Colorado, Iowa, Nebraska, and Minnesota. It became evident that Blumberg had carefully researched what he intended to steal. For example, three complete sets of seven volumes each of an academic library's catalog holdings in Western Americana were marked with checks in pencil. He was arrested again in 1988 at the University of California-Riverside and fingerprinted and photographed before he jumped bail. One can only speculate as to whether Blumberg used such catalogs as shopping lists so that he could add marked items in them to his personal collection.

How do libraries make discoveries of thefts and mutilations? In many cases, of course, they simply don't. But in 1994, a survey went out to about three hundred libraries victimized by Blumberg. The first question asked was "How did you first discover that Blumberg stole books from your library?" About 77 percent reported that they first learned that something was amiss when the FBI contacted them after Blumberg's trove of purloined volumes was examined. One institution was contacted by local police, three happened to read publicity about

Blumberg in the library professional journals, and two heard from another library to which their books had been mistakenly returned by the FBI. Only a very few had discovered some evidence of theft in their buildings on their own. A few other libraries said that they were unaware that Blumberg had ever visited them, and that the survey must have been sent to them in error. From all this, the statistical evidence confirms what anecdotal evidence first suggested: Libraries are often unaware that they have been victimized, or at least say that they are, for whatever reasons.

Gildea

> In March 1998, the United States Attorney's Office in Boston, Massachusetts, announced that Kevin P. Gildea, 42, who had last resided in Quincy, Massachusetts, had been indicted by a federal grand jury for the theft and subsequent concealment of "objects of cultural heritage" and with theft and subsequent concealment of government property. Four stolen rare books were returned to the Adams National Historic Site amid a flurry of favorable publicity. "This was not simply a theft of priceless books," said the FBI agent in charge of the case. "It resulted in a piece of this nation's history being ripped out of Quincy. John Quincy Adams would have been pleased with the professionalism and dedication of the FBI, the Quincy Police Department, and the U.S. Park Service in cracking this case."
>
> The charges relate to four priceless books that were taken on November 11, 1996, during a break-in at the Stone Library on the grounds of the Adams National Historic Site at 135 Adams Street in Quincy. All were part of John Quincy Adams's personal book collection and are further described as follows:
>
> - An English Bible published in 1838 in the United States, which was given to John Quincy Adams by a group of Mendi tribesmen from what is now Sierra Leone, West Africa. It was given in commemoration of Adams's representation of the tribesmen before the U.S. Supreme Court in a case relating to their mutiny while aboard the slave ship *Amistad* (an episode recently the subject of Steven Spielberg's movie *Amistad*).
> - An English Bible published in 1772 in England, which had belonged to John Quincy Adams's wife
> - A Latin Bible published in Germany 1521, which was the oldest book in John Quincy Adams's collection

- A book of hand-painted illustrations of fish published in Germany in 1785 and printed in French.

The fate of Gildea, the alleged book thief, is still undecided. If convicted, however, Gildea faces a maximum penalty of ten years' imprisonment and a fine of $250,000 for each charged offense. Although he was at liberty at the time of the theft of the books in November 1996, Gildea is currently serving a five-year term of imprisonment. That sentence was imposed in March 1997 for violation of the terms of his probation in connection with an unrelated federal case.

Lessons to Be Learned

Amid the great loss and destruction of valuable items, the Blumberg case, among others, may have had several useful consequences. Perhaps publicity from it encouraged libraries to keep a closer eye on their books. Perhaps it alerted law enforcement agencies to the potential seriousness of book theft. Perhaps it helped change how libraries and universities behave when they are robbed. It is obvious to anyone that opportunities for vandalism and theft of public collections are multitudinous. Even areas not open to the public can be entered, often easily, through stealth, bravado, or chicanery. At issue, however, are individual rights to personal privacy versus library security. Habitual and intelligent library thieves, well organized and frequently working from personal shopping lists, will work with tireless determination to achieve their nefarious goals. They must be met with equal and opposite zeal if we hope to protect our valuable property.

Penalties for stealing from libraries, while appearing stiff and severe, are not always enforced due to lack of resolve or time on the part of the victims. In Michigan, the state penal code classes theft of any library materials as a mere misdemeanor. In 1992, one thief, Robert Martin, stole hundreds of books from at least eleven libraries, including public libraries, the state library, and a major university. Despite being convicted of "larceny by conversion under $100,000," he spent only four days in jail. It appears that, given the magnitude of the offense in such cases, the punishment rarely fits the crime.

Perhaps more stringent laws and stricter sentences for library thieves are required. In a feature article (*Los Angeles Times,* 1988) following the conviction of notorious book thief Charles Merrill Mount,

David Zeidberg, head of Special Collections at the University of California, Los Angeles, pressed for more attention to library theft and the need for quick and decisive action:

> When the aberrant few among us take advantage of the free access to collections by stealing materials, they are stealing our cultural heritage from us all. Let's call thefts of the magnitude of those described here what they are: felonies. Let's call the people who perpetrate these crimes what they are: criminals who must be made accountable to society.

Clearly we make theft too easy in libraries. False identification cards, aliases, open stacks, and staff innocently and unwittingly helping criminals make our libraries too open to theft. Unless we study the motives of those involved in thievery—be it monetary gain, the desire to possess what does not belong to one, the challenge of stealing, or mental illness—and attempt more effectively to deter theft, our collections will shrink, our patrons will be unhappy, the costs of providing library service to the community will go up unnecessarily, and our potential donors will look elsewhere for secure locations for their bequests.

Thieves normally find libraries pleasant places in which to ply their trade. There is nothing to stop them from entering and no barrier to pass or requirement that they stop, show identification, discuss anything, pay an admission charge, or do anything else that might call attention to themselves or cause people to remember them later. And you can't always tell who the thieves are. Thieves do not wear signs that say, "I'm not here to do library work; I'm on a shopping spree." They don't necessarily look suspicious, either. Many of the most successful thieves, in fact, are attractive, well dressed, well spoken, and confident. That's no doubt part of the reason they are so successful.

Part of the problem is that people tend to let their guard or innate wariness down inside a library. The street smarts that serve them well in urban communities are sometimes put aside or deactivated in the sedate and quiet precincts of a library reading room. That represents an opportunity for the clever thief. In fact, the library seems so "safe" that after the thief strikes, the victim may actually feel betrayed by the library because something was stolen. "It's not the way it's supposed to be," more than one patron has said in an aggrieved tone when reporting lost items.

Deterrence of Library Theft

> In Australia there is apparently a public notice that reads, "In other states, trespassers are prosecuted. Here, we shoot the bastards!"
>
> —J. Steven Huntsberry, veteran security officer

Prevention of crime and other antisocial acts in libraries before they occur would be the best thing, but failing that, deterrence is possible, and in most cases, it begins with attitude adjustment (see figure 2.2).

- Theft and loss occur less often when staff use and check existing locks and alarms regularly.
- There is less theft and loss when staff visibly or physically perform inventory regularly.
- There is less theft and other loss when the staff demonstrate that they care about protecting valuables.
- Theft and loss are always reduced when staff apply the business principles of risk management to their institution.
- Theft prevention is less expensive than the cost of legal recovery or replacement.
- Missing items are found more often when they are immediately reported as missing.
- Old locks usually have too many keys in circulation. Every library should change locks and keys from time to time as a matter of good business practice.
- Thieves choose to commit the easiest or safest theft; you can at least encourage them to go elsewhere by improving the appearance of your security.
- Most thefts occur because of simple or common oversights of caretakers of valuable property. Regularly examine the basic means you use for protection.
- Private areas of buildings need clear separation and marking from public areas, with locks or control of entry and exit to them.
- To avoid theft and other losses, managers should ask insurance specialists and other protection professionals for advice.

(Continued)

FIGURE 2.2
Important Considerations for Prevention of Theft of Library Property

FIGURE 2.2 *(Continued)*

- Theft is best prevented by physically separating valuables from those who would remove them, using nonwalk spaces such as pits, platforms, and height before using ropes, railings, and glass.
- Theft and loss are often prevented when staff consider looking after the property as if it were their own.
- Some thefts will inevitably occur, but 99 percent of them are preventable.
- Fewer thefts occur when staff close, lock, and frequently check existing doors—a small inconvenience in comparison to the result of actual loss.
- Thefts inevitably occur through carelessness or neglect.
- Thefts from public or government property are viewed as acceptable to some people. The key is to make library thefts appear as thefts from the "people" or "heritage" of the country, which may arouse a sense of outrage in a largely indifferent public.
- Thefts for *any* purpose are not acceptable—cultural thieves have no higher motives than other thieves.
- Thefts by outsiders or staff are still thefts. Prosecute all thieves.
- Employee thefts occur less often when ethics codes are known and respected by all staff.
- Thefts by outside persons are often assisted by staff, even without their knowledge. Be careful with sensitive or security information.
- Theft also includes embezzlement, forgery, misappropriation, extortion, and hijacking.

Why Is Theft Such a Problem?

The public must be educated and reminded of the possibility of theft. Most people would not leave book bags, purses, or coats unattended at a restaurant table while they use the rest room or pay their bill, yet many people do just that when using libraries. They leave all sorts of personal belongings alone "for just a minute or two" while browsing the shelves, using the copiers, rest rooms, telephones, catalogs, and so on. Patrons often seem quite surprised and angry when they find their belongings missing. Staff are entirely within their rights to demand to know who is using the library. Libraries are also businesses; specifically, the library is in the lending and information business. And, like other businesses, we must know how to get in touch with our customers. To qualify for library services, a valid identification card with address and photo may be necessary, and it is reasonable to expect people to produce such documents upon request.

People who reside outside the library's governmental jurisdiction or who have no permanent residence could be hard to track down if materials are not returned. Sometimes patrons refuse to provide this information, for a variety of reasons. Signs, brochures, and staff guidelines are necessary, and acceptable behavior policies are imperative. In short, we must be vigilant and diligent about educating both our public and our staff. This proactive approach will go a long way to cut down on complaints and misunderstandings and improve public relations.

Research has shown that magazines and other periodicals constitute the number one target of opportunity for library thieves. Also high on the petty larceny hit list are such commonly ripped-off materials as automobile repair manuals, newspapers, adult magazines, and sports magazines. Like so many other problems, this is not unique to libraries. Libraries, in fact, are comparative novices in protecting their materials, especially when compared with high-risk private purveyors. There is much librarians could learn, for example, from convenience stores regarding loss. How do the managers and employees at 7-Eleven and other similar stores attempt to dissuade or deter would-be thieves and robbers? It's a valid question, worth asking. By one estimate, libraries, regardless of type, are being pillaged of 2 to 5 percent of their book collections annually and 5 to 25 percent of their audiovisual collections (primarily videos and CDs). The sheer total of loss and destruction of material in various types of physical and electronic collections has grown into a major national and international problem.

From a public relations standpoint, such losses are very bad for the library's image as well. There is nothing sadder than having a patron need something we think we own and being unable to provide it because it is lost, stolen, strayed, missing, or simply unaccounted for. The illicit removal of physical objects from archives, libraries, museums, and collections has always presented a problem for their owners and guardians, whether they are private individuals or public administrators. Securing material is much easier in a private collection that is completely inaccessible to anyone except the owner than it is in a large library or museum whose very existence is predicated on serving the public. Libraries' responses to materials' disappearance can range from naive laxity or indifference to extraordinary vigilance bordering on paranoia.

As an example of both extremes, consider the experience of Robert Hauptman, editor of the *Journal of Information Ethics.* In 1987, Hauptman visited the New York Public Library for the purpose of examining Carson McCullers' correspondence, so that he could produce a more informed biographical account of her life and works for the *Dictionary of American Biography.* Formal permission to enter the collection was immediately granted; once inside, a pleasant woman quickly retrieved the appropriate folder, handed it over to him, and turned away. Hauptman pointed out that he preferred not to be left alone with these irreplaceable documents, and so the librarian reluctantly stood there while he briefly perused them. When he was finished, he was let out of the building without examination of his property or person.

Five years later, Hauptman again had occasion to visit the New York Public Library print collection. Formal permission was granted. He buzzed and a young woman unlocked the print room door, allowed him to enter, and then relocked the door, taking the key with her (which Hauptman noted was a safety hazard in an emergency). Thus ensconced, he was given the scholarly research tools he needed, spent some time reading, and then asked to be let out. During this and a subsequent visit some minutes later, Hauptman reports that he felt as if he were being carefully scrutinized by the somewhat overly officious attendants. Such an atmosphere obviously produces anxiety, guilt, and a desire to flee to some safer, less tempting haven, but the trade-off of such measures tends to be that fewer books disappear or become mutilated.

Why Librarians Are Hesitant about Security

Most libraries seek to take some middle road between these extremes. This path allows them to avoid continually losing valuable materials, yet prevents their countermeasures from alienating patrons. Among the most popular and affordable security measures is the use of narrow strips of magnetic tape inserted into the spines of print materials. Tattle-tape was a revolutionary idea when it arrived on the scene many years ago. Thousands of the nation's libraries began putting magnetic devices into books that trip sensors if the volumes are not properly checked out at the loan desk. The idea caught on, as library systems tried desperately to improve security without escalating costs. Thousands of libraries that were financially able scrambled to secure print holdings in this way. Using minimum-wage or student workers, "tattling" all books could render collections of half a million or more books secured within a matter of weeks. Librarians then figured that they could now relax, since their precious holdings were protected from theft. Or so they thought and hoped. At least initially, the statistics bore them out.

All security countermeasures eventually meet with new threats, however. These lead to improved countermeasures and so on in an endless chain. It didn't take potential thieves very long to figure out how to beat the tattle-tape system; they did, and still do, en masse. Statistics are difficult to obtain to verify the actual security of holdings when tattle-tape is used; libraries are typically if understandably disinclined to discuss their shortcomings. Yes, the alarm usually does ring and a waist-high gate may even lock when a patron tries to leave the library with material that has not been desensitized, presumably signaling an attempted theft. Sometimes, however, the alarm may ring for other reasons, or for no reason at all. Unfortunately, the alarm often rings when a desensitizing machine malfunctions. If this happens enough times, staff may simply come to ignore it. Busy workers at counters also make the common error of not desensitizing material that has been legitimately checked out, a human error difficult to control or correct. And even if the material has been checked out, and if a functioning desensitizing machine has been used appropriately, the alarm may *still* sound! This can be a traumatic or intensely irritating experience for the conscientious and law-abiding patron who checks out books in the prescribed manner and still sets off the alarm. An ongoing complaint against tattle-tape, in fact, is that it has a surprisingly high error rate.

Despite its ubiquitousness, perhaps the most condoned crime in the community and on campus is theft of library materials; this work of unscrupulous or indifferent people is costing libraries millions of dollars yearly. An Ivy League university reported a few years ago that it had experienced a major loss from one of its valuable collections of rare materials. It didn't know about the missing item until a thief, under the guise of being a library security professional, tried to sell them a security system. To close the deal, the thief even pointed out what was missing already to demonstrate the potential for future theft. More than a few book thieves have actually stolen books and offered to sell them right back to the library from which they had pilfered them. Minnesota authorities once raided a house that contained so many historical records that they described it as appearing to be a large private museum, complete with "Do Not Touch" signs.

Recent studies show that theft from libraries may run as high as 20 percent per year, yet few libraries conduct regularly scheduled inventories because it is boring, labor-intensive, and too costly in staff time. What's more, they make little attempt to identify security problems and often refuse to prosecute those individuals caught in the act. In this sense, we are often our own worst enemies, giving aid and comfort to the potential enemies who would steal from us. Why? It is often a matter of attitude. Among the attitudes of librarians expressed in questionnaire responses are frequently found statements like these:

- We don't have the time or personnel to do anything about theft.
- Theft of materials comes with the territory and we have to live with it.
- We only want our books returned. Preventing future crime is not a librarian's role.
- Why publicize our thefts? Potential future donors will think our security is poor.
- If we do publicize thefts, maybe new people will begin to look at the library as a target for their future crimes.
- We're afraid. If we help put these people in jail, when they come out, they're likely to come back here, looking for some payback.

Such typical arguments and evasions, while understandable, only serve to encourage the would-be library thief. Doesn't anyone care that our written records are being taken from us by artful thieves who practically have the red carpet rolled out for them? Ralph Munn, while director of the Carnegie Library in Pittsburgh during the Great Depression over sixty years ago, wrote an article concerning non-return of books and mutilation of library materials (Munn, 1935). He described two major concerns that are still germane: (1) Librarians worry that publicizing theft will give the idea of thievery to others, and (2) they fear the reaction of library boards, political officials, and the public when thefts are made known. "My experience is that the public takes a realistic and reasonable view of the problem," said Munn. "Surely we must justify this reasonable attitude by doing everything possible to reduce thefts, rather than by attempting to ignore and hide them."

Treating Theft as Disaster

> A book is a fragile creature; it suffers the wear of time, it fears rodents, the elements and clumsy hands. . . . So the librarian protects the books not only against mankind but also against nature, and devotes his life to this war with the forces of oblivion.
>
> —Umberto Eco, *The Name of the Rose*

One immediate and inexpensive way to attempt to reduce incidents of theft in libraries is to post simple signs cautioning people to mind their belongings just the way they would do outside the building. This may serve as a reminder to the public—and a possible legal defense for the library—when victims report a purse, a laptop, or a jacket missing. Signage and patron education are both required. "We are not responsible for lost or stolen items" signs are common, even in coatcheck areas of restaurants and other commercial establishments. Libraries need similar signs to warn and inform people of a potential risk, problem, or condition, and whose responsibility it is when something is stolen. Signs may seem obvious, but they do help remind people of the problem of theft. They further serve to protect the library when problems arise and those who have been ripped off are looking for someone to blame or sue for their losses.

Even without talking about the intervention of thieves and vandals, library losses each year are significant due to the natural processes of wear, humidity, heat, ill use or abuse, or just plain aging. But when people get into the act, the losses are staggering. How serious is it? One or two books at a time missing is probably not major. In a very real sense, however, the cumulative effect of theft or mutilation of books or other property from a library is a disaster like an earthquake, a hurricane, or a fire. The result, from the library's standpoint, is very similar—the only difference is one of degree.

Books, however, tend to disappear from the library one or two at a time, meaning that, unlike other types of disasters, this one sneaks up quietly and without attracting undue notice. In fact, you may not notice its scope until you perform an inventory and total up your losses. Unfortunately, with library budgets what they are and with the increasing emphasis on serving the public, many libraries never get around to performing any form of inventory. They just resign themselves to living with their losses. The resulting disaster from theft or mutilation, however, may be as devastating as any natural disaster for an institution's collections and staff morale, even if nothing life-threatening occurs.

Library books—the good ones, anyway—lead hard but frequently short useful lives. Many disappear, their whereabouts unknown. Others get lost, stolen, or stray. More than a few lose pages or are returned minus their front covers. They develop broken spines, grubby covers, or pages like prune skin, the result of falling into the tub while being read by bathers or being used as shelter during that sudden rainstorm. Just as water-soaked or smoke-damaged materials caused by a hurricane, flood, or fire are lost forever if timely action is not taken to treat them, so stolen materials are lost forever if timely action is not taken to attempt to recover them. In the process, action must be taken to stop thieves from any future activity. Preventing theft and incorporating attempts at theft prevention into a disaster plan should be ranked with natural disasters as threats to the library's security, the collection's integrity, the community's intellectual heritage, and the taxpayers' burden.

Questions about Book Theft

Now that the incidence and pervasiveness of book and other material theft are well established, several questions arise in this context:

- How can one assess or estimate the magnitude of the current problem of theft from libraries?
- How do thefts and mutilations occur? What are the principal methods used by thieves and vandals to appropriate and make off with public property?
- How do incidents of theft and mutilation come to light? That is, in what way do we discover and report our losses?
- Why is library theft not taken seriously by the public? How can we get people to take this problem seriously and get tough about attempting to solve it?

True, the ravages of time and use are enemies of libraries. But a much greater threat exists in the ample evidence that people like us have a nasty habit of swiping the things they want or need and not bringing them back, or perhaps bringing them back only when they feel like it. Sometimes what appears at first to be theft may in fact turn out to be mutilation or a freelance stab at censorship. For example, in 1994 a state university library staff found that things were missing from the collection of women's studies materials in the periodical stacks. Librarians at first thought they were dealing with theft. Later, they found the missing materials in a sadly mutilated condition hidden behind shelved materials elsewhere in the library. In that case, the motivation of the perpetrator seemed to have been neither greed nor the desire to own things without paying for them. Instead, the crime seemed to have been committed by a person or persons opposed to feminism and women's studies and their aims and objectives.

Sometimes the target is not books but equipment. One glaring example was described by columnist Louise Yarnall in the *Los Angeles Times* (Nov. 5, 1997, sec. B8, col. 1). She reported that a UCLA library building was cleaned out of more than $70,000 worth of computers in a smoothly orchestrated theft. The thieves reportedly pulled a van behind the library and systematically removed thirty-two computer processors, laptops, and multimedia computers. Rifling through desks, they found master keys to twelve rooms. The theft effectively halted one UCLA class with more than sixty library science students and postponed another course for three months. The theft may have been an inside job. A faculty member commented, "Technology has become so integral to every aspect of what we do that when it's not there, we realize the new vulnerability we have."

Yarnell added that such theft represents the tip of a chronic problem for universities in the Information Age. In recent years, rings of computer thieves have preyed upon academic institutions, which typically provide students with easy access to technology. The financial loss in these crimes quickly adds up because of the high cost of each computer. The wave of campus computer theft nationwide has been called devastating by the *Chronicle of Higher Education* (June 20, 1997, p. 4).

What Can We Do to Stop Thieves?

As has been made clear, library theft is quite common. The misdeeds of a large number of professional book thieves have come to light.

While much of the evidence is anecdotal, certain threads can be woven together to create a profile of the habitual library thief and prevailing modus operandi. But even that pattern is subject to wide variation.

J. Steven Huntsberry, the Washington State University police detective who solved the Blumberg case, sees no reason why we should just throw up our hands and let it happen. He offers four simple suggestions for preventing any future Blumbergs, Mounts, or Witherells from plying their destructive trade:

- Do not depend on only one line of defense.
- Make things as difficult as possible for potential thieves.
- Protect access and keys.
- Inspire all personnel to be caring, wary, and cooperative.

But despite eternal vigilance, the nation's rare and valuable books are still reported missing at a frightening and depressing rate. For example, you can still read many of the Library of Congress's journals of nineteenth-century expeditions and its rare old botanical encyclopedias and bird books. You just can't see very many of the pictures. Nearly 27,000 valuable maps, engravings, and hand-colored illustrations have been cut out and, librarians suspect, fenced to unscrupulous or unwitting dealers. The stolen plates, worth an estimated $1.75 million, are feeding a burgeoning U.S. market in rare prints and engravings. And approximately 300,000 books are missing from LC, according to the latest tally, which accounts for the new, harsher policy of stack admittance now in force. Many of the Library's books are rare, old, richly illustrated, and salable. Their loss or mutilation is emblematic of a more general hemorrhage for public, private, university, and governmental libraries across the nation as poorly protected, irreplaceable older materials disappear.

Thieves are becoming more sophisticated, using technology to achieve their purposes. If a thief is careful, the odds are still pretty good that he or she will not get caught. So what else can we do to slow this bleeding away of our libraries' life's blood? Here are a few ideas:

Treat all materials (e.g., books, periodicals, media, equipment) with stop-loss preventives, such as indelible property marking if possible. Sometimes a simple property stamp and an ink pad may serve to protect and identify library property and deter those who would steal it.

Security equipment and staff should be a significant part of the library's operating budget.

Security expenditure should be the same proportionately for all libraries. The goal in every case is good security.

Good security for materials also helps to deter nuisance incidents and in-library crime against people.

In addition, library staff may have to disabuse both visitors and staff of the long-standing notion that the library is a "safe haven," despite the possibility that awareness of this reality may negatively affect both circulation figures and library visits. Posting a highly visible warning sign to the effect that library users should be vigilant against purse snatchers and other thieves may help remind patrons of inevitable dangers and risks without occasioning undue alarm.

Keep Current on Theft

Because many rare book librarians are hesitant about reporting their losses out of embarrassment or fear of frightening donors, other librarians cannot keep up by reading the professional literature. That's why we need to publicize and be willing to talk about our losses. If we don't talk to one another, individuals or gangs—some working from shopping lists of desiderata—and occasionally assigning roles to confederates (e.g., one or more to distract library personnel while the thief is taking things) will keep on stealing books and manuscripts and selling them to shady collectors or fences.

Make Security a Priority

Perhaps it's a question of priorities: Is the primary concern of the library to ensure unlimited access to the library collections or is it to enforce rules such as making the existing collection available on demand, even if that means restrictions on personal liberties within the building? One way to look at the problem, of course, is to embrace the argument that book theft is actually a *tribute* to the value and utility of libraries and that if no one ever stole or mutilated anything, it would demonstrate the lack of need for libraries. Such a view may offer us a modicum of cold comfort when we finally get around to inventory and discover that we've lost vital chunks of our collection.

Security precautions are a price to pay for having material when people want it or need it. Patrons must be made to see that precautions are for their benefit. Historically and even ironically, the worst repeat offenders are scholars, students, and faculty members, legitimate library users whose activities are above suspicion and impossible to monitor. Effective security, however, means that *no one* has unlimited access and no exceptions are made. Commercial stores don't allow such unlimited access; why, then, should libraries?

Are library materials in public institutions community property? Is taking an item from a public or university library a crime against "everybody"? What does the word "public" actually mean? Until we can answer these questions and figure out how to deal with transgressors, we will continue to be plagued. The sad but inevitable bottom line emerging from all the foregoing documentation is that the dedicated, resourceful, and accomplished thief will be successful if he or she wants to badly enough. There is no such thing as perfect library security. Technology, no matter how sophisticated, can be defeated—it's people and their attitudes that must be overcome.

Keep Track

How do thefts and mutilations come to light? Slowly, in a majority of cases, and never in all too many. Frequently, a library is unaware that materials have actually left the premises until a telephone call or Internet message from an alert book dealer or law enforcement agent arouses suspicion. Recovery of stolen materials often becomes the first signal that something is wrong. On the other hand, evidence of forced intrusion or apprehension of a person in the act may abruptly signal a theft or mutilation. More subtle indications such as altered bibliographic records or substitutions may be the signal that a staff member has stolen valuable materials—another example in the rich tapestry of inside jobs.

It is possible that regular inventories may reveal a systematic pattern of loss without providing any explanation whatsoever. The most difficult discovery to grapple with is what insurance adjustors call "mysterious disappearance." That is when an important and valuable item that is seldom used from a rare book collection may one day be missing when it is called for without any sign of intrusion or other irregularity. This may be the hardest type of theft to detect because feelings of denial must be overcome before the librarian is emotionally able to take positive action. The mutilation of bound periodicals and art books also may not be discovered until someone tries to use them, and then it's too late to do anything about the problem.

Library Security Officers

As a first recommendation, every library director or board should appoint a Library Security Officer (LSO) and establish a Security Planning Group. The LSO and this group should work with the institution's public relations personnel and establish contact with local law enforcement before any problems arise. It is also important to establish contact with local book dealers to alert them to ways to identify stolen materials. If an institution is an academic or independent research library, the name of the LSO should be reported to the ACRL-RBMS Security Committee for inclusion on the LSO list available from the ACRL office. This also makes the library eligible for participation in the LSO distribution list, which reports incidents of theft. It was established in 1994 and is still published by the ACRL-RBMS Security Committee. A list of other preventive measures might include:

- Ensuring that collections are indelibly marked in some way that displays proof of ownership.
- Maintaining accurate catalog or other records of ownership.
- Eliminating cataloging backlogs.
- Reviewing collections to identify rare or vulnerable materials in open stacks areas.
- Conducting regular inventories of collections.
- Following careful and ethical hiring and management practices.

Ideal Remedial Measures

In reaction to evidence of the deliberate and widespread theft of library materials, some research libraries have taken steps to strengthen their security with the aim of thwarting future Blumbergs. Some of the better endowed already boast of a state-of-the-art system, designed to thwart and frustrate would-be library thieves. Such a security system would have all or most of the following parts:

A zoned perimeter and closed-circuit TV system, including an after-hours combination of motion detectors, closed-circuit television (CCTV) monitors, and VCRs, with video display monitors hooked up to CCTV cameras and video recorders, and a video switcher selecting what to display on the monitors.

Emergency fire exit protection at all entrances, which includes magnetic door contacts and a closed-circuit TV monitor permanently trained on each exit, with the video camera automatically activated whenever the door is opened.

A Halon (or other oxygen-removing) fire suppression system and water detectors for all special collections areas and vaults.

A fire detection system including sprinklers in all rooms except special collections vaults.

A panic button that silently notifies local police or campus security, located on the staff side of the main service desk.

Every desk supplied with a detailed floor plan showing the location of security devices and zones.

Rekeying of the entire library, with employee signatures on file for all keys.

Special collections areas accessed only through locked doors. The outer door is always kept closed unless being used and is locked at closing. The inner door is always locked as well. Entrance is gained by a buzzer answered by a member of the curatorial staff who secures, authenticates, and retains the ID card of the patron until all materials are returned.

One option for libraries—not without a variety of costs—is a high degree of tight security such as that boasted by government and military installations, even though many patrons find such measures to be intimidating and highly user-unfriendly. For example, what if the library decided that, in order to get serious about security, it would institute the following measures commonly found on active military bases?

- Guards at all access points (armed or otherwise).
- Photo ID for admission.
- Retinal, fingerprint/palm print, or voice recognition scanners.
- Passwords for computer use (changed frequently).

- Need-to-know basis for information.
- An authorization code for use of equipment and materials.
- Public and certain knowledge of penalties.
- Surveillance cameras.
- Intrusion alarms, heat sensors, motion detectors, etc.
- Searching of belongings at exits to the building.

Other Measures

But even with such harsh, expensive, and labor-intensive measures, it's a good bet that things would still continue to be missing, albeit at a somewhat slower pace. Sadly, and perhaps more to the point, a competent and clever library thief probably will be successful—sooner or later—in defeating even these measures designed to "bulletproof" your library's security. But bowing to the inevitability of loss doesn't in any way imply that we are powerless to stop thieves from preying on our libraries. At the very least, we can take several steps to make their task more difficult, which may even have the happy effect of deterring them completely.

Read the literature of library theft. Don't assume you know all the answers or have even thought of all the questions. For example, does acquiring multiple copies of items frequently stolen reduce theft? Do slow growth rate collections experience a higher rate of loss? Would putting sought-after items in reserve collections under tighter control dramatically reduce losses? The answer is usually "no" to all those questions! Sadly, the major deterrent to such theft is reducing access to our collections by outsiders. Only our immediate patron population should be granted direct access. All others should be required to use interlibrary loan. It's a sad commentary on the world that such steps are necessary, but there it is. And very little can be done to prevent a trusted employee from subverting the process and making off with whatever he or she likes.

Library staff members universally cringe at the very thought of the tiresome chore of inventory shelf reading. Anyone who has performed this odious task knows just how time consuming and boring it is. It is, however, still the most effective device in identifying what is missing and which subjects require greater surveillance. Hand in hand with surveillance goes the shelflist catalog, which many libraries either poorly maintain or have completely abandoned.

Well-advertised prosecutions of those caught red-handed can help, too. California's Alameda County Library in 1985 started referring delinquent patrons to the district attorney for criminal prosecution of theft, averaging two to five cases a month. One borrower who had thirteen overdue books and ignored all warnings was charged, fingerprinted, and sentenced to a week of community service in the library. One family tried to start their own cookbook collection, often visiting several of the county's libraries and taking out over 100 books a week. When they were caught, they pled guilty and were billed for $1,200. They quickly returned over half the items and worked out a schedule to pay the fines.

In 1990, Massachusetts enacted a law for people who steal, deface, or fail to return library materials. The law provides for fines up to $25,000 and five years in jail for library materials valued at more than $250 that are stolen or mutilated. For overdues, there is a maximum fine of $500 and no jail sentence. But such measures can backfire. The reaction to prosecutions under the Massachusetts law—outrage by some more vocal members of the public—was mocked in the press. But despite both criticism and satire, there was a good and demonstrable need for this law—it was estimated that Massachusetts public libraries were collectively losing $1.1 million yearly in library materials. It was pointed out that one small-town library, serving a population of 23,000, was losing $12,000 in missing books yearly.

Researchers often find library procedures cumbersome and detrimental to their needs. They become frustrated with tiresome routines, and their frustration can result in theft. It has been suggested that professors cue their students about visiting distant libraries: They need to call or write ahead of the visit and alert librarians there concerning the scope of their research. Libraries need to provide special space and services to serious researchers. Historians have complained of nonexistent or inadequate space and of long waits for library staff to locate needed documents. One major library requires twenty-four hours notice to provide historical material. Researchers complain of being limited to a few items at a time, of having to complete many borrowing forms, of the lack of microfilming or photocopying facilities, and so on. There needs to be a better understanding of the problem of theft by researchers and of the frustrations of busy researchers by librarians. Many researchers view librarians as impeding scholarship rather than assisting or promoting it. And getting tough with those who do not play by the rules, while often mocked or derided, at least will go a long way toward ensuring that the book you want will be in and available to you when you want it. A cartoon appearing in the *Saturday Review* for November 1980 shows a librarian talking on the telephone as she stands before library bookstacks, on one of which the sign "Quiet!" is posted. Next to her, bound and gagged, and securely tied to a chair, sits a young child. The caption reads: "I'm not kidding around anymore, Mrs. Whitman. You have our book. We have your son!"

Library Rules

Suppose we decide that we are through hoping and wishing for a better world, and that from now on, we are going to protect our collections by creating and enforcing a set of universal rules designed to reduce or even stop library crime. Among these might be the following:

Upon entering, a patron presents identification to a security officer. This identification card is retained until the patron leaves the building.

Outside the reference or reading room, all coats, briefcases, notebooks, envelopes, and so on are placed in lockers.

The patron must show and surrender his or her identification card for entry to the reference or reading room if that was not done upon entering the library.

The patron is limited to one box of material or book or folder open at a time. All materials used must be in plain sight, and placed flat on the desk, not tilted on edge.

Library staff will be encouraged to walk among library users, actively paying attention to what they are doing and unconcerned with whether they are perceived as being snoops.

After the patron has used protected materials, his or her belongings will be searched.

When exiting the room, the user's identification card is returned by the security officer.

The trade-off implicit in such rules poses a question for the general public, which might lead to different answers from different library users. Assuming that the library could afford such labor-intensive procedures, would the public accept such harsh measures? In other words, would library users voluntarily give up some of their present privacy and confidentiality rights and liberties in exchange for a reasonable expectation that the enhanced security is ultimately beneficial for everyone who uses the library?

Some logical and precautionary recommendations include the guidelines from the ACRL's Rare Books and Manuscripts Section Security Committee shown in figure 2.3. These steps can be taken to help maximize the library's ability to keep its books, or at least help the library pursue them when they are removed without authorization.

- Before thefts occur, appoint a senior staff member Library Security Officer to represent the library with legal counsel and campus security forces.
- Form a library security committee.
- Work with local administrative and community law enforcement officials to decide who is responsible for apprehension and prosecution.
- Establish networks and good relationships with book dealers and others involved in rare books.
- Pay constant attention to improving all aspects of library security.
- When a theft is discovered, protect the scene of the theft or loss to preserve evidence. Insist that no one contaminate evidence left behind.
- Notify the appropriate local police, sheriff, and investigation departments as soon as possible. The longer you wait, the less chance there is for recovery of missing materials.
- Cooperate closely with law enforcement.
- Take advantage of the new federal crime bill that makes any museum theft over $1 million value a federal crime, warranting FBI attention.
- Gather documents, descriptions, and photographs of what is missing. Provide police with a list of what is missing as soon as possible.
- Help police understand who traffics in those items and where and how to make a positive identification of the items.
- Use press coverage to your advantage. Control press information through one or two persons. Use publicity to pressure thieves and motivate recoveries. Note that ransoms are only marginally effective.

FIGURE 2.3
Rules for Optimizing the Recovery of Lost or Stolen Materials

- Notify stolen cultural property files:

FBI National Stolen Art File	202-324-4192
Interpol—Washington, D.C.	202-616-9000
Art Loss Register	718-879-1780
Interloc (books and manuscripts)	Interloc@shaynet.com
Canadian Heritage Information Network	can-service@immedia.ca
Ex Libris (rare books and manuscripts)	exlibris@rutvml.bitnet
AB Bookman's Weekly (books and manuscripts)	201-772-0020
Journal of Field Archeology (archeological)	617-353-2357

- Follow up on police notifications and investigations. Report suggestions and new information. Periodically check progress.
- Internet users may use a new resource called TARGET, a list of cultural property protection materials. (The name is an acronym for Tools And Resources Getting Extremely Timely.) opsl.listond@ic.si.edu

The Law

Perhaps more stringent local, state, and federal laws and stricter sentences for library thieves are required. Much ado about nothing? Perhaps, but it is worth repeating that when the aberrant few among us take advantage of the free access to collections by stealing archival materials, they are stealing our cultural heritage from us all. Let's call thefts of the magnitude of those described here what they are: felonies. And let's call the people who perpetrate these crimes what they are: criminals who must be made accountable to society.

Circles of Security

There is normally no unified or consistent security apparatus between libraries or among libraries, booksellers, and law enforcement agencies. E-mail networks have been created for members to communicate and for posting warnings. Closer working relationships between librarians and antiquarian book dealers would help by promoting the sharing of information. The ACRL's Library Security Committee has promulgated guidelines for what to do before, during, and after theft problems. Model legislation for ensuring legal and law enforcement support is either on the books or pending in about forty states, which have enacted measures in the last ten years dealing with library theft and library violence.

Libraries must form and join electronic networks of their own and talk to one another. Patterns may develop and lead to arrests. One problem with this form of communication, however, is that libraries don't really like to talk about their losses for fear of alienating the public, discouraging potential donors, and having to confess the embarrassing facts of lack of due diligence and vigilance. Many security experts advocate, instead, concentric circles of security. The master plan is to impede and frustrate the suspect to the extent that he or she either becomes discouraged or makes a mistake. The concentric configuration should begin outside the building, and as the thief moves closer to the heart of the rare materials or other valuables collection, it becomes more difficult to penetrate the library's defenses.

Despite the predatory nature of some patrons, libraries should do all they can to keep materials available. There is, however, lack of consensus among staff members as to what the balance between access and protection should be. Some staffers will say that it is preferable to take one's losses while guaranteeing availability; others think that safety and security outweigh the desires and needs of patrons.

Effective deterrents to theft and mutilation exist, but lack of funding may preclude their purchase and implementation. Even when funds are available, there is sometimes lack of commitment to security enforcement at administrative levels. Without the firm dedication of city, county, university officials, and library administrators, there is little chance for the library to do what is necessary to make it difficult for thieves and vandals to ply their trades.

Of course, just catching thieves and others who have misappropriated library property is only step 1. Step 2 involves follow-through, which may include willingness to press charges in court. There is often a lack of awareness or indifference to the problem of library theft on the part of the criminal justice system, whose officers may feel they have more serious things to worry about. In many communities, moreover, librarians must also contend with general public indifference to library theft and mutilation as a crime. If people outside of libraries view library crime with an attitude of "These things happen" or "What's the big deal about a few stolen books?" attempts to avoid or combat theft and mutilation are going to be difficult.

Why prosecute, then, since going to court to recover materials or punish thieves necessarily entails publicity, and the risk of others deciding that preying on libraries is a high-profit/low-risk way to make money? We must be mindful not to set precedents that will lead people to think they can take advantage of us. We should be well mannered, but we need to be tough. The seriousness of library theft has reached a point where people agree we must start publicizing it and be more aggressive about it. What's at risk is too great for us to sit passively, wishing that people wouldn't swipe our books. We have to be willing to fight to hold onto them.

CHAPTER 3

Problem Behaviors in Libraries

Crime costs Americans at least $450 billion a year, according to the most comprehensive survey ever done on the price of violence. The report, done for the Justice department, is the first to try to measure the cost of intangible factors, with crimes like murder, rape and robbery.

—*New York Times,* April 22, 1996

The objectives of this chapter are to:

- discuss the various aspects of public safety in libraries, including issues of public access and personal safety
- review various methods of preventing library violence
- discuss the library's reactions to the special plight of problem homeless patrons
- explain the elements in a workable master security plan for the library

The Public Safety Problem

This chapter discusses problems, preparedness, and precautions for personal safety in libraries as public buildings in the hope and expectation that readers, acknowledging their potential difficulty, will be at least forewarned and forearmed.

Thankfully, most people's mental concept of a library does not entail jarring images of violence, risk, danger, fear, or anxiety—or they'd never show up at all. Libraries are normally perceived as tranquil places, where one may spend quiet hours in contemplation and study, and may feel free to find—or lose—one's way. Demonstrably, however, library staff and patrons are increasingly at risk. The sampling of violent incidents reported in this chapter should show that while library crime against people is rare, it does occur with alarming—and depressing—frequency.

Libraries, whatever else they are, are also workplaces. A study of violence in the workplace conducted by the National Institute for Occupational Safety and Health (NIOSH) revealed that 73 percent of workplace homicides reported in the United States in 1993 were robbery-related, and 53 percent of victims did not know their attackers.

Are libraries, then, unsafe places to be? Not really. Generally, crimes committed in libraries are isolated incidents, and libraries are normally safe, secure places both to work in and visit. However, while safekeeping of a library's collection and equipment is obviously very important, personal safety is even more important, for the lives of staff and patrons may be at stake.

Therefore, security precautions are necessary and should be considered as part of the price to be paid for working with people. Such precautions may be annoying and will often slow down procedures, but all staff and patrons must be made to see that the precautions are for their benefit, and that without the precautions, they'd be more at risk and vulnerable. Unfortunately, in this imprecise and often risky world, there is no such thing as absolute library security. Librarians and library staff can never have an absolute lock on personal safety for their patrons or staffs, but there are still ways to increase the odds of deterring or preventing incidents.

Clearly, there's a basic trade-off between individual liberties (e.g., totally open, unsupervised reading rooms and stacks) and restricted access to information (e.g., restricted access, closed and secure areas, sign-ins, surveillance cameras, security guards). In addition to posing restrictions on personal freedoms, such a trade-off involves choices between what we can do to deter crime and the demands such measures make on the library's budget, normally stretched thin enough as it is. This also means a trade-off between money spent on library services and materials and the growing share of the budget that goes to protecting people and materials.

The library literature over the last two decades has contained numerous stories dealing entirely or in part with safety and security concerns of those who work in, manage, or visit libraries. Taken out of context, such anecdotal evidence could create in the reader's mind a frightening mosaic of risk, peril, and danger. The following are but a few violent incidents reported over the past several years:

- 1993: A Georgia librarian was murdered while working alone in a small-town library. The next day, a sixteen-year-old youth from a nearby town was arrested and charged with armed robbery, murder, and felony murder. His motive, he explained, was the desire to possess the staff member's expensive jewelry.
- 1993: A patron killed two reference librarians in a branch of a California public library. The gunman was a transient, homeless person who was wounded in a subsequent shootout with police and fell to his death from the roof of the building. He was described as a regular patron of the library. He entered just before closing, carrying a handgun. Without warning, he opened fire on several employees, fatally wounding the two librarians. The assailant was described as having no criminal or psychiatric history, but it was subsequently revealed that he'd had a grudge against the county, saying he had suffered extreme emotional and mental distress after being falsely imprisoned for twenty-eight days when mistaken for a fugitive from another state.
- 1994: A gunman, carrying a pistol and what he said was a bomb, took eighteen people hostage at the Salt Lake City Public Library and created a very real threat of massive loss of life and property inside the building. An alert off-duty deputy, who managed to sneak in among the hostages, subsequently shot and killed the gunman. Luckily, no hostages were hurt, despite a tense five-and-one-half-hour standoff, but the bomb found on the dead man's person proved to be "live" and big enough to blow up the whole building.
- 1997: A library clerk working in a branch of a West Virginia public library system was beaten to death by a young man who had been harassing several of the women on the library staff by making obscene phone calls and exposing himself to female staff members. The victim had complained to police a week earlier that the man had been harassing her.

Such news items, taken out of context, could lead to the unwarranted conclusion that libraries are not places where one may feel safe to spend one's energies on the intellectual or recreational tasks at hand without undue concern for personal safety. Perhaps the situation is analogous to reading an isolated clipping concerned with an air travel disaster and concluding that getting on a plane is so risky as to be tantamount to suicide. Publicity is all a matter of scale. Some people—including noted celebrities—live in abject terror of flying because of well-publicized tragedies that occupy the front page of every newspaper for weeks after every airliner tragedy. They prefer to make their way more slowly by using ground transportation. They infer from lurid accounts of such incidents that they happen all the time. And just as people fear being in airliner crashes because every time one falls out of the sky it's a page-one story and the lead item on every television newscast, so library crimes tend to be long remembered because they are so rare and thus so widely publicized. Yet one does not read very much about security-related incidents of crime in libraries precisely because incidents of trouble are so rare. It's only the newsworthy and, all too often, sensational events that get publicity.

Are libraries, then, unsafe places to be? While the above reports of library crime are isolated incidents, and libraries are normally safe, secure places both to work and play, they are still public buildings and workplaces. And workplace violence is demonstrably on the rise all over the nation. In chapter 1, we were careful to distinguish between crime against library materials or other property and crime against people in the library. In the sense of removing library materials without following procedures, or keeping them beyond their borrowing period, the public is occasionally guilty of crimes or at least misdemeanors. But if one considers physical or violent crime in the library —crime against people—the magnitude of the offense is much greater, and the transgressor is normally a member of one of the following four categories of people:

- Patrons disgruntled or enraged with library policies or with staff members' attitude or behavior.
- Persons with irrational behaviors, mental problems, domestic disturbances, sometimes augmented and exacerbated by drug or alcohol abuse.
- Former employees, seething with resentment and looking for a payback for being demoted, passed over for promotion, fired, or downsized.

- Criminals with or without weapons intending to use violence to achieve their goals.

As a public institution in an increasingly violent society, every library must take steps to create a safe environment for staff and patrons. And while no library or institution of any size is immune to threats, prevention of most violent events or threats is possible with careful planning and cooperation from employees. Should violence or an unplanned emergency take place, minimization of the subsequent damage is equally possible if staff will learn and bear in mind some rules.

The problem of violence in public places, of course, is not confined to libraries. (Post offices come to mind as much more unsafe, particularly for the postal workers themselves.) Workplace homicide is now the third leading cause of death on the job, with an estimated 1,400 people killed at work each year, according to the National Institute for Occupational Safety and Health. In New York, 69 percent of the 177 workers reported killed on the job in 1991 were the result of homicide, mostly by handguns. Why do crimes take place in library buildings? Library buildings are no more immune to violence than other public facilities. In fact, their unique characteristics may actually invite or create a favorable environment for violence:

- They are normally the only public buildings open evenings and weekends, and that fact attracts people who have no place else to go.
- Few libraries have metal detectors installed at the front doors, and little ability to search visitors.
- Many libraries cannot afford security staff or off-duty police officers on-site. In the absence of such controls, criminals feel free to do whatever they like.
- Evening staff also have to deal with patrons leaving the library late at closing time, knowing that they must follow the patrons out ten minutes later.

Preventing Violence in the Library

What can be done to curtail or at least reduce the risk of violence in the library? There are precautions that can be implemented that may serve to lessen the threat of violence. For example, the library could install metal detectors at all public entrances to the building. Why not? They're already part of the interior landscape of every airport, and while they may slow down the procedure of getting to one's plane, they are universally accepted now as the price of feeling more secure. Libraries (with few exceptions) have no metal detectors at their doors; anyone is free to enter with anything they happen to be carrying concealed or in plain sight. But metal detectors are both expensive and labor-intensive in that they require personnel to spring into action when a weapon or other suspicious metallic object is detected. Also, they are psychologically problematic in that some people resent the intrusion and the corresponding implication that they are not to be trusted. Finally, they are not foolproof. An umbrella, a cane, or even a library book, for example, may be employed as a lethal weapon, yet it is quite easy to enter a library with one, or, in the latter case, to find the place filled with them. So, given that potential weapons are everywhere and no attempts to prohibit them are feasible or possible, what else can a library do to improve its security posture?

Hire Security

One preventive against unbridled misconduct is to hire security guards and charge them, among other duties, with examining the property of those entering and leaving the building. Sometimes security guards may require patrons to check their bags and other possessions in lockers; in others (this, too, is labor-intensive and thus stressful on stretched budgets), they may be granted the right to search briefcases, book bags, and other luggage on demand. Besides being a considerable expense, security guards tend to be more intent on finding books and other library property leaving the building illegally than they are on discovering concealed weapons being brought into the building, although both are important. Additionally, depending on local laws and ordinances, library employees may have no legal right to search the persons or belongings of their visitors, and insisting on doing so may leave the library legally vulnerable to lawsuits.

Restrict Access

Another action that makes good sense is to establish and maintain areas of restricted access. Such rules may be used to keep all unauthorized people out of some areas, or to prevent certain groups of people from entering off-limits parts of the building. While crime may occur anywhere on the premises or on the surrounding grounds, the largest proportion of library crime actually takes place in the non-public areas where perpetrators are not supposed to be. Keeping the public out of unauthorized areas by making it impossible, or at least difficult, for them to enter will help reduce library crime.

In some libraries, only borrowers who can produce and display valid and current borrower's cards are privileged to use the building. In other libraries, a current ID must be produced before the patron is granted admission to stack areas. Every little bit helps. Closed stacks, for example—still standard operating procedure in some academic libraries—curtail the right to browse freely, as only authorized people have the right to do so. The question then becomes whether it is worth giving up individual rights in favor of enhanced personal safety. As said before, it's a matter of trade-off.

Be Aware of Building Flaws

In contrast to commercial establishments, libraries are usually easier places for criminal or deviant behavior. There are several reasons for this. Libraries are first of all deliberately free for all to enter. Additionally, many libraries are housed in old buildings with poor lighting. Many newer structures have been intentionally designed to provide charming, sequestered, out-of-the-way nooks and other places for quiet reading, contemplation, and study. Even if older buildings are rehabbed or renovated, aisles and alcoves are often secluded because people like them that way. There is limited constant hustle and bustle because people favor quiet in libraries, and quiet contributes to a place to concentrate undisturbed.

In the past, most libraries were designed to house closed stacks, and were not intended for the public to browse; therefore, stack security was not much of an issue. Closed stacks, however, meant that staff members had to get items for patrons to take home or use in the reading rooms. The stacks did not have to be short enough to see over, around, or through, since they were intended for staff use only. Patrons had to submit call slips and wait for their books, while the stack areas were the province of speedy runners who were the only ones normally allowed into the book storage area.

Gradually, due to changing times and changing user expectations, the stacks of almost all public and academic libraries were opened to the public. Thus they became ideal hangouts for thieves, thrill seekers, sexual cruisers, vandals, and others bent on mischief or mayhem. In seeking to become more accessible to their users, libraries opened their stacks to browsers, which necessarily reduced the overall security level in favor of open access. Can libraries with open stacks afford to staff each level or patrol the building's areas and spaces constantly to deter unwanted behavior? Clearly, the answer is almost always no. So the stacks have become great places to hide. Even unwarranted spying, surveillance, and monitoring of activity in the building may not actually overcome the ability of determined persons to commit violent acts. Even a library equipped with multiple surveillance cameras cannot expect to be able to monitor everyone's behavior everywhere in the building at all times.

Library design is another unfortunate factor in encouraging some types of problem patron behavior. Some of the newest libraries feature recesses, alcoves, study carrels, and other remote spots where surveillance by staff (or even security guards) is infrequent, unlikely, or just not possible, especially when the library is short-staffed. Another reason that libraries attract potential criminals is because they do not charge admission. Everyone is free to enter without challenge, interrogation, or proof of financial solvency. Nor can most libraries afford frequent security patrols—the cost of employing security guards is prohibitive for smaller libraries and difficult even for larger ones. Because library buildings are so accessible, in fact, they invite problems. They provide a free, safe haven for those who want to read or study or think, but they also cater to people who seek convenient places for their criminal, antisocial, or deviant behavior.

Establish Rules

It is a fact of life that no one in a library building is completely safe from attack by determined or demented individuals bent on doing mischief or harm to others. It is, after all, in the librarian's professional nature to want to meet, interact with, and help patrons. But the bad guys are out there, and sometimes in here among us. Every librarian at one time or another has uttered words to the effect that, "This would be a really great place to work if we didn't have to unlock the doors every morning at nine o'clock to let the thundering herd enter." But public service entails public access, and an element of danger comes with the territory. In essence, we sacrifice a measure of our personal safety in exchange for the free and open interaction of a public agency. That may be our decision, but keep in mind that we sacrifice the potential safety of our patrons, too. Libraries cannot afford to be cavalier about public safety, figuring that patrons enter at their own risk. They must place the welfare of their visitors at the top of the list of imperatives.

In today's society, library workers can find themselves subjected to public abuse, and they may even become the target of actual or threatened violence. In addressing this problem, many library ideals for providing aesthetically pleasing and easily accessible libraries may have to give way to more practical safety considerations. What are some preventive measures that may be useful in enhancing building, staff, and internal security measures? First of all, you must specify what constitutes unacceptable conduct or behavior within the building. Figure 3.1 represents one large public library's attempt to specify prohibited or proscribed behavior:

Your cooperation is requested in refraining from:

- Loitering or sleeping on library property.
- Gambling, soliciting, or campaigning on library property.
- Eating and drinking in the library.
- Use of typewriters and playing of radios, tape players, and televisions without use of personal earphones in authorized areas.
- Fighting, running, or "horseplay."
- Use of loud, obscene, or abusive language.
- Smoking except in authorized areas.
- Bringing in animals other than guide dogs.
- Inappropriate dress, for example, bare chests and feet.
- Carrying of weapons or dangerous objects.
- Public drunkenness or use of alcohol.

FIGURE 3.1
Rules of Conduct for the Detroit Public Library

- All sexual acts and sexually deviant behavior.
- Mutilation or damage of library materials, equipment, and property.
- Use of drugs, hallucinogens, and other chemical substances.
- Placing feet on library furniture.
- Leaving children unattended.

The above constitutes a decent attempt at a list of prohibited behaviors, perhaps, but do you notice what's missing? Look more closely and it'll probably come to you. The list, comprehensive as it may otherwise seem in its coverage, says nothing at all about odor (an issue that will be returned to later in this book), which may prove to be a serious lapse in spelling out intolerable behaviors.

Prepare a Security Manual

The most fundamental and inexpensive precaution in personal safety in libraries is an explicit, nondiscriminatory code of acceptable conduct that recognizes the rights of patrons and the enforceable laws regarding aberrant behavior. Building security procedures must be explicit and thorough enough to deal with problem patrons, yet sufficiently flexible to cover unusual situations and ways in which staff are expected to react. There is no simple template for what your library should have in a security manual (which should be drawn up in conjunction with legal counsel), but at minimum, it ought to include the following:

- the rationale and procedures for security guard training
- a program for surveillance of the library building at regular intervals, either by security staff or a designated staff monitor
- selection criteria for security guards and monitors
- studies of staffing patterns and procedures
- behavior guidelines and other appropriate library policy statements
- where affordable, theft detection, security alarms, and other preventive systems.

Problem Behaviors in Library Patrons

Plus ça change, plus c'est la même chose. (The more things change, the more they remain the same.)

—Old French saying

Some things never seem to change. It's a pretty safe bet that, thousands of years ago, on the day that the world's first library opened to the public, one of the first guys through the door was a problem patron of one variety or another. Volume 1:5 of *Library & Archival Security* (1975) contained a brief article listing "Staff and Patron Safety: Eight Most Common Problems."

- Perverts
- Youths threatening malicious mischief
- Loitering and vagrancy
- Incidents between the library building and people's cars, or in a nearby parking lot
- Patrons sneaking into restricted areas
- Mentally unbalanced patrons
- Threat of personal injury
- Muggings

The sad lesson learned from reading this old list is that, after all the years of technological triumphs since its publication, conditions and problems haven't really changed very much. Nor have they changed significantly in well over a century. The noted nineteenth-century English author and critic G. K. Chesterton once wrote of his conviction that every London-area family with a madman among its number must drop him off in the sedate precincts of the British Museum for the day; otherwise, how could so many bizarre and eccentric people congregate in one spot every afternoon?

In Western society, all public and most academic libraries are intentionally open to all who seek to enter them—which constitutes both the best and worst feature of the institution. That is, the best thing about the library is that anyone—regardless of race, creed, age, gender, ethnicity, wherewithal, stated or unstated reason for the visit, property ownership, or identification—may enter and partake of the services and collections. At the same time, the sheer extent of that freedom can be the worst thing about the library, because not everyone who enters does so with the intent of using the building, its facilities, and its materials for accepted, library-related purposes. In fact, many public libraries have become—if not by charter, then by custom and usage—magnets for the troubled, havens for the homeless, and social gathering places for legitimate and illegitimate activities. The public library is commonly seen as a place that welcomes all comers and cannot legitimately turn them away, so long as they refrain from objectionable behavior, do not snore while they sleep, and fake it well enough to look as if they are reading when someone observes them. Even severely offensive personal odor or lack of a permanent address do not seem to be universal criteria for exclusion or expulsion, as recent court cases have proved. Yet, because of this very openness, libraries may be frequented by thieves, vandals, disturbers of the peace, drug users and vendors, firebugs, sexual deviates, the mentally ill, and all those with a nasty attitude they want to take out on the world. And while the vast preponderance of a library's problem patrons are not bent on harm or destruction of human life, many of them visit the library only to prey upon and destroy our collections, which hurts all of us.

But aggressive or violent behavior is even more of a threat. To the end of combating such behavior, a good, comprehensive behavior policy is mandatory. A behavior policy provides guidelines for determining and managing unacceptable behavior. It protects library patrons and staff from abusive actions of others that undermine the purpose of the library. If it's done right, such a policy is at the same time easy to understand, consistent, equitable, and fair. Having a written policy also provides safety and security officials with the authority to intervene when called to the library, and it may be used as a reference document when individuals challenge rules or seek to fight their expulsion. The purpose of such a policy is to ensure that all problem behaviors are defined and lawfully prohibited, with subsequent actions and reactions prescribed. Specific issues to be addressed in such a policy will vary with the library's circumstances, and can be facilitated by consulting staff, campus police, and other officials, and by examining other libraries' successful policies and procedures.

> We ought to get hazard pay and wear firearms. . . . We try to forewarn new clerks about what to expect, but there's really no way to prepare them for what it's like. People yell vulgarities and

> threats at them. Some jump up and wave their arms, conducting an invisible orchestra. Others talk to themselves. We get people who are infested with vermin, who smell so bad that it makes us sick to our stomachs and who chase our legitimate patrons out of the room. . . . You never know when one of these people is going to flip. One man threatened to strangle me. I never did figure out why. They don't need any reason. . . . The subject has been the profession's skeleton in the closet.
>
> —Carol Eaton, *American Libraries,* October 1977

Problem behaviors may reasonably be divided, according to the severity of the activity, into two broad classes: threatening and non-threatening. It would be nice if there were a clear-cut line of demarcation between those categories. However, since the distinction between them is frequently blurred, a beleaguered or highly stressed staff member may guess wrong about which is which, or a given individual may be both at the same time, or first one and then the other, as a confrontation escalates.

Class 1 Problem Patrons

Nuisances/Non-Threatening Behaviors

- beggars
- hustlers and freelance salespersons
- idlers, loafers, loiterers, and vagrants
- drunks (the peaceful kind)
- eaters, snackers
- finger tappers or knuckle crackers
- laughers, loud talkers, loud yawners
- coughers, wheezers, singers, hummers, sleepers, snorers
- hyperactives
- loud whisperers
- persons who appear to be talking to themselves
- pet owners who bring animals into the library
- pick up artists and those who "hit on" people minding their own business
- malodorous but otherwise innocuous persons

monopolizers of staff time
lonely seniors desperately craving human contact
mutilators and defacers of library property
censors who seek to remove objectionable parts from books or magazines
moralists, preachers, and proselytizers
voyeurs, starers
public telephone monopolizers
thieves and pickpockets
compulsive rearrangers and tidiers
latchkey children with nowhere else to go
neckers, persons engaged in inappropriate (but legal) amorous pursuits
persons seeking consensual sexual contact
those who won't leave quietly at the close of the business day
practical jokers
graffiti artists (also called "taggers")
rule breakers (e.g., defiant smokers, fire-alarm pullers)
the homeless (who may be any or all of the other types)

What do these diverse types of "Class 1" patrons have in common? While all the listed behaviors can be extremely annoying, most of the individuals committing them in the library can safely be dealt with by unarmed staff members, even if all such people cannot necessarily be considered harmless, and thus worthy of being either indulged or overlooked.

Class 2 Problem Patrons

Safety/Security Threats, Behaviors That Pose a Serious and Real Threat to Staff and Other Patrons

drug sellers, buyers, and users
fighters and those looking to pick quarrels with others
angry or aggressive people
delinquents, who may or may not be gang members
the mentally disturbed

weapon carriers
sexual deviants or sexual predators
exhibitionists
verbal abusers
persons who use profanity aloud
arsonists
extortionists
vandals
child molesters and pedophiles
touchers
fetishists
paranoids, who may also be schizophrenics
those who use public rooms or telephones to conduct illegal business dealings

Unfortunately, even when a person may be classified as belonging to the latter category, a clear sense of what to do (or do first) about his or her behavior is not always obvious, or even agreed upon. Most problem patrons are of the Class 1 nonviolent variety, and, however annoying they may be, will not commit violent acts on others. But can we assume the essential harmlessness of every patron with obnoxious habits or bizarre behaviors? Not if we want to keep ourselves, our staffs, and our patrons safe while they are in the library. Library staff members should become a little paranoid, perhaps, and learn to watch everybody for problem behaviors. As a preliminary step, they should first anticipate problems with the public by attempting to define and ban or deal with in a recommended way specific problem behaviors, and to post their lists of prohibitions prominently.

L'Affaire Kreimer

Not all threats to library security (a broad, amorphous term, admittedly) involve either fear of material theft or imminent personal danger. Sometimes intimidation and terror, as opposed to violence, are the perpetrator's objective. Consider as an example the case of Richard Kreimer, a frequent visitor to the Morris Free Library in Morristown, New Jersey. Kreimer, homeless by choice, displayed such a one-two punch of offensive lack of personal hygiene and objectionable behavior that it made library staff want to throw him out of the building with a stern injunction never to return. When they finally couldn't stand it anymore and decided to do so, however, Kreimer, who was an educated and intelligent man for all of his strangeness, was canny enough to employ legal remedies to challenge his ejection.

Kreimer lived on the streets with no fixed or given address. He spent most of his days in the local public library, where he treated his fellow patrons to the full benefit of his unwashed body and clothes, his piercing stare, and his fondness for following young females through the stacks. There he sought to stand very close to them, though he was careful never to touch them or say or do anything that could be defined as crime or even harassment. He just stared and shambled along behind young girls as they searched out their books, his penetrating gaze causing them to react with terror, which was probably the whole idea.

When ordered to leave because his smell and his behavior were upsetting others, Kreimer adamantly refused. He claimed that he had just as much right to be there as others did, and that he was breaking no rules that he knew of. The staff, of course, consulted the library's existing library rules of conduct straightaway. True enough, the rules contained no rule or law (whether library, city, county, or state) that prohibited either smelling bad or staring. At the time, "stalking" had not yet become a punishable offense in New Jersey. So Kreimer, upon being forced to leave the premises despite his protests, turned to the law to defend him, seeking legal remedy and damages. What is really frightening is that—initially, at least—he made his point and won!

The magistrate who heard the case, in finding for Kreimer, pointed out that he did so not out of sympathy for the man, or even in the name of First Amendment freedoms or justice, but because the library had failed to define or describe in its rules of conduct the man's specific behaviors as transgressions that merited eviction. Kreimer was therefore entitled to enter and use the library just like anyone else, despite his perceived personal hygiene or motivations. In his lawsuit, he won a sizable sum of money in compensatory and punitive damages. So back he came, into the library, victorious, vindictive, and still unwashed. One can imagine that the library's security personnel, informed of the judge's decision, were silently urging Kreimer to go over the line and commit a crime—anything defined as a crime—so that they could roust him with impunity.

How could this miscarriage of justice—favoring the rights of one citizen to do as he pleases over the rights of all other library patrons and staff in the building to be free from his behaviors—have occurred? The presiding judge, in defending his decision, pointed out that there was no "rule" on smelling bad in the library's existing code of conduct, or even a guideline governing malodorousness that everyone could agree upon. How bad do you have to smell to be classed as bad enough to be given the old heave-ho? Just as it is impossible to attempt to define speeding as "driving too fast," the judge pointed out, so it is impossible to define "offensive odor" such that everyone will agree on how bad it has to get before a patron has to leave. In both cases, there is plenty of room for different opinions and interpretations of what the expression means.

The judge in the Kreimer case said he was unable to support the efforts of a library to throw a malodorous patron out and keep him out because the library had not defined the offense in such a way that everyone could agree on whether the homeless man had crossed the line into unacceptable behavior. Behaving in ways that made the man highly undesirable to staff and patrons clouded the issue but was deemed as irrelevant to the odor problem.

Some libraries have attempted to deal with the problem of smell in more quantifiable terms than merely calling it "bad." Security guards sometimes attempt to grapple with it by making up rough rules of thumb. One library security guard explains that "If I can smell a patron's body odor at a distance of six feet, that patron is fair game for eviction," implying that any lesser distance means the offense is not severe enough to merit removal from the building. Does such a criterion work? Hardly. Such a definition is assailable as arbitrary and vague, due to a host of variables, such as the guard's olfactory acuity, differing perceptions of "six feet," the room's ventilation system, the day or time in question, and the nature of the odor emitted. Moreover, it is doubtful whether such a criterion, if challenged, would ever stand up in a court of law.

Giving off a foul and offensive odor in a public building can, without a doubt, work all kinds of mischief on others who happen to be nearby. We have all been in the presence of persons whose aroma can cause us symptoms ranging from nausea to respiratory problems to stinging eyes. But exactly how bad do you have to smell to be considered malodorous enough to be expelled from a public building for it? That's a very difficult matter to codify and quantify. And then there's an ancillary question: Is unwashed body odor the only criterion of "smelling bad"? What about cologne, hairspray, and perfume, for example? Many people experience reactions from severe headaches to nausea to asthma attacks when they breathe such chemical odors.

Odor aside, staring or following people around the library, which Kreimer also did on a regular basis, hadn't been specifically listed as transgressions in the library's list of rules, either, and were thus also not deemed valid reasons for his expulsion. All right, then, what about his malicious and probably lascivious intent? What he was thinking when he followed young girls around wasn't too hard to guess. Wasn't he on a deliberate campaign to frighten them? Possibly, but staring while walking around in the stacks was not prohibited by the library's code of behavior. Since Kreimer never touched anyone, and only rarely spoke, he was guilty of nothing expressly listed in the library's code. And the New Jersey state penal code is clear on this point: You can't prove intent until after the man does something specifically prohibited.

But there's a larger question here. Shouldn't the rights of the majority outweigh the rights of one lone person? Shouldn't prompt and forceful action be taken against a person who, by exercising his personal freedom, makes everyone else disinclined to enter or remain in the building? By and large, the public still thinks that coming into a library is like entering a zone of tranquility. They don't expect to be hassled once inside. Such expectations may be at odds with the reality of today's services and staff capabilities, but they are users' expectations, nonetheless. Some patrons come wanting nothing more than an old-fashioned reading room with a "personal librarian," only to find a computer-driven information factory that makes them feel out of place. These patrons may respond to change or the new reality in a fashion that we find unexpected or even unacceptable, but these are not normally true problem patrons. They may, however, present an opportunity for patron education in library use, or may require a different manner of service from other users. It's the "bad actors" that we're worried about, however, and many libraries have to worry about them every day.

Other Problem Behaviors in Libraries and Some Solutions

There are people (like Kreimer, perhaps) frequenting libraries every day, seemingly for the obvious purpose of following young women around or otherwise terrorizing fellow visitors. Once undesirable activities are suspected, patrollers are able to observe and follow these people, to deter—or if that is not possible, to observe and report—their objectionable behaviors. Local police or campus security may be called in to deal directly with these individuals based on staff security members' observations. On occasion, these people may be officially barred from the library, or even from a college campus. But almost inevitably, most show up in the library again, often within hours of their exile. In these instances, security staff have the duty of making quick identification of these recidivist problem patrons and the obligation to monitor their behavior until the police come to intervene.

A myriad of other possible scenarios involve problem patrons. Unless it's a clear case, easily determined to be a police issue, we should carefully examine each situation before determining that a problem patron is in our midst. Here are some examples of this ambiguity, with discussion and suggested strategies for solving the problems:

> A pair of patrons uses the library's index tables to play chess every afternoon. Sometimes conversation over the chessboard turns to argument and becomes quite raucous and heated. After several warnings, the players are asked to leave. They protest and refuse to leave quietly.

RECOMMENDATION: Unless or until a solemn promise to behave can be extracted from each of the chess players, they should not be permitted to re-enter the library building and make use of the chess tables. Even promises, however earnest the intentions of the promisers, often cannot be kept. In calm moments, people find it easy to promise that they'll be good, but when you think someone is cheating you at your favorite game, it is very easy, in the heat of passion or outrage, to forget your vow. Given the relatively mild nature of the infraction, however, a good deal of tolerance is recommended.

> An elderly woman, recently widowed, comes into the library daily just to visit with staff and other patrons. She's clearly lonely and chatters constantly to everyone she encounters about all sorts of things.

RECOMMENDATION: This is a difficult type of problem patron, because, in light of her recent tragic loss, staff tend to be disinclined to offend or upset her by asking her to be quiet or to go elsewhere for her conversations. Unless other patrons complain that she is bothering them, there is little the librarian can do about her behavior. If she's bothering you, however, a gentle reminder that you are extremely busy may do the trick without unduly hurting her feelings. Suggesting alternative recreational opportunities outside the library may not be amiss.

> A homeless man comes into the library to sleep and snores, disturbing those around him.

RECOMMENDATION: In such a case, many librarians and security guards follow a personal sliding scale of reactions. The decision may be, thus, a function of such variables as (1) the loudness of the snoring, (2) whether the snorer's behavior (or personal odor) are driving others away, and (3) weather conditions outside on the day of the infraction. While it is probably not a good idea to touch him, he should be awakened, however, as gently as possible. If speaking to him ("Excuse me? Sir? Sir? Please wake up!") doesn't get the job done, try forcefully slamming a book down on the table next to him. But stand well clear. The first reactions of sleepers startled by a rude awakening are very hard to predict.

> An elderly patron suddenly, and at random intervals, emits a high, barking, maniacal laugh, with no apparent cause or reason. Some other patrons report that they are uneasy or afraid and want you to deal with the laugher.

RECOMMENDATION: Sometimes mental health institutions advise their clients to hang around public libraries as part of their pathway of reculturalization and reintegration into society. The person exhibiting such behavior may therefore be merely eccentric or may be mentally ill, and must, in either case, be treated with care and delicacy. In this case, a good place to start would be to ask the person politely to refrain from such conduct. Sometimes that's all it takes. Upon a second incident, however, you may wish to warn the person sternly that such behavior will not be tolerated. At the third reported instance, most libraries would be held blameless for evicting the person, who is disturbing the peace of all those around him.

> A patron complains that a tablemate in the reading room keeps humming to herself, distracting others.

RECOMMENDATION: Here there are two immediate and workable solutions to an annoying yet not serious problem: (1) Request that the complainer change tables or relocate to another part of the building.

Usually, he or she will have figured this out. (2) Speak to the hummer, telling him or her that the behavior is annoying others, and ask that the behavior cease. In the event of persistent humming, whether unconscious, compulsive, or deliberate, it may be necessary to modify the library's code of conduct to justify the expulsion of the guilty party. Sometimes the hummer will continue to do so—and even ratchet up the volume—just to get even with the complainer, or it may be an unconscious resumption of an old and ingrained habit. But it is easy to apologize for something of this sort one minute and then forget and begin to hum anew in the next. Tolerance is the watchword here.

> An elderly man is behaving oddly, sticking his tongue out at other patrons. Some people around him take it personally.

RECOMMENDATION: Mentally disturbed people are free to enter library buildings like any other patrons, and some of them are actually encouraged by their physicians and counselors to visit the library, meaning that bizarre behavior can break out at any time. As provocations go, this one is relatively innocuous, but still it cannot be ignored. Possibly the man is exhibiting signs of mental illness. If, upon request, he refuses to stop such behavior but does nothing further by way of provocation, a telephone call to community mental health services might be in order.

> A self-styled preacher, calling himself a messenger of God, seems to be deeply and earnestly religious. He frequents various rooms of a large city public library, shouting scripture at the top of his lungs. When asked to desist his harangue by a staff member, he shouts about "sin, sinners, godlessness, the blood of the lamb, unrepentant evildoers, unbaptized heathens," and a list of others bound for hell.

RECOMMENDATION: While the man's shouting undeniably can disrupt everyone's morning or afternoon, let us assume that he does not seem prone to violent behavior. The aim, therefore, is principally to get him to stop what he is doing, not to avert a tragedy. This raises an interesting and problematic question of rights: Does this preacher have a constitutional right of free speech that allows him to say whatever's on his mind, or does the right of everyone else in the area to be let alone outweigh his individual right? In this case, using a soothing, calm manner of speech, while neither agreeing nor disagreeing with the man's message, may cause him to subside. You may not know at this point whether he is a fervent religious zealot or merely a madman. In any case, he cannot be allowed to continue to preach if it annoys others. He should be told to leave the building, even if he threatens one and all with eternal damnation for such effrontery. No one enjoys being placed under a curse, but taking such risks comes with the territory.

A man arguing about an overdue fine becomes verbally abusive.

RECOMMENDATION: Maybe he's just blowing off steam, in which case, he may respond well to a warm smile and soothing words. Staff must attempt to remain calm and reasonable in the face of verbal abuse. But there is a point at which even the most serene of us will have had enough. Sometimes asking another staff member to deal with the man will solve the problem. If the man becomes louder and more abusive, however, security or law enforcement must be informed immediately, and the man must be treated as potentially dangerous to others. It is also advisable to leave the man a clear path to the door, should he wish to leave the building.

The above examples are illustrative of the rich and varied tapestry of problem patron scenarios that librarians may encounter every day. There are many others. The solutions suggested are only advice. There are many approaches to each problem. We can only hope that, when such troubles occur, the librarian has the luxury of time to consider options and choose the best and safest of them.

Sexual Behavior in the Library

> Why do we come here to do it? I'll tell you why. Because it's a lot cheaper than the Holiday Inn, that's why.
>
> —Statement made to police by a man arrested for having sex with his girlfriend in the stacks of a public library

Some people use the library for sexual behavior ranging from blatant exhibitionism to actual acts of love. Why do people have sex in the library? It's an interesting psychological problem, but one simple answer is that it's undeniably a lot cheaper than going to a motel. For another, the coast is usually clear because many libraries have no security force at all, while the security personnel of others are stretched thin, and are thus able to spend very little time observing human behavior.

How should library staff and security personnel deal with egregious or criminal sexual behavior? After all, there is usually a delicate and rather subjective line between what is actually criminal and what is merely offensive or in poor taste. Consider these typical examples. You're the librarian in charge and must deal with the following situations:

> A young couple sits, side by side (fully clothed), in adjacent library chairs, necking furiously, seemingly lost in each other, and oblivious to the stares, sniggers, and comments of those around them.

RECOMMENDATION: Is this a case of bad taste? Certainly. Inappropriate? You bet. But this is not normally punishable behavior or anything that warrants calling the cops. In most cases, a stern warning that they are engaging in inappropriate behavior, they must desist their amorous activity or be banished from the library unless they conform to the rules, will suffice.

> A female library patron reports that she has observed a man in the stacks, squatting down and pretending to consult books on low shelves, while actually, she believes, looking up the skirts of young schoolgirls.

RECOMMENDATION: Looking at other library patrons is no crime, even if it makes others uncomfortable. Even if a security guard sees a man looking up the girls' skirts, he is taking a considerable legal risk should he detain him and accuse him of it. The suspected "peeper," after all, is likely to deny the charge hotly, and evidence is impossible to provide. But the guard has various options, nevertheless. He can, for example, speak to the man, warn the girls, attempt to ignore the situation, alert the security force, call the police, or notify his superiors. In one case a discussion with the young girls of what they were innocently inviting stopped the problem cold, at least for a while.

> According to a deeply disturbed and alarmed patron, a man is opening his pants and exposing himself to women in the stacks.

RECOMMENDATION: First the security employee should attempt to verify such behavior personally. If it is observed, a call to local police can resolve the situation because indecent exposure is against the law in all communities. If no such behavior is observed, options range from warning the man about the illegality of what he is suspected of doing to notifying one's superior, attempting to sneak up and catch the man at it at a later time, or trying to ignore the situation. In the latter case, of course, you may have a public relations problem should the complaining patron perceive that you're doing nothing about her complaint.

> A male patron uses the library building to meet other males who may or may not be interested in his sexual passes.

RECOMMENDATION: There are several choices: Ignore him? Evict him? Call the police? If such behavior is observed in public areas, guards may wish to speak to the man, warn him that the library is not a pickup bar and that he is under continual observation. Here, it's all right to attempt to be intimidating without any suggestion of threat or violence. Should the offending patron attempt to conduct his erotic business in public rest rooms, or appear to be forcing his attentions on others, however, immediate eviction is called for.

> A guard, making his tour of the building, discovers that the door to a conference room is unlocked. Curious, he looks in and finds a couple engaged in an apparently consensual sex act on the carpeted floor.

RECOMMENDATION: Among options for the guard are (1) chase them out of the building, (2) detain them and call the police, (3) interrupt them (possibly with a cough or throat clearing), giving them time to put their clothes on again and leave, and (4) lecture them on their outrageous and inappropriate behavior. The choice is a matter of the guard's instructions, but under no circumstances should the miscreants be allowed to think of their actions as a joke, or they'll be apt to return to do it again.

The Special Plight of the Homeless

The plight of the homeless is already at epidemic proportions and growing. Many homeless persons, with no place else to spend their time, find the library a more comfortable ambiance for their daytime hours than the streets, and a much more affordable one than any other spot in town. While homeless persons in the library may present severe problems, they are—first and foremost—patrons of the library, and should be treated to the extent possible like everyone else who enters the building. Similarly, they are subject to the same rules and regulations as are persons with homes.

In keeping with both law and tradition, homeless people, regardless of their degree of personal hygiene, receive the protection of the First and Fourteenth Amendments to the U.S. Constitution, just as do the Methodist minister, the mayor's wife, and the high school girls doing their homework after school. In other words, as long as they are violating no established building or municipal rules, the homeless are not eligible for eviction. Yet there are so many of them in our city libraries, with so many undesirable traits and conditions! How did they get that way?

Even though the homeless comprise only a segment of those people we lump together as problem patrons, they are the ones we most worry about and have trouble accepting, frequently because of their lack of personal hygiene. In times of homelessness, people with nowhere else to go naturally gravitate to public buildings as a haven from the streets. These places offer warmth, shelter, public rest rooms, and quiet rooms where one can read, socialize, and, on occasion, sleep without the requirement of paying for the privilege or worrying about being assaulted or robbed. Along with homelessness, of course, come other related problems, stemming from lack of access to or interest in proper sanitation and hygiene, and, due to economic and societal problems, mental illness.

All of these worries affect the library directly, of course, as well as all who spend time in it. As homelessness is a great social and personal tragedy, the consequences and ramifications for libraries are immense. The homeless generally fall into the amorphous library classification of problem patrons, along with thieves, exhibitionists, and persons whose behaviors are annoying and worrisome, yet completely legal. It is, however, important to remember that not all homeless persons are problem patrons, and correspondingly, not all problem patrons are homeless.

When the homeless weary of the streets and seek the shelter of buildings where they can warm up and maybe snooze a bit in a relatively clean, well-lighted place, where can they go? The public library comes readily to mind. After all, the rules are easy and the safety factor is normally high. Many homeless people enjoy reading, and where else can you read books all day long without the necessity of buying something? Yes, the library is tops on the short list of places for the homeless to go. It is easier to list the places they can't go. In every city, downtown commercial buildings have security personnel whose routine responsibilities include that of shooing away undesirables.

The homeless obviously vary in their potential for problem behavior, and library staff and security personnel are frequently required to make impromptu and subjective distinctions among such poorly defined terms as eccentric, highly emotional, emotionally disturbed, and even psychotic. In the absence of on-site and immediate psychiatric evaluation of individuals, in fact, most such classifications become nothing more than snap judgment calls, which will accordingly vary with the individual observer.

Still, there are forms of triage, which security and staff can apply with a degree of consistency. A person classified as physically ill may require only a routine call to 911 or help by staff until paramedics arrive. The condition of being mentally ill, however, is much harder to define and much more troublesome for staff to diagnose and deal with. However intuitive or trained he or she might be in human behavior, the library staff member is not always given the time and opportunity to analyze facts and render a measured judgment. Sometimes, in fact, an instant, on-the-spot decision becomes necessary, and everybody has to live with the consequences.

It's important to remember that homeless people cannot be classed as a monolithic entity. Just as they are unique in their appearance, they do not all act, react, or think the same way. Some are, admittedly, seriously and dangerously ill, and that illness may be physical, mental, or emotional. They may be drunks or substance abusers or clean and sober. Others are quite normal, in the sense of being average in intelligence or perception and free from obvious substance abuse. What they frequently share, however, is a syndrome of conditions from which they cannot easily escape. Like everyone else, the homeless get hungry, they experience too much cold or heat, dampness and dryness, and most feel almost constant fear and anxiety for their safety.

Despite lurid headlines in both the library journals and the general news media about crimes committed by a handful of homeless people, most of America's homeless are merely persons down on their luck, seeking only to warm themselves or have daytime respite from the weather, predators, police, and boredom. While they are generally harmless, even if they are considered nuisances by library staff and other patrons, many are unable to avoid—or are uninterested in controlling—extreme body odor, which may present a severe problem for others in the library building when they enter or move around.

Library literature is full of news items concerning the conflicting rights of persons to have free access to library materials and other persons seeking the same access in non-toxic air.

The homeless tend to feel suspicion and sometimes anger toward police and social workers, or the variety of people who approach them offering help, seeking to rehabilitate their bodies, their work skills, or, sometimes, their souls. A sense of hopelessness is often pervasive among them, and it takes more than either charity or policy to make that feeling go away. Through bitter, firsthand experience, the homeless are often disinclined to trust "do-gooders" beyond accepting charity when it is offered. Many are proud, disdaining charity, and subsisting on only what they can provide for themselves. Others have a talent for panhandling and telling hard-luck stories to affluent passersby or other library patrons, making a surprising income through preying on the generosity, guilt, or discomfort of others.

Feeding themselves adequately is often a daylong occupation of the homeless, and alcohol, when available, is both a comfort and an enemy. The homeless make use of the public library as shelter from the streets; within its walls, they can, depending on the prevailing weather, warm up, cool off, sleep, use clean rest room facilities, and simply spend the day. Some of them actually read or use library materials, while others use those materials as props, as a justification for their presence in the library. Most homeless people feel a sense of entitlement to the library as citizens and former or occasional taxpayers, and see no reason why they should be treated any differently from other visitors to the building. With a few exceptions, they are meek and inoffensive, knowing that their continued ability to enter and use the building has a good deal to do with their comportment and behavior. Many, if they could choose, would become transparent or invisible, free to enter and move about the library without attracting the notice of staff, guards, or other patrons. Only the troublesome few who come in angry, defiant, flouting the rules, or threatening others grab the headlines, but most wish to be left alone in anonymous silence.

Can the library just ignore the homeless and their demonstrable lack of personal hygiene? That, too, depends. For the most part, homeless patrons (who cannot always be identified as such) must be treated just like those with homes. The library's set of rules for behavior, demeanor, attire, and personal hygiene must apply to all visitors to the building, regardless of their economic status or residence.

But what arguments can be advanced for leaving them alone, or, for that matter, for throwing them out of the building with the stern warning not to return until they are cleaned up and presentable? Figures 3.2 and 3.3 present complementary (and to some extent competing) lists of arguments both for compelling undesirable, malodorous, or otherwise obnoxious persons to leave the library and those in favor of toleration—just grinning and bearing it—as best one can.

Some Vexing Questions

Many difficult questions remain concerning the rights and privileges of visitors to the library. Such questions may be legal, ethical, merely practical, or even all three.

- The library exists to satisfy the information and reading needs of its patrons in a pleasant, comfortable atmosphere. Anyone not demonstrably in the library for such purposes is fair game for expulsion.
- Any visitor to the library who seriously interferes with the normal functioning of the facility, whether as nuisance or threat, is a problem for all and may be dealt with in the same way as other nuisances or threats.
- Unwashed persons, because of their smell, can make using library materials difficult for others. One malodorous patron can prevent most of the rest of the building's visitors from entering a room. Why should one smelly customer be permitted to foul the air of many others who keep themselves clean?
- Mental or emotional illness is often part of the homeless person's history or condition. Public safety concerns permit libraries to eject persons who misbehave, even if they are not misbehaving at the moment.
- Library staff do not have the same luxury as patrons to leave a building to escape from offensive people, if they choose. Employees are stuck in the building without the option of flight. Dealing with the homeless on a daily basis may arouse negative feelings in employees, leading to high turnover and a decline in morale, and a demoralized staff is an inefficient one. Moreover, listening to complaints about the homeless and being unable to do anything about them is extremely stressful on staff members.

FIGURE 3.2
Arguments in Favor of Barriers to the Homeless

- The homeless have the same rights as anyone else, and it is unfair and discriminatory to treat them any differently because they are unfortunate or lacking the creature comforts of others.
- Because it is possibly illegal to treat homeless persons differently from the rest, the library could be in jeopardy from lawsuits demanding both compensatory and punitive damages if homeless persons are denied or ejected from the library.
- Libraries are centrally located, climatized, and inviting places that attract the homeless. Community agencies who deal with the homeless and their problems are often severely overtaxed, short-staffed, and hamstrung by laws, rules, and citizen complaints. Urban police complain that they have higher priorities in their workdays than rousting nuisance patrons from libraries. Besides, the police who arrive to deal with the situation may be understandably disinclined to place smelly vagrants in their police cruisers for transport to shelters or jail.
- The library can perform an important community service by identifying and reporting apparently homeless persons to proper authorities, thus preventing needless suffering and even death.
- Recent trends in mental health treatment have prescribed library visits for those persons classified as harmless among the formerly institutionalized, providing them with the opportunity to associate and intermingle with normal people as a form of therapy. The public library thus serves as a link in the chain of rehabilitation and reintegration of such persons into the mainstream of society.

FIGURE 3.3
Arguments against Barriers to the Homeless

- When does tolerable eccentricity become abnormal behavior that justifies or necessitates some kind of action? Where do you draw the line? What criteria should be used, and who makes the judgment call?
- When does the enforcement of reasonable rules become harassment of individuals?
- Is it an appropriate application of the need to accommodate rights in conflict to designate a room for the homeless and require that they confine themselves only to that room while in the library building?

- Do library staff have the right or responsibility to speak to homeless persons about their perceived lack of compliance with the rules of acceptable conduct or appearance? If so, what are they allowed to say?
- Does denying equal access to the information contained in the library to any subset of the community equate to discrimination and denial of group members' civil rights?
- How literally should the meaning of the word "public" in the name of the public library be taken? Does public mean that anyone is entitled to be in the building?
- Should "informational need" be the criterion of admission to the library? Who is qualified to determine the nature and scope of an "informational need," and whether specific behaviors qualify as such?
- Is there a difference between access to information and access to the library itself, and how and by whom is this determined? How does this impact the homeless?
- What about persons who are obviously loitering in the library all day?
- Are there psychological barriers to access to libraries for the homeless along with physical and legal ones? How should this affect their treatment?
- Can a library that deals harshly and decisively with its homeless honestly say that it is "reaching out" to its public?

The foregoing list makes no claim to being exhaustive; it is intended merely to illustrate some of the nettlesome issues connected with dealing with the homeless in the public library. Inevitably, with lists like the one above, there are more questions raised than answered. It is still valuable and useful, however, to consider the questions. In any event, more research on the homeless is both necessary and desirable, facilitating better, more equitable, and fairer decisions. An appropriate balance between recognizing the rights of homeless patrons and the need to provide for security for staff and patrons is highly desirable and can be achieved in most situations. Safety and security threats lie in the realm of the wider society, and both government and the civic society have the responsibility of addressing the problem. Librarians should be part of initiatives that work closely with community structures to address community-based social programs.

A Workable Master Plan for Library Safety and Security

Understandably, those entrusted with protecting personal safety in libraries have differing opinions concerning the appropriate level of freedom that the public should enjoy. There are several points of almost total consensus, however. It is generally agreed by writers on building security for libraries that every library should perform as many of the following actions as possible in assessing and preserving its security posture:

- *Monitor crime patterns in the community,* especially in the surrounding area of the library. Find out what's going on from talking to people, from reading the newspaper, watching local television stations, and so on. Many newspapers carry some type of police blotter with records of crime by locale, which should make tracking crime relatively easy to do.
- *Analyze the library's present security posture.* Take a walk around the library to see if there are areas where augmented lighting; moving stacks, equipment, or furniture; or installing mirrors could make a difference in sight lines. The assumption here is that those intending to commit violent, hostile acts against others will be less likely to do so in bright lights and in plain view of staff.
- *Evaluate design flaws.* The old Carnegie library buildings had built into their basic design a generally universal feature: good visibility down sight lines emanating from the central desk in the rotunda. This made it possible for a librarian or desk attendant to see who was up to what without having to stray very far from the front desk. Today, however, many libraries have interior architecture deliberately intended to afford readers and browsers privacy in secluded nooks and carrels. And while such little alcoves may be ideal for quiet reading or study, their presence may also be asking for trouble.
- *Hire police or security guards.* The presence of designated security officers is highly desirable, but many libraries find their employment financially impossible. There is a big distinction—both legal and in the minds of the public—to be made between uniformed security guards (who normally do not carry weapons, but often have communications devices and the authority to handle disruptive situations) and off-duty uniformed police. Were hiring

police not so expensive, it might, in fact, be the remedy of choice. Nothing is so reassuring to library visitors and so daunting to violent people than the presence of a uniformed cop. Without funds to hire off-duty officers or a security force, of course, library staff must assume security duties in addition to their primary and other assigned responsibilities. The major disadvantage of this is that such staffers have less time to fulfill their primary duties when they are performing security duties, and most are not trained for appropriate reaction to trouble. Sometimes untrained staffers get in over their heads in situations they cannot resolve.

- *Purchase security equipment or augment surveillance technology.* Some devices, such as surveillance cameras and silent alarms, are likely to cost serious money, of course, but steps in this direction are recommended as money permits. Even if the library's surveillance cameras are unwatched or without film, their conspicuous presence may deter those contemplating a crime or creating a disturbance.
- *Devise and implement a security checklist.* (A model list is provided in chapter 4.) The purpose of such a list is to see if your library's security posture measures up to established minimum standards for keeping people safe and secure. It's also a convenient way of finding out what your weaknesses are and what you can do to remedy them. Items on the list but not present in your library create a "wish list," in the event that the library receives a windfall or bequest.
- *Put a comprehensive security policy in place.* Discuss it with all staff members. Develop or update safety policies and procedures. Prepare a risk assessment study for the entire library and locate trouble spots that require more frequent monitoring or changes in staffing or design. No policy or manual, of course, will be able to anticipate or cover every emergency with step-by-step instructions, but everyone—from the director to the custodian—should be familiar with safety rules, know when to call the police, when to evacuate the building, and when all an angry, recalcitrant, or nonconformist patron needs is a "good talking to."
- *Train all levels of staff in the elements of security and crisis management.* This may involve internal training on library security policies as well as safety training by police officers or other safety experts.

- *Designate personnel as security monitors.* Every library, no matter how small, should put one person (a Library Security Officer) in charge of security concerns and dealing with security officers or police. This person must be able to use good judgment under pressure, be cool under fire, and be willing and able to make difficult decisions rapidly.
- *Screen future employees.* While looking into the character or background of present employees may cause problems for the library administration, the best way to guard against a staff person erupting into violence is to be extremely careful when hiring. Compelling evidence shows that a significant proportion of library crime—including stealing books and other materials—is committed by staff. It is easier, of course, to screen prospective employees than to evaluate the trustworthiness of existing staff, but the library administration should attempt to do what it can to monitor all staff to evaluate them from the standpoint of such things as substance abuse, emotional balance, and mental health.
- *Post behavior policies in conspicuous places in more than one location.* These signs should alert patrons who read them to what is and is not acceptable behavior. Be specific, and use plain, unambiguous language. Clearly, this step is more a legal shield than a real defense against threats to personal safety, but it may serve to deter some bent on mischief. If people know what is forbidden, yet proceed to do it anyway, they are then subject to sanctions and punishment by law.
- *Have liability insurance coverage.* No library should even open its doors in the morning without a current and claimable all-risks policy of comprehensive insurance. Only in that way can it hope to survive a lawsuit by a member of the public who feels that his or her injury was the result of negligence on the part of the staff or the governing unit or jurisdiction. Such a policy may not prevent crime, but it will go a long way to helping pick up the pieces after an event takes place.
- *Network and maintain continual communication with other institutions who share your security risks and problems.* These may include other types of businesses in the area or other public buildings such as museums and art galleries.

- *Do conspicuous monitoring.* Whenever staff have reason to be suspicious of any individual, they should gently but firmly let the people know that they're aware of them and watching them closely.

The purpose of all the ongoing activity is, ideally, to guard against outbreaks of violence against others in the building. A worthwhile subtext, however, is to make would-be felons and those contemplating mischief so uncomfortable in your library that they move along to another target of opportunity.

Laws, Rules, and Guidelines

Our actions or reactions regarding people causing trouble are safest when we have a book, brochure, or document that addresses the specific problem behavior and specifies recommended action. In situations involving problem patrons, it is useful to ask ourselves several questions, initially:

- What tools do we have to guide us?
- What documents are in place, bearing on the problem?
- Do we have guidelines that describe the specific types of behavior permitted and not permitted in the library?
- Does an existing document specify permitted (and forbidden) use of meeting rooms, etc.?

Angry, disturbed, and problematic people are as free to enter a library building as are considerate, normal people, every day and every evening. Libraries—especially public and permissive ones—are often ideal outlets for their acting out their anger and other antisocial behaviors. Security patrols help, of course, but even libraries with uniformed security report failure to control behavior everywhere in a large building. Can libraries with open stacks afford to staff each level or patrol them constantly to deter unwanted behavior? In most cases, the answer is no, so the stacks have become great places to hide. Surveillance cameras and closed-circuit television have proven to be helpful, but they cost significant amounts to purchase and install as well as extra money for staff to monitor them.

As already stated, library design is another important factor in dealing with some types of problem patron behavior. Libraries, because they do not charge admission, tend to attract all manner of weirdos and people bent on misbehaving. Most libraries cannot afford frequent security patrols, and thus provide a free, safe haven for those who seek places for their criminal or deviant behavior. Guards and staff members entrusted with security, of course, work in existing buildings of finite size and dimensions, where responses to requests for revised architecture range anywhere from difficult (and expensive) to impossible. Within existing buildings, however, there are steps that can be taken with a minimum of remodeling and expense to enhance the library's security posture. These steps and other suggestions are elaborated as lists in chapter 4 of this book.

Dealing with an angry patron is not easy, nor is it fun. Yet most angry patrons are merely normal people who need to let off steam in order to cope with their frustrations. The question is, how much "letting off steam" must we tolerate before we go into action to restrain an angry patron? In many cases, an angry person cools down after his or her anger is expressed, but sometimes meeting with a passive response merely serves to enrage the stressed-out individual further. Candidly, sometimes anger may be justified if staff members have been rude, incompetent, or unhelpful. But some people's anger is chronic or pathological and beyond limits.

When judgment is called for, there are no absolutes. On very cold, snowy, or rainy nights, for example, a librarian or security guard may permit various forms of non-threatening behavior (e.g., sleeping, snoring at the reading tables) that would not be tolerated on fine summer evenings. As an example, exiling a drunk from the library building on one of the coldest days of the year could lead to his or her death from exposure or frostbite. A security guard may therefore reason that the best course of action is to let the unfortunate person sleep it off in the library, lest he or she turn into a popsicle outside and not survive the night. But such a decision may have unintended and unpleasant results: If word gets out that the library tolerates drunks, it could become marked as a haven for alcoholics, resulting in a sudden and alarmingly unruly influx.

A sensible recommendation is to factor in the circumstances before deciding on a course of action. The library should seek to adapt policies that are flexible but still meet consistent safety standards. In order to achieve this, however, staff need to be clear on what behavior they should and should not tolerate, and what to do when there clearly is a problem. Such lists should be in writing, circulated to all staff, and prominently posted in the library for the public to see. Remember that all decisions have consequences. It is frequently very difficult to anticipate just what those consequences are going to be, especially when dealing with human behavior. No one ever said that working in a public place was easy, and part of the salary of every public employee compensates him or her for having, on occasion, to make difficult or distasteful choices regarding other people.

Problem patrons not only bother staff but deter law-abiding patrons from visiting the library. What can be done to minimize the disruptions caused by problem patrons? The cornerstone to dealing with such people when they become difficult or dangerous is a strong and supportive administration that is willing to back up security measures with enforcement when necessary. In too many problem patron scenarios, nothing useful can be done by the staff because they have no support from the administration, who may fear adverse consequences if they give security staffers freedom of action. If the library administration takes the same approach to problem patrons as ostriches are said to do to danger—heads in the sand—problems will continue and perhaps escalate. First and foremost, therefore, there must be administrative support.

Both administration and staff need consensus on which behaviors are problematic, and decisions that will apply to everyone should be written into a security policy. Sometimes, however, just what is or is not a problem may be very difficult to codify and put in writing. Staff members and security personnel meeting and talking potential problems over before they become crises is one of the most effective forms of deterrence and is strongly recommended for all staff at all levels.

Crisis Prevention

Clearly, the best way to deal with a crisis—of whatever kind—is to prevent it from happening in the first place. In that vein, we quote the following "10 Tips for Crisis Prevention," provided by the National Crisis Prevention Institute:

- Be empathic (try to show respect and not to be judgmental).
- Clarify messages (make sure you understand what is being said).
- Respect personal space (don't stand too close for comfort).

- Be aware of body position (don't stand straight in front of him or her or appear to block his or her avenue of escape).
- Permit verbal venting where possible (let him or her blow off steam).
- Set and enforce reasonable limits (state what you will permit).
- Avoid overreacting (strive to remain calm, rational, and professional).
- Use physical techniques only as a last resort (pushing, grabbing, etc., can only make things worse, and may lead to subsequent lawsuits).
- Ignore challenge questions (do not respond to challenges to your authority, training, intelligence, policy, etc.).
- Keep your nonverbal cues non-threatening (the more an individual loses control, the less he or she listens to your actual words).

In order to know what to do about potentially troublesome patrons, it is often wise to attempt to engage them in conversation, in the hope that they will explain complaints, motives, intentions, and goals. Getting an explanation at least offers you an opportunity to understand the perpetrator's motives and may provide clues to ways you can defuse the situation before it escalates. For such conversations, fig. 3.4 offers some guidelines for eliciting maximum information while ensuring public safety.

What constitutes unacceptable behavior? There is no standard form, nor is there agreement on what to include on the list. Each library, in fact, may designate its own list of prohibitions. In 1992 in the aftermath of the Kreimer incident in Morristown, the New Jersey Library Association (NJLA) took a stab of its own at making a list of rules of acceptable and unacceptable behaviors. The NJLA list is interesting for the ways it both mirrors and goes beyond the Detroit Public Library's list (see figure 3.1). The NJLA list is presented in fig. 3.5.

This list, like the Detroit Public Library's list of prohibitions found earlier in this chapter, is fine as far as it goes but contains no definitions of certain terms (e.g., misuse, disruption, interference), which could have legal implications if challenged. Moreover, in the wake of the Kreimer verdict, it still contains nothing about odors, personal hygiene (these two are especially difficult to define), staring, following library patrons around, using a library for other than library purposes, loitering, panhandling, or swearing. These may be constitutionally

- Listen carefully to the person's words; ensure that he or she knows you're paying attention.
- Use firm, assertive (but not aggressive) language.
- Avoid a tone of voice or the use of phrases that might be considered judgmental, moralizing, or condescending.
- Respond in a calm, reasonable, and friendly manner.
- Use common sense in dealing with the problem situation.
- Try not to show anger, fear, disapproval, or disgust.
- Explain your position and that of the library in a calm tone of voice.
- Stress your responsibility to the collection and to other patrons.
- Do not allow yourself to be sidetracked or angered by personal insults or threats.
- Repeat your position as often as necessary.
- Suggest realistic alternatives—provide the patron with choices, if at all possible.
- If the patron demands to see someone "higher up," comply, but first insist on having the time to explain the situation to the supervisor in realistic terms and a calm manner.

FIGURE 3.4
Guidelines for Speaking with Problem Patrons

protected behaviors in some localities, and library staff are urged to consult with legal representation before codifying and posting a list of rules.

Weapons in the library must be strictly prohibited, except as authorized or permitted. The New Orleans Public Library (one publicized example of a burgeoning trend) has now installed in its downtown facility airport-style metal detectors at the front door, in hopes that this move will reduce the number of incidents of shooting within the library. This move is being closely watched to see if the prohibition should be recommended and adopted elsewhere. Even if statistics demonstrate that the number of gun incidents declines in that building, however, whether such a reduction will be permanent or a brief blip on the charts will still be unknown. But you've got to start somewhere, and reducing the number of weapons in a library building is a commendable beginning!

- Eating or drinking.
- Playing audio equipment so that others can hear it.
- Smoking.
- Carrying a weapon into the library unless authorized by law. Any patron authorized to carry a weapon must notify library staff that he or she is carrying a weapon in the library.
- Bringing animals into the library, except those needed to assist a person with a disability.
- Misusing the rest rooms (i.e., using one as a laundry or washing facility).
- Leaving a child under the age of seven unattended in the library.
- Talking loudly, making noise, or engaging in other disruptive conduct.
- Interfering with another person's use of the library or with the library personnel's performance of their duties.
- Shoes and shirts must be worn.
- Library privileges may be limited for the following reasons:
  a. damaging library property
  b. stealing library materials
  c. physically harming staff or patrons.

FIGURE 3.5
Activities Not Allowed in the Library

There is no single set of rules and recommendations that applies to all situations in all libraries. A few coherent guidelines are in order, however, and constitute fig. 3.6.

Since your institution wants to provide the safest facility for visitors and workers possible, you will want to know when any illegal, violent, abusive, or threatening behavior occurs on library premises in order to take action to prevent injury, damage, or interruption of operation and prevention of further occurrences. The library should not tolerate any unauthorized person carrying firearms, deadly weapons, or clearly dangerous materials into the building or having them on the premises, in accordance with local laws. The library should attempt to detain and turn over to police authorities any visitors or staff members who violate criminal laws or who display a serious or immediate

- When confronted with the threat of actual physical violence, your first responsibility is to protect your patrons. Don't be indecisive: Call the police or 911 immediately. Then, quietly go about removing as many people from the area or the building as you and other staff can safely manage in order to get them out of harm's way.
- Before a problem occurs, develop contacts with local mental health and social service agencies to work out referral procedures. Librarians are not psychiatrists. Don't expect to know what to do about every problem patron or person exhibiting unusual behavior, and don't spend too much time trying to put a name to what's wrong with a person acting unusually. In any case, it is risky to attempt to "pigeonhole" people, trying to make them conform to established types. Go to the experts; consult with a specialist.
- Don't try to detain or reason with a perpetrator who is holding a deadly weapon, unless you're using the chance for discussion as a cooling-off period or as a means of getting away. Be sure to leave the person a clear path to the door.
- Attempt to assess the seriousness of the situation as early in the confrontation as possible. The best course of subsequent action will depend on the accuracy of the assessment.
- Try to distinguish between problem and merely eccentric behavior, and act accordingly. While both types of behavior may appear strange, problem behavior is potentially dangerous, potentially destructive, and suggests malicious intent. Eccentric behavior is generally not dangerous or destructive, and usually stems from no malicious or larcenous motive.
- Teamwork, where at all possible—the consensus of multiple minds—is recommended. Consider and discuss as a group how a staff member can decide whether he or she is confronting a problem, and what to do about it.
- Provide regular training sessions to allow staff members to think problem situations through and discuss alternative approaches and their consequences. Case studies are especially good at providing "role-playing" experiences, which offer realistic situations for discussion without the threat of immediate real-world consequences.
- After an incident occurs in which someone has committed an offense against others, follow through to get the malefactor punished. Criminal behavior (as defined by laws and statutes) is still criminal behavior, even if it happens in your quiet library. File charges, even if it means going to court, hiring lawyers, and missing staff time on the job.

FIGURE 3.6
General Rules for Dealing with Problem Behavior

threat to themselves or others. This is for the protection of the public, the institution, the staff, and the continuation of facility operations.

The institution must not tolerate illegal, violent, abusive, or threatening behavior, and each individual must be held accountable for his or her actions on library premises. Staff must require perpetrators to leave, even if the offense is not deemed serious or immediate enough to pose either a threat or a violation of local law. One can never predict human behavior to any degree of certainty, and there are the lives of others present to think about. Violent, abusive, or threatening patrons may, if you see fit, be warned once to immediately cease these behaviors and sternly warned not to exhibit these behaviors again on library premises, or face being barred from the building. Security or staff must intervene in each situation that is construed as an illegal act, that disrupts workers or facility operation, or that threatens to do so.

Because the library needs to provide each visitor and staff member a safe facility, the governing agency (e.g., city, county, college, or university) must provide facilities, regulatory procedures, and inspections to promote safety and security. The library must therefore respond to each report of concern and seek to improve each questionable condition to everyone's satisfaction. Any violent, abusive, or threatening behavior by staff members must be seen as cause for disciplinary action up to and including dismissal. Managers and supervisors are accountable for taking appropriate action to prevent threatening behavior from occurring, to know when it occurs, and to take reasonable actions to protect life, property, and facilities on the premises.

CHAPTER 4

Preparing for and Reacting to Security Incidents in Libraries

As violence and the fear of violence increasingly disrupt our workplaces and drain our resources, libraries must take steps to create a safer environment for staff and patrons. While no library or institution of any size is immune to threat, prevention of most events is possible with careful planning and cooperation.

—Stevan Layne (from the brochure for his talk on library security to the ALA Annual Conference, 1996)

The objectives of this chapter are to:

- provide ideas and recommendations for preparing the library to deal with security problems before they arise
- provide suggestions that the library can use in creating and implementing a workable comprehensive security plan
- provide a thorough checklist by which a library can analyze its security posture
- discuss workable solutions to library crime
- discuss training for library security, including the hiring, supervision, and instruction of staff and security guards
- discuss possible reactions to several common security problems

Risk Management

All security is basically risk management, and consequently, the role of all security precautions and actions is to manage and minimize the risk of security problems occurring. Naturally, it is preferable to prevent incidents from taking place rather than seek to repair the damage subsequently. There are three types of security with regard to libraries as public buildings:

- physical security of occupants of the building (ranging from stairways inspected for safety to protection against assault)
- a master plan consisting of operating procedures for staff, security personnel, and the public to follow
- security personnel

The sources of risk to libraries are theft or damage to its collection, violent behavior perpetrated against others in the building, and physical damage to the building or facilities by vandalism, accident, or one of a number of other events. As a library staff member, you have an obligation to all who enter the building to provide a safe environment for them to use the facilities.

Comprehensive Planning

Careful planning for comprehensive library security is a sequential process involving several factors, which should follow a logical progression:

Assets to Be Protected

Asset definition is a good way to begin the process. Ask yourself what is to be protected and what level of security is needed for each type of asset. Such assets include property (all library collections, materials, furniture, equipment), information (e.g., computer records, which could be lost, destroyed, altered, stolen, or vandalized), and people (members of the public and library staff).

Threats to Assets

Once assets to be protected have been defined or at least described, we then move on to defining some of the potential threats to each asset and who would be likely to act them out. It is important to ask what means people might use to threaten our assets (e.g., vandalism, burglary, robbery, assault, or sabotage). It is equally important to calculate how likely such threats are to happen. The foregoing should assist the library in figuring out appropriate steps that can be taken to reduce each threat.

Formation of the Library's Security Team

This team, headed by the member of the staff designated as Library Security Officer (LSO), should meet periodically to discuss and deal with such matters as security responsibility (guards, key control, crowd control, fire drills, alarm systems, etc.). Designation of a Library Security Officer from among existing staff and writing a situation-specific building security manual are paramount. Preparation also involves the team's anticipation and discussion of security and safety problems. The point is, where possible, to attempt to deter or discourage perpetrators before they commit their crimes. Knowing the appropriate laws and rules and what security officers are permitted or supposed to do is equally important and may require consultation with legal officers or representatives.

A security team is highly recommended for every library of every size and type. The team should either personally conduct or delegate someone to conduct a security audit of the entire building. In performing such an audit, staff members will do well to anticipate just how criminals will come "at" the library by attempting, to the extent possible, to think like criminals! Ask yourself how, as a criminal, you would get in, commit your acts, accomplish your goals, and get out again undetected. Several access issues will surface during this security audit stage. (For example, Who has access to keys to what? How is access controlled? How is crime reported, and to whom?)

The Building Security Audit

Security deals with the possible, not the ideal. Since total security is an unobtainable goal, the object of a periodic security audit should not be an attempt to make the library absolutely safe—just safer! The security team should consider and analyze various types and levels of security measures possible, with projected costs. Initially (and regularly thereafter) the library security team should conduct some form of "walkabout" with a view to assessing the building's vulnerability, including identification of potential problems, itemization of alternative solutions to those problems, and an estimate of comparative costs of enhanced security against costs of potential loss.

The building audit should pay special attention to such matters as entrances and exits, other means of access, (e.g., tunnels, skylights, windows, roofs, internal access to restricted areas), and security screening devices. In conducting the audit, the team should ask itself what, if any, are the design or redesign implications of bolstering security in the library, how much remodeling will be necessary to upgrade the library's security posture, and what it will cost.

Other matters associated with improving security may include:

- Surveillance strategies (how best to keep people under observation, both by mechanical and human means), including ethical and legal aspects of that surveillance.
- Managing risk and legal liability (e.g., compliance with all existing rules, laws, insurance, costs of deterrence).
- Effective deployment of forces available (who and what assets are in place to assist in managing the risk of occurrences).
- Options for improving the library's security posture. (This may profitably entail a literature search to ascertain what has worked well in other institutions, and with what result.)
- Boundaries, constraints, and limits of security (costs and other factors that may hinder the library from achieving the highest level of personal safety).
- Finding the money—how to demonstrate need, sources of extra funding, and how best to allocate it.
- Psychological factors. (Important is not just the safety of all building occupants but their perception of safety. There is normally trade-off between high security and personal freedom; we want the library to be secure, yet not fortresslike.)
- Political factors. (These will be different for each community and thus for each library.)

Other variables the library may or will be forced to deal with include such issues as ongoing maintenance contracts, metal detectors at doorways, armed versus unarmed security forces, staff training for security operations, surveillance cameras inside and outside the building, glass breakage detectors, video surveillance, door and other intrusion alarms, delay devices, thermal sensors and alarms, duress alarms, scream alarms, and fire alarms.

The Comprehensive Security Plan

The library's security plan document should be designed to make criminal behavior so difficult that it occurs infrequently or not at all. Here are some steps to preparing a security and public safety plan:

- Analyze the potential for unauthorized access to non-public areas.
- Discuss with staff various responses to armed or dangerous intruders.
- Install or upgrade access controls and surveillance equipment.
- Regularly review the effectiveness and roles of security personnel.
- Distribute an up-to-date security and safety checklist to all staff.
- Work on improving and clarifying communications lines among staff and with police, fire department, and so on.
- At least once a year, involve all employees in a full-scale simulated practical exercise to rehearse their roles in an incident involving a threat to public safety.
- Orient new employees to emergency procedures.
- Train new employees in emergency procedures as part of their orientation.

While public safety is—and should be—everyone's job in the library, there is frequently lack of consensus or disagreement among administration and library staff on several points. Among these are:

- Lack of agreement about the balance between access and protection.
- Different views on funding priorities (e.g., more materials versus a certain percentage spent on deterrents to library crime).
- Lack of commitment on the part of city, academic institution, or library administrators to enforcement of safety procedures.
- Lack of coordination among library staff, security force, and police.
- Lack of awareness in the criminal justice system to the problem and magnitude of library crime.
- Lack of resolve or knowing what to do on the part of staff members in dealing with non-violent (but still unsettling) people and incidents in the library.

The difficulty of achieving consensus on appropriate action is that there is so much variety in humanity. There's just no telling who is going to walk through the front doors next. It is natural that people are going to exhibit a wide range of problem behaviors, each requiring a different approach, none guaranteed or foolproof. In other words, what works with one difficult individual on a given day may not work on other individuals on the same day, nor will it necessarily prove effective with the same individual on a different day. Complicating the problem is interpersonal divergence on exactly what constitutes "appropriate action" at a given time. We must therefore frequently rely on a mix of instinct, rules, preexisting guidelines, and a healthy dose of common sense in coping with problem situations.

Still, knowing what to do can be very difficult. For proof of this assertion, let's say for the sake of convenience that there are four alternative solutions (actually, there are many more) to a problem behavior in the library:

- Ignore the behavior and encourage others to do the same.
- Gently talk to the offensive party and try to persuade him or her to stop.
- Firmly request or demand that the offender stop or you will call security or the police immediately.
- Call security or the police immediately.

Developing the Library's Master Security Plan

There are various important security considerations with regard to libraries as public buildings: physical security of occupants of the building (ranging from stairways inspected for safety to protection against assault). The master plan, consisting of standard or recommended operating procedures for staff, security personnel, and the public should address each of these problems to the extent that they can be anticipated. Security personnel, where present, should be consulted and included in planning procedures. The sources of risk to libraries are theft or damage to its collection, violent behavior perpetrated against others in the building, and physical damage to the building or facilities by vandalism, accident, or any of a number of other events. Every library staff member has an obligation to all who enter the building to provide a safe environment in which they may use facilities with a minimum of risk.

It may be useful in planning library security to remember that while tight security is antithetical to the free-access philosophy of most modern libraries, a good level of security is achievable at reasonable cost. Good security, however, is going to be expensive, and very good security is going to be very expensive. Some workable compromise between tight security and no security at all is possible and must be found so that (1) the public is comfortable with any inconvenience and (2) materials and people are reasonably protected from harm, intrusion, or loss. Security personnel and various anti-theft devices are highly recommended, but while each of them has its costs, each offers its own rewards.

Anticipation of Emergency Situations

The old aphorism about the relative values of an ounce of prevention and a pound of cure is right on the money today and constitutes one of life's great truths. Deliberate and thoughtful planning for emergency situations in the library is very important and should be accomplished to the extent possible before such situations occur. While no one can predict or anticipate every problem that may befall a library and its staff, there are steps that any library can take to prepare so a response will swing swiftly into action at the time of emergency. According to the Smithsonian Institution's "Guidelines for Library and Archives Security" (1996), every library, as an institution open to the public yet entrusted with the protection of valuable property, should enact policies and procedures with regard to such matters as:

- fire protection
- emergency protection
- physical barrier and lock and key protection
- security staff protection
- personal access and property control protection
- security alarms and electronics protection

Security policies and procedures should be carefully thought out and discussed with all library staff, involving such concerns as minimizing risk; rapid, firm, and consistent response; remaining calm; drill evacuation procedures; a "telephone tree" to alert other departments; the role of security guards; and role-playing games and simulated emergencies to elicit and evaluate possible responses to threats. Here's the bottom line: Because everyone is potentially affected by security problems, all library employees must be serious about building security. Management must endorse and support both the goals and the strategies of interdiction and discouragement of potential perpetrators.

Most of the following actions can be taken immediately by most libraries and have the additional advantage of not requiring much in the way of new funding:

- Safety seminars, workshops and in-service training sessions should be scheduled on a regular basis to train all staff for dealing with confrontation and recognizing and knowing how to cope with threats, attitudes, and warning signs (in fellow staff as well as the general public).
- A crisis management plan should be in place and reviewed with all staff members.
- Liaison with local law enforcement agencies (such as community and campus police) should be maintained or upgraded, where possible.
- All rules pertinent to library security should be posted in conspicuous places.
- The library should affirm its willingness to prosecute in cases of crime committed against people or property.
- Monitoring of rest rooms should be a daily part of staff duties.
- Well-marked emergency phones or communications devices should be placed outside the libraries (e.g., along walkways and in parking lots).
- Staff photo ID badges should be worn.

Even the most vigilant library, however, cannot be prepared for emergencies or sudden problems. By definition, unexpected and/or unanticipated events occur with little or no notice ahead of time. That's why participation of all staff in training exercises and discussions is so important. Security is everybody's business because it affects everybody's safety.

However we might wish it otherwise, library crime exists and is going to continue to exist as long as there are libraries. It therefore behooves us to do what we can to prevent crime as a preferable and cheaper alternative to dealing with crime's outbreak or its aftermath and repercussions. The combined attempts of library staff and others can go a long way toward mitigating the potential for breaches of normal safety and security. Such mitigation activities are designed to reduce the degree of long-term risk to human life and property from natural and manufactured hazards alike. Among these preventive steps are:

- strict adherence to building structure and safety codes
- compliance with occupational safety and health guidelines
- disaster insurance coverage
- well-thought-out emergency plans
- properly functioning fire and intrusion alarms and other warning systems
- good relations with local police and firefighters
- training and exercises for all personnel, including simulated emergency drills conducted once a year, at the very least

A Checklist for Library Building Security

Figure 4.1, which follows, provides a checklist for assessing library building security. It contains matters to consider and methods to prepare a library for anticipated problems of security and safety. The checklist is intended to be of use in deciding what security is needed and how it should be allocated, given stringent resources. It may serve as a template or model for evaluating a library's security posture, where prior policies are absent.

It is strongly recommended that library administration attempt to get a clear idea of the recent crime rate in the library's community and immediate vicinity. If presented in statistical format, this may help those who fund libraries appreciate the magnitude of the problem of security. Knowing such things will not necessarily serve as a predictor of when and where crime will strike, but it will furnish a timely warning of when increased vigilance is necessary. It is also useful to know the specific kinds of crime that are common nearby and something about the people who commit them. All of these factors will assist in evaluating what is necessary in the area of security to handle the problems that are likely to come up. Beyond these considerations, check the following list of questions to ask during the security analysis:

- What is the library's distance from a police station?
- What is the library's proximity to the nearest school?
- Are there many teenage patrons (especially in areas where gangs are in evidence)?
- Is there proximity to an agency serving indigents (e.g., homeless shelters, halfway houses)?
- Is the library isolated from other buildings?
- Can a potential criminal approach the building without being seen?
- Are there evening hours of public service, especially in winter?
- Are staff members frequently working alone?
- Are money and other negotiable valuables or items of high value kept in the building at night, especially in drawers or in desks?
- Are there signs posted warning of surveillance and describing penalties for specific crimes?

FIGURE 4.1
Library Location and Community Characteristics—Factors That May Contribute to Increased Risk of Crime in a Library Building

Management of Materials, Property, and Building Contents

- Is cash out of patrons' reach in secured containers (and, if possible, out of their sight)?
- Are rare items and those of considerable value kept in locked rooms or cases with alarmed doors or gates?
- Are displays in public areas arranged so that missing items can be readily noticed?
- Is there a schedule for checking inventory often enough to detect ongoing theft?
- Are all desks in the building lockable and kept locked?
- Is valuable equipment (e.g., computer terminals and printers) either bolted to desks or secured in safe places at night?
- Are personal belongings kept in locked areas to which only the staff has normal access?

Doors, Keys, and Locks: Entry and Interior Space Control

- Is door security such that no patrons should be able to enter or leave the building undetected?

- Are door locks durable heavy-duty dead bolts in good repair, with secure hinges that make them difficult to pick or damage?
- Do all entry points to the building have adequate and functioning alarms?
- Are master keys to the building—plainly marked "Do Not Duplicate"—distributed to as few staff members as practicable?
- Can the library afford break-resistant windows with strong security locks or alarm systems?
- Are all fire escapes, vents, ducts, and skylights—potential access points for intrusion—protected in the same manner as doors and windows?
- If the "walkaround" audit revealed blind spots and "secret places," has an attempt been made to get rid of them?
- Have administration and staff discussed and considered the ramifications of not allowing patrons to carry bags and other materials into or out of the building without being stopped? This is, of course, a privacy issue, but most people will consent to checking their belongings once they realize that it's for everyone's safety and security, and has the extra bonus of keeping the cost of library restocking minimal.
- Are designated staff or guards given the responsibility for inspecting bags and other materials carried into and out of the building?
- Are doors to all staff areas locked with peepholes drilled into solid doors?
- Are display cases kept locked?
- Is anything being done to prevent people from loitering or "hanging out" in rest rooms and private or restricted locations?
- Is the library willing to consider limiting access to rest rooms (e.g., key access with one person at a time permitted to have the key) and elevators?
- Are staff members not left to work alone on floors or in remote locations?
- Is it feasible to leave "peepholes" in library stacks by leaving sections of shelving empty?
- Are all library records securely stored, including lockdown files and password-only accessible computer programs?

- Is there periodic maintenance and repair of locks, hinges, and door closers?
- Are emergency exits clearly identified inside and out?
- Does the library have some form of internal communications system, accessible to all staff?

Windows

- Are all windows either made of break-resistant glazing panels or covered with secured grilles or screens to prevent easy break-in?
- Are all ground-level or below ground-level windows key-locked?
- Are all duct openings secured from the inside?
- Are upper-level windows, doors (including roof, stairwell, and elevator penthouses), roof hatches, and other openings inaccessible from fire escapes, balconies or porches, adjacent building windows and rooftops, high walls or fences, attached ladders, trellises, vines, trees, or utility poles?

Barriers/Fencing/Gates

- Is the exterior of the library well lighted after dark with bushes and shrubbery small enough to prevent hiding?
- Are fences and shrubs placed and trimmed so that they do not block visibility?
- For the sake of perimeter control, is it possible to avoid or get rid of hidden locations outside such as weeds, vines, bushes, and close trees?
- Is it possible to get rid of dark or hidden spots in the library's parking lot?
- Do local or campus police patrol on an unpredictable schedule, both during normal operating hours and at night and on weekends?
- Are padlocks securely attached to fences or gates, with hinge pins difficult to remove?

Lights

Over and over again, studies of crime have shown a positive correlation in public places of lighting with safety. The more there is of one, the more there is of the other. Few potential criminals are willing to attempt their deeds in well-lighted places where the risk of being seen and identified is high. These are questions for the self-examining library to ask concerning the placement, level, and adequacy of lighting within and outside the library building:

- Is there adequate lighting in all public areas of the building?
- Are study areas, carrels, shelving, and stacks arranged for maximum visibility?
- Are master fuse and lighting panels operated only through key switches?
- Are fuse and switch boxes kept locked and as vandal-proof as possible?
- Are all bulbs and fluorescent lighting tubes covered and locked?
- If electrical failure occurs, is there an instant and automatic power backup system?
- Are emergency lights inaccessible to the public and secured?
- Does the library have a program of periodic testing of all light fixtures?
- Are elevator lights controlled by vandal-proof and theft-proof key switches?
- Is there provision for adequate and automatic after-hours security lighting that is adequate and practical, not just aesthetic?
- Is there periodic review and discussion of changes in lighting due to building alterations or changes in traffic flow?
- Do all staff understand what to do in the event of a light or power failure?
- Does the library have a contract for periodic maintenance and repair of lighting?

Intrusion and Fire Alarms and Protection

The purpose of most alarms is to alert staff and authorities to emergencies. It is assumed that fire alarms are required by state or local ordinances for public buildings, but intrusion alarms are expensive systems that the library may wish to get along without. They are expensive purchases often requiring equally expensive service and maintenance contracts. Asking yourself these questions will help you decide whether your library needs such alarms.

- Has it been determined that burglar alarms are necessary (e.g., the identification of something valuable in need of protection)?
- Does the library's insurance provider insist upon or give a discount for intrusion alarms?
- Are silent panic alarms necessary and feasible at entrances and remote areas?
- Are audiovisual signal alarms necessary to monitor door openings or pedestrian traffic?
- Are emergency and exit doors provided with alarms?
- Are interior alarms installed on exhibit cases, rare document displays, and drawers for petty cash?
- Are alarm monitors always secured, tamper-proof, and away from mainstream traffic?
- Are explicit written instructions on the operation of alarms and the action to be taken in the event of a problem printed on or near alarm signaling devices?
- Is a sprinkler system installed?
- Is there an adequate system of fire alarm devices? Does the fire department generally respond to alarms promptly?
- Are street fire alarm boxes nearby?
- Are adequate fire extinguishers present on all floors? Are they of the appropriate type? Do they get tested and serviced on a regular basis?
- Are there written procedures for fire alarms, drills, and evacuation, revised as necessary?
- Are all staff aware of a systematic fire or other emergency evacuation plan?
- Does the library conduct periodic fire drills?

Stack Access

Most American libraries, especially those in public buildings, provide public access to open stacks. This is a convenience for the public, permitting browsing and exploration. It is also a risk for those who use open stacks. So the library must first consider the pros and cons of closing the stacks. When the library follows an open stack policy, here are some questions to consider:

- How can the library's physical arrangement be altered for better surveillance and room and stack monitoring?
- How much surveillance can be achieved by librarians from their desks or workstations?
- What is the best method of floor patrols for stack areas?
- How can surveillance be augmented by librarian assistants while shelving and retrieving?
- Would increased lighting in stack areas help reduce opportunities for crime?
- Before admitting people to open stacks, how can the library inspect briefcases, packages, and other belongings without unduly delaying, irritating, or inconveniencing the public?
- Can the library afford strategically placed cameras, mirrors, and microphones for spot surveillance by staff?
- If the decision is made to keep stacks closed, how will the public be kept out of stack areas (e.g., closed doors with signs, locked doors, access granted to certain employees only)?
- If the decision is made to close previously open stacks, how can the library best seek to persuade the community that the move is desirable and necessary?
- Will those permitted to enter closed stacks require passes?
- Will staff use coded or photo employee ID cards?
- Will the closed stack library staff control access by maintaining a log of visitors who must sign in and out?

Security Gates

Security gates are designed to prevent the disappearance of uncharged books via the front door. Once installed, they will protect the book stock to a certain extent, but all library staff should be aware that such gates have their obvious limits. In the first place, it doesn't require a sophisticated knowledge of electronics for a person to figure out how the magnetization system works and then to defeat it by removing the magnetized strips before attempting to make off with books. Secondly, books may be removed in other ways, such as being slid under or sailed over the gate's effective field, or may simply be removed through an unguarded staff entrance, an openable window, or with a cooperating staff member.

Older security gates are frequently subject to so many false alarms that staff grow inattentive when alarms sound and do not question or detain people who set them off. Finally, a clever thief will sometimes conceal two or more books on his or her person, and, when the alarm goes off, sheepishly give up one to reproving library staff, while walking away with the other undetected. Such gates, moreover, can do nothing to protect most magazines or to ward off mutilation of library materials.

Here is a checklist to follow for libraries using magnetic security gates in the attempt to safeguard their property:

- Are all public exits from the library (except for required fire doors) gated?
- Is it possible for would-be book thieves to throw books out open windows?
- Are security gates "on" at all times during normal operating hours? Are they in proper working order?
- Is the magnetic field of the gate sufficiently sensitive that the alarm will always go off when an unmagnetized strip passes through it?
- Are the gates tested periodically to ensure that they do not malfunction?
- Have all books in the permanent collection been fitted with magnetized strips?
- Are magazines and newspapers magnetized?
- Are circulation and security staff properly trained in the procedure to follow when the gate alarm goes off?
- Do all staff know what to do when it appears that a patron has attempted to exit the building with an improperly checked-out book?

Proactive Solutions for Security Problems

In general terms, the simplest way to reduce security problems is to make the most likely trouble spots (those that receive the most complaints or look like ideal targets for the bad guys) less attractive to thieves, sexual deviants, and others bent on crime or mischief. Specific remedies may be to add lighting that cannot be altered (e.g., bulbs that cannot be unscrewed, switches that cannot be turned off); to move or create an employee work area or staging area for shelving in or near these areas; to arrange some sort of activity in the area that is also productive for the library, like shelf reading, bar coding, or shifting shelves to make room for new books.

If space permits, a library may find it prudent to leave gaps at eye level or to lower stack shelving so that it is not taller than most patrons—maybe four feet in height, maximum. Perhaps most important of all, persons caught violating laws should be prosecuted, regardless of who is caught, and their prosecution should be publicized. It must be made known that this behavior is not condoned by the library administration, will not be tolerated, and those caught will be prosecuted vigorously. Further, the public should be aware that library theft or mutilation has real-world consequences severe enough to deter would-be criminals or opportunists from contemplating adding the library to the short list of their favorite haunts and hangouts.

A proactive library is one that has prepared itself for quick reaction to security problems. Sometimes, however, legal statutes or existing guidelines can impede efforts for that reaction to be instituted. It is important to know where the library stands—both legally and practically—regarding problem behavior by members of the public. Ask yourself these questions:

- Does your library have a policy or procedure manual approved by the political or administrative jurisdiction?
- Does that document contain a statement of admission criteria?
- Does it contain a building usage statement?
- Does it have patron behavior guidelines?

If no such documents exist, you're likely to be hard-pressed to identify persons you do not have to or wish to admit, or whom you wish to evict, and the reasons for such actions. If such documents do not exist, it is recommended that they be created immediately. If you have some of these policies but not all, create the remainder. If you have them but they were written a long time ago when conditions in your community were different, they may need to be reviewed and updated to reflect changing circumstances.

There are, of course, limits on what a library staff may reasonably expect to put up with in the way of patron behavior. Libraries open to the public exist to serve the public but usually can define their public and the services to be rendered as they see them. For instance, some services, such as borrowing privileges, may apply only to those who can prove residency within the taxing district. Some libraries allow a nominal initial borrowing of only a few items, as a safeguard against untrustworthiness, in case they never see their materials again. The actual library card is mailed to the patron at the address stated on the application. If it comes back, the library's loss is limited to those items checked out initially. Some libraries issue membership cards only if the card-seeker brings in a recent utility bill or other official correspondence with his or her name on it. This is only good sense and protection of the public interest. After all, when library materials are purchased with tax dollars, the whole community has a financial stake in their cost. Librarians lend, but do not give, materials to patrons. They expect these materials to be returned in a timely fashion or renewed. Like all other custodians and guardians, librarians must be accountable to their funding source (the public) for the proper management of the items in their charge. Sometimes missing articles can be recovered, but recovery of overdue and lost items can become problematical in a number of ways, and it is normally safer and saner to make a serious attempt to hold on to things before they walk out the door than it is to try to get them back afterward. This is yet another proof of the adage about the ounce of prevention, and it is good business sense as well.

Libraries are, after all, businesses, and should be run accordingly. What kind of business is a library? Specifically, the library is in the lending and information business. Like any other business, the library must know how to get in touch with its customers. To qualify for availing oneself of library services, a valid identification card with address and photo may be necessary. People who reside outside of the library's governmental jurisdiction, or have no permanent residence, will be hard to track down if materials are not returned on time or at all. Nonmembers of the library's community may be extended privileges, but fairness requires that they incur charges commensurate with the taxes paid by residents of the jurisdiction for their borrowing privileges.

Sometimes patrons refuse to provide personal information. When such patrons are notified that we view them as risky borrowers, they become problem patrons if they begin arguing with the desk staff over procedures and policies. Many unpleasant incidents, however, can be averted or avoided if we have spelled out ahead of time just who is entitled to what, and do not deviate from established policy no matter who is concerned. Whom do we serve? This question needs to be answered in writing for us by our administration and our board.

It is also unwise (and possibly legally actionable) to keep the rules hidden or to make them up as you go along to suit the situation. Sometimes patrons actually ask to see the rules in writing or ask how long and why a particular rule has been in effect. We should have positive and prompt answers to these questions ready for them. Above all, the rules must apply uniformly and evenly to all who enter the library—whether it's a homeless man or the mayor or the dean of Arts and Sciences—or we're going to have problems and possibly be charged with discrimination.

We need to keep in mind that patrons come from a variety of backgrounds, experiences, and levels of literacy. However we do it, we must find ways to communicate the rules. All patrons need to know about them, and we cannot assume that the public knows anything about us or what we do. This is why it is important to review, distribute, and reiterate the rules of our library to all. Just as examples, we must remind people how to dress, if that's one of our requirements. We must require them to bring appropriate identification, if we use it to determine borrowing eligibility. We must let them know ahead of time the penalties that they will incur should they fail to return materials on time. It is also important to post rules and board-sanctioned policies concerning proper conduct within the library's walls. Conspicuous signage, brochures, and printed sheets of rules are imperative because they can be used to explain or uphold challenged policies. In short, we must be both vigilant and diligent about educating both our public and our staff. This proactive approach will, in the long run, serve to cut down on complaints and misunderstandings and to improve public relations.

The cornerstone to solving the problem patron issue is a strong and supportive administration. There are too many problem patron scenarios in library literature in which nothing useful could be done by the staff to address the problem because they had no authority or support from the administration. If the administration takes a blasé or cavalier approach to problem patrons, behavior problems will continue or perhaps even multiply.

Change is one of life's only constants. Entire neighborhoods can change in a year or two, and libraries may find themselves behind the curve in keeping up. Being proactive means that we cannot wait until a problem occurs and then develop a policy. If the library does have a policy and/or patron guidelines document, review it annually to see if it is still up-to-date. If it was written five, ten, or even more years ago, chances are that things have changed to the extent that changes are needed in the policies. Perhaps teen gangs did not harass patrons at the library some years ago but have begun to do so now. Newer phenomena like skateboarding and roller blading were not problems a decade ago, but they are in library buildings today. They may have to be mentioned specifically in lists of proscribed behaviors. Some parents have always used the library as a baby-sitting or day-care service, but in times of economic uncertainty, their numbers grow. Panhandling, theft of personal property, sexual harassment, and indecent display may not have occurred to the policy/guideline writers of a generation ago as problems, but they are often more problematic today. What's our policy on food and drink in the building (e.g, what action should we take when we spot someone having a snack in a reading room)? Do we permit using library tables for playing games? How do we feel about patrons sleeping on couches and chairs? These and other situations ought to be discussed by staff and administration, and rules concerning them should be clearly spelled out. And the best policy is to have the rules in place before an incident occurs, rather than to try to write one to fit an action that has already transpired.

The policy and guidelines cannot list each and every possible offense, but both should be worded in such a manner as to be broadly inclusive. For instance, does our policy clearly state that the library is solely intended for the use of persons making use of library materials? And what, does it warn, will happen to those judged to be using the building and its facilities for non-library purposes? The language of your library's behavior policy will reflect not just your conditions, objectives, and goals, but something in the rules ought to state that any person in the library whose behavior falls outside the guidelines may be asked to leave by library personnel, be evicted from the premises by security officers, or be subject to arrest by police.

The behavior policy document should set the parameters of acceptable behavior and indicate who has the ultimate responsibility of deciding whether behavior is unacceptable. In public libraries, this language should be consistent with relevant provisions of local municipal civil and criminal codes. Academic institutions may have a code of student conduct that governs behavior on campus, which will normally apply to library users as well. These are good sources to start with because they should delineate prohibitions and rights. Academic campuses, in addition to having their own rules, are not exempt from state or federal laws that cover all other citizens. If certain actions like theft and vandalism are against the law in a specific locality, they are equally against the law on campuses and within academic library buildings such as libraries.

If necessary, library security officers may need to discuss these issues with local police to find out which behaviors are not allowed in public; what laws exist, apply, and are enforceable; and what recourse is available. This takes time, but it will save aggravation later. It is equally important to educate the public. Do not hide the rules. Post them, pass them out, and display them, along with the hours of service. While a policy document cannot prevent all undesirable behavior, it will at least present a clear guideline for making decisions and choices. Most people—even when they do not like a decision in sorting out a dispute—will respect fairness and impartiality where it is detectable.

As staff members, we should be acquainted with our rights as public employees. Every library worker at a public workstation will hear many times during a long career some aggrieved member of the public protesting, "I pay your salary!" True, in a sense, but we have the right to work in a safe environment. Allowing free entry into our library building does not constitute passive consent to an "anything goes" range of behaviors. Does our state or municipality or campus have rules governing behavior in public settings? Are those rules enforced? And if we do enforce the rules, and a member of the public still persists in objectionable behavior, who can we call for backup? A library that maintains a good rapport with local police and social service agencies is more likely to get a quick response to its requests for assistance than one that has never bothered. If no amicable ties to law enforcement have been developed to date, they should be pursued by whomever has the authority to do so.

The Library Security Staff

As stated previously, every library, regardless of type or size, should appoint someone from existing staff as Library Security Officer (LSO), and that officer should be charged with coordination of building security and handling of problem situations. The LSO's coordination of staff efforts should include compilation of inventories. This may simply be noting the loss of a few items, or it may mean an extensive inventory of the entire collection, which may take months. Each authority notified is likely to ask at least the same two questions: "What is missing?" and "What is its value?" Therefore, arrangement for appraisals of lost or recovered materials must also be made. The FBI may not be willing to enter a case unless the value of the missing material can be judged sufficiently substantial that felony charges can be anticipated in the event an arrest is made. Prompt and candid communication to staff about progress on the case is also a good idea. And finally, creation and maintenance of internal records of actions followed during the progress of the case must be undertaken. Names, telephone numbers, and addresses should be included when appropriate. This will prove to be a valuable record later as memory fades. Document everything relevant to the case. You never know when it might be helpful later. Information, even in jotted notation format, can be used to assure trustees and insurers that appropriate actions have been taken or are in the works. And each new law enforcement officer or detective assigned to the case can be brought up to speed quickly by reading such journal entries. If the case drags on for a long period of time and institutional personnel change, it may become the only accurate record of what occurred at the time the theft was detected, what action was taken at that time, and with what result.

Library theft is serious business. It needs legal prosecution like other transgressions and infractions. One can only hope that librarians will take their concerns to their state or provincial legislatures and demand improvement where inadequate state laws exist. Our lawmakers ought to be encouraged to review the inadequate treatment of theft from libraries as it appears in many state codes. This proposed legislation should no longer classify theft from libraries as a mere misdemeanor, punishable by a proverbial "slap on the wrist." The proposed model legislation, in fact, should recommend that theft of materials valued at less than $500 be classed as a misdemeanor, $500 to $5,000 be a Class I felony, and theft of more than $5,000 be a Class II felony, with appropriate punishments prescribed for convictions. Once we prosecute book thieves as common criminals by equating the monetary value of what they have stolen as we do the value of other stolen goods, then the criminals can be prosecuted fairly, and equal justice will prevail. This will probably entail some consciousness-raising in the public sector as well. The library's publicity staff (if there is one) should get busy writing appropriate copy to acquaint the community with the reasons for the desired legislation.

Summing up, librarians must press immediately for the revision of antiquated state laws to make the prosecution of book thieves an acknowledged punishment for criminal behavior. The clever library thief or vandal knows that some times are better than others for carrying out criminal work. Library buildings in which service areas are spread over several floors, and whose architecture includes study carrels, alcoves, nooks, and crannies, may be conducive to quiet study but may equally facilitate covert activity.

A library's staffing may leave its security at risk, too. During evening and weekend hours, student assistants may be the mainstay of library services. Weeknights, full-time library employees may work only at the reference and government documents desks until 9:00 P.M. Circulation staff members may rotate evening and weekend duties, and might be the only full-time staff available in an emergency situation. Clearly, the library cannot be monitored by such a skeleton staff while continuing to provide library services.

Security Guards

Security guards are responsible for securing the library at closing and are trusted with access to keys normally unavailable to other library workers. These duties require the maturity to assume responsibility and authority and to make quick, accurate judgments in an emergency or problem situation. Guards may have served in the military or even be retired from the police force. They should project a self-assured appearance. We prefer those with a mature, outgoing demeanor who demonstrate good communications skills over those who are seeking control over patrons. The ideal guards are responsible, reliable people who are willing to work as a team to enforce library rules and provide security on a night and weekend schedule. See figure 4.2.

Staff Training and Supervision

Staff training and supervision are imperative to good security.The primary objectives of such training are to teach normal operating and closing procedures, to learn emergency procedures, and to become familiar with library public service areas. First, the patrollers must be familiar with library rules and know how these should be enforced.

- Is a security staff deemed necessary? (It should be, in any library.)
- Should the library hire on contract or hire its own security employees?
- Are background and reference checks performed before guards are hired?
- Are guards uniformed?
- Are guards permitted to carry firearms, nightsticks, or other weapons?
- Are guards provided with a good communications system and equipment?
- Are guards thoroughly trained before assuming their duties and then supervised on the job?
- Is there a written code of instructions dealing with the duties and responsibilities of security staff?
- Is a security officer's performance spot-checked?
- Do library security staff have a system of liaison with local police?

FIGURE 4.2
Security Staff Selection—A Checklist

They should be given a copy of pertinent policies and procedures. The library security specialist should discuss these with the new recruits at length, giving examples of problems and how they should be addressed. Next to be learned is the layout of the buildings, including which doors should be locked at all times; location of emergency exits, fire extinguishers, alarms, and house telephones; and operation of security gates. This stage of training is reinforced by assigning the trainee to accompany a veteran patroller or the security specialist on rounds and at closing. Known library security risks, such as remote areas or open windows, should be discussed as they are encountered on the rounds.

Emergency procedures such as fire alarm evacuation, tornado warning procedures, and so forth, call for a somewhat different training approach. Since an emergency requires communication and team effort, the security specialist must delineate procedures to be followed and discuss possible scenarios with each team. This approach establishes a group understanding of both the team's and each individual's responsibilities in an emergency. To reinforce this understanding, about once a semester, the security specialist will arrange a library fire drill with the city's, county's, or academic institution's public safety division. After this surprise exercise, the patroller team will reconvene to discuss problems and concerns about the procedures.

After an initial training period, the LSO has several ways of checking the thoroughness of the student patroller's understanding and compliance with procedures. First is to accompany the student on rounds and at closing, having the student explain the procedures as he or she proceeds. Second is to have the student use a watch clock, checking to make sure all key stations are recorded on the paper dial. The third method of checking falls under the heading of unobtrusive study, such as attempting to hide at closing or leave a door unlocked to see if the student patrollers can be caught off guard. The students find this last method to be challenging, almost a game, although some feel threatened or resentful when they discover that they're being tested in what they perceive as a "sneaky" manner. They also may build a team rapport, trying to "outfox the fox." The security supervisor may wish to reward the team when they find the traps set for them by treating them to a pizza or donuts at the end of the shift, providing positive reinforcement for this potentially demoralizing checkup.

An aware, alert library staff is often the best deterrent to library crime. The issue of proper training as a means of making staff aware of their responsibilities for security is very important. Security supervisors should have regular and frequent training meetings with the library staff. In these sessions, the library staff should discuss their expectations in detail. The sessions should include a walk-through of the library to highlight what security monitors are expected to do when they patrol, including checking the alarms on all emergency exits. Evacuation procedures should also be covered. The supervisor should perform spot checks throughout the year, especially during evening hours after most staff have left the building. As additional deterrents, the library staff may wish to institute such crime prevention measures as leaving warning notes on unattended belongings, designing crime awareness bookmarks to be placed in books at checkout, or placing crime awareness and library rules posters throughout the building.

Staff training covering various forms of reaction to security problems and matters of public safety should be part of every library's orientation for new staff and should also be required of all staff at least once a year via in-service workshops and programs. Dealing with sudden illness and injury, including the basics of first aid, should also be part of continuing education programs for all staff, in addition to education and discussions of responses to patron behavior.

As examples of situations that may arise, staff should discuss such matters as what to do when you suspect a heart attack, an epileptic seizure, a stroke, and so on. Another important question is when—if at all—is it permissible to touch a patron, whether to loosen clothing, search for identification, or rummage for medications? The important thing is that the library will want to be on the safe and legal side in all such occurrences.

Some other specific questions to ask yourself concerning staff training are:

- Have you developed or been given a clear procedure including forms for reporting crime?
- Have all staff been trained in the elements of crime prevention and reporting?
- Working with a legal officer, can you develop a set of guidelines for prosecution of thieves?

When should your security forces go into action against suspected infractions? When is it acceptable to ignore certain behaviors, wait and observe, or let a suspect off with a warning? Ensuring that all patrons are using the library as a library is what preparedness is all about. Anyone perceived as using the library for library purposes deserves a degree of latitude about possibly eccentric or even bizarre behavior. How much latitude? That will vary with the prevailing rules and the temperament of the staff member making the observation. To the extent that the person with unusual behavior is using library materials or services and harming no one else, it is probably a good idea to leave such a person alone. Naturally, your best judgment concerning what the person is likely to do next should guide your reaction to what he or she is doing at the moment. Experience is a great teacher, and years of observing human behavior will often permit security-minded library staff to develop a "sixth sense" about who must bear careful watching. When you are in doubt, however, one obvious but helpful suggestion is to inform your superior in the library hierarchy and let him or her make the call in problem situations.

Surveillance in Preventing Library Crime

Surveillance in one form or another is very useful in libraries seeking to discourage people intent on sexual behavior in public buildings. The object of all types of surveillance is not just to keep an eye on everybody, but to make would-be perpetrators of sex acts or other proscribed behavior so uncomfortable or so fearful of being discovered that they will elect voluntarily to go elsewhere. Surveillance is expensive when it entails cameras, film, and people paid to watch several banks of cameras, correctly interpret what they see, and act swiftly and effectively to clamp down on the behavior. The simple expedient of having large, baleful security personnel follow "suspects" around the building may accomplish the same end.

Deterring such crime in library rooms and areas is definitely a commendable goal. Service stations and public buildings in urban areas commonly resort to locked rest rooms, whereby the person desiring admission must ask an employee for the key. This practice, however, has several drawbacks. It is, first of all, labor-intensive; handing out the key to the rest room is just one more annoying chore for the staff members. More importantly, how do they secure its safe return? When giving out the rest room key, how can the staff member know whether the rest room is going to be used by one person or more and whether it is being used for its intended function?

Better lighting in stacks and other public areas will help a lot, and at comparatively minimal expense, as contrasted to other solutions. This may go a long way to deterring offenders who shrink from exposure to bright light, but what will it do to stop the public exhibitionist?

Admittedly, some patrons visit library buildings with the intention of committing acts of vandalism, mischief, misconduct, or even crime. The bottom line, however, is that the prevention of crime is much easier than the apprehension of suspected criminals. The object is to dissuade those who come to libraries for immoral or illegal purposes from accomplishing their goals. The combined efforts of security staff, library personnel, and cooperating police authorities may not deter or prevent all crime, but they should make it riskier for those inclined to such acts to continue than to stop.

More, more frequent, and better-trained guards and patrols are an obvious solution, but full-time security doesn't come cheap, and such a line in the budget may be deleted by cost-conscious library trustees or the politicians down at city hall. Uniformed guards, who project a no-nonsense attitude, who look and act like law enforcement professionals, and who appear to be conscientious and to take their work seriously, are still probably the most workable solution to the problem.

The best advice for a library administrator serious and intent on preventing library crime is to walk through the building, trying as much as possible to think like a bad guy. Take a walk around with another staff member and analyze your library's security posture from the point of view of a person intent on ripping off, walking away with, or stealing something. Look for weak points, dark areas, remote alcoves, and other places where surveillance is infrequent or absent. Ask yourself "How could I make off with something without being seen or heard?" The answers to a question like this should lead to (1) an awareness of where your library is vulnerable to theft, mutilation, and concealment of library materials, and (2) ideas on how to prevent such action or at least make it more difficult. Some countermeasures cost a lot of money to institute and deploy, but some, such as having thorough patrols of all library areas at irregular intervals, may not.

It was stated earlier in this chapter, but it's worth saying again: Security is everybody's business, especially that of library staff. Any loss of materials is unacceptable and weakens libraries at the same time. Solutions to the various problems of library crime begin with good space planning and architecture that optimize visual surveillance. Knowing who's up to what in the library's public rooms and stack areas is essential to good security.

Recommended Procedure When a Loss Is Determined

The Smithsonian Institution's National Conference on Cultural Property Protection, held in Raleigh, North Carolina, in February 1997 (and at which the author was both an attendee and a presenter), offered the following guidelines for dealing with the loss of important library materials:

Protect the scene and notify your local police, sheriff, and investigation departments as soon as possible. Use press coverage to your advantage. Post rewards but pass ransoms to police.

Determine the last time the lost objects were seen and what happened in the area or to the objects since then.

Gather documents, descriptions, and photographs of what is missing and tell the police what they are looking for.

Do not hesitate to report both direct losses and losses that have occurred over time. You do your colleagues a disservice by not reporting.

Follow up on police actions and investigations to ensure that everything possible is being done.

Each of the following agencies keeps a lost or stolen file and can be contacted. Work with your local law enforcement agency who keeps the case active.

National Stolen Art File, Federal Bureau of Investigation	(202) 324-4192
Interpol—U.S. Washington, D.C. National Central Bureau	(202) 616-9000
New York City Police Department, Special Frauds Squad	(212) 374-6850
Art Loss Register, International Foundation for Art Research, Inc. (IFAR)	(718) 879-1780
Special Agent in Charge, U.S. Customs Service, New York City	(212) 466-2900
Bookline Alert, Missing Books and Manuscripts (BAMBAM)*	(212) 737-2715
Antiques Market, *Journal of Field Archeology*	(617) 353-2357
Internet's Interloc*	interloc@shaynet.com
Internet's LIBSAFE.L	mailserv@bvc.edu
Internet's LSO-L	sallen@hobbes.kzoo.edu

*required to list loss

In conclusion, here are several more checklists that may be profitably used by a library seeking to upgrade or maintain its security posture:

Each Staff Member Must . . .

- be responsible for his or her own behavior
- interact courteously and ethically with visitors, supervisors, and other staff

- be alert for evidence of violent, abusive, or threatening behavior that he or she personally witnesses, or planned violent or disruptive behavior of which he or she has knowledge
- quickly report such a situation to his or her supervisor, management, security office, or human resources/personnel administrative office/employment assistance counseling program staff

Each Supervisor and Manager Must . . .

- be responsible as staff members in the manner defined above
- assist in a swift and effective response to each situation that poses a serious threat to life, property, or facility operation
- when an illegal, violent, abusive, or threatening behavior occurs, seek advice from a representative from security or other member of the crisis management team and inform your supervisor or manager of the actions recommended or taken
- when an illegal, violent, abusive, or threatening behavior occurs involving staff under your responsibility, take reasonable steps to intercede to preserve life, property, and facility operation, and prepare to take corrective and disciplinary or other administrative action to prevent further disruptive behavior or threat of such behavior
- keep evidence and logs and interview those involved in any incident
- be alert to undesirable or unexplainable changes in behavior that may indicate hostility or require further supervisory action, using advice from appropriate staff

Managers Must . . .

- provide legal advice to managers and supervisors regarding appropriate actions to take and their possible effects
- evaluate the risk and damage to individuals, the institution, the facility, and the facility's operation
- involve other institutional offices as necessary, such as personnel, assistance programs, public affairs, and union representatives
- be aware of your responsibilities through training. Be responsible for educating and supervising your subordinates

Security in Academic Libraries

The term "academic library" conjures up visions of quiet contemplation: students sitting silently, cramming for finals, poring over volumes or indexes, cranking through rolls of microfilm, and reflecting on the origins of humanity, what lies beyond the stars, or some other equally deep philosophical topic. It is inconceivable to many that any sort of criminal activity could possibly take place in such a cloistered environment. However, crime has indeed become an issue in academic libraries, especially those in urban settings. Because of naive and often misplaced trust, most academic libraries are easy targets for crime, including theft or damage to collections, theft of personal or library property, deviant behavior, and personal abuse of library staff.

Most academic libraries share certain characteristics that make them especially vulnerable. The very nature of the function of libraries, in fact, lends itself to criminal activity in that the library expects its assets to be taken off the premises free of charge and brought back at a later date. Even more problematically, academic libraries tend to be open beyond normal business hours and are accessible more hours than other buildings on campus. Most have large open stack areas and are sparsely staffed after the end of the business day and on weekends. Study carrels may dot the stack areas, and these are ideal places for various forms of crime. The fact that libraries are usually rather pleasant places, with normally friendly staff, makes academic libraries, especially those in or near urban areas, attractive to the homeless and mentally ill.

First among alternate security options would be the employment of uniformed police to patrol and maintain a presence in the building during all hours of operation. If this is prohibitive economically, the next best option would be to contract with an outside agency to employ uniformed security guards. Even one uniformed professional security guard provides a psychological level of security and a deterrent to opportunists as well.

But private security may have problems, too, including high turnover, inadequate training, inconsistent supervision, sleeping or reading on duty, and being out of sight for long periods of time. In addition, one library reported thefts by the security guards. On one remembered occasion, I observed that the library's "rent-a-cop" did little else during his nightly four-hour shift beyond flirting and conversing with the female clerks at the circulation desk. What effect his uniformed presence might have had on thieves and other criminals in the building is unknown, but his presence in the library was quickly dispensed with when it became known to the board that he was receiving $10 per hour for talking with library staff and precious little else.

University libraries often are empowered to station security employees in their buildings. Failing that, many have utilized student security officers. They are normally paid at substantially lower wages than career security guards but are taught skills to deal effectively with unruly or belligerent persons and to look for suspicious circumstances and persons. Their duties include random interior patrols, external checks of the building, and a preclosing security check. Such patrols, provided that selection is careful, can be a successful deterrent to theft, mutilation, and rule violation. Student security monitors are often contracted through campus police departments that may hire, schedule, train them in basic security procedures, provide uniforms, and supervise them. The library and the campus police should jointly develop a detailed job description for use in training the monitors in specific library procedures.

In addition, such monitors—especially those wearing uniforms—provide a "presence" by being easily recognizable as security personnel. By regularly being seen throughout the buildings, they act as deterrents to potential violations of library policy and/or the law. They should be trained to handle problem situations such as loud talking, eating and drinking, and other annoying activities. They can also investigate deviant and potentially threatening behavior and coordinate obtaining police assistance, if needed. They may be used at closing to check the outside exits to make sure they are locked and properly secured. Additionally, at closing, monitors clear unstaffed areas of the library and assist public service staff in clearing and securing their areas. In addition, student monitors can be expected to check the integrity of the alarms on all emergency exits on a monthly basis, and to assist in the evacuation of the buildings during emergency situations.

The hiring and deployment of student security monitors, however, is not without its problems for many colleges and universities. A persistent problem stems from the lack of library control over the monitors, who work for campus police. While there is a method of reporting problems, the library has no way of ensuring that action is taken to correct them. Some monitors don't appear to receive adequate training. Each of them is given a packet of information, but frequently, no one goes over it with them.

All too often, two monitors may decide to patrol together. They share a conversation, their attention not on their duties, even though one is supposed to patrol the building while the other remains at the desk. When times are slow, monitors study, sleep, or sit for long periods of time, reading while on duty instead of patrolling. Less conscientious monitors may disappear for long periods of time after they sign in so that no one knows where they are. Many academic libraries have taken repeated measures over the years to remedy such situations but the problems persist.

By way of solution to such problems, a very specific checklist of duties should be compiled by library staff and sent to campus police, along with the library's evacuation plan, copies of which should be distributed to all security monitors. An hourly head count may be required so that the monitors have to walk through the library to all the public service points at least once an hour to count patrons and have public service staff initial their head-count sheet.

The ideal situation—if affordable—would be to hire security guards as members of the library staff to be on duty during all hours the library is open. The advantages of this plan for the library include the opportunity to make hiring and firing decisions; the ability to employ library performance standards, including merit raises or other rewards for good performance, as well as immediate reprimands; and control of training. Employee loyalty because of long-term employment is also a benefit. Since they are library staff, uniformed officers may also be trained to help out at circulation and in the stacks when necessary, where their contracts do not prohibit such practices.

Security in Public Libraries

College and university libraries frequently cite student handbook provisions or campus rules as justifications for decisions about who is permitted access to the building and what visitors may not do once inside. Campus police, moreover, are normally entrusted with the right to question, search, and even apprehend those who do not belong or who are caught doing things against the rules. Public libraries, however, unlike their academic counterparts, do not normally have the luxury of prohibiting people from using their facility, and their guards must be extremely circumspect in what they are allowed to do in dealing with suspicious patrons. As a de facto, if not de jure, public building, the public library is open to all who walk through the doors. Most people who use a public library employ it for "library purposes" —reading for recreation or information, studying, and so on. It is the minority of people who do *not* use the library for "library purposes" who cause headaches for the library's staff.

Many public libraries, as previously mentioned, simply do not have security staff, for the simple reason that the hiring of such employees is beyond their budgets. The public library's security staff should, where funds permit, carry walkie-talkies while they are on duty. This permits them to converse with each other and makes them easy to reach and to summon police quickly if they need help. The primary responsibility of library security staff is to check bags, backpacks, and similar items to prevent theft. Such responsibility is especially important on school days. During the hours between the time when school is dismissed and closing time (which may be well after sunset), monitors should patrol the library. They are instructed to be alert for noisy or disruptive people, vandalism attempts, harassing or stalking behavior, and other possible threats against library property or users. While they can deal with minor problems (boisterous young people, children playing on the elevator or stairs), they should be empowered to call the police if violations of the law occur. To this end, the library staff should seek to establish good rapport with the local police department. Periodic meetings help maintain lines of communication. Having uniformed police visible from time to time on the library's grounds deters many potential troublemakers from coming into the library, while having police patrol the building on no fixed schedule will go a long way to deterring crime.

Still, like other urban facilities, city public libraries still have problems with criminal activity. Drug dealing is the most common infraction, and when the practice is observed, staff should call police immediately and not attempt to deal with such behaviors themselves. Although gang members and "wanna-bees" may loiter on the public library grounds, they usually do not bring their battles into the facility, for which we should all be grateful. Fortunately, libraries are not normally declared a specific gang's "turf," although "showing of colors" goes on all the time in urban libraries, and that could lead to incidents within the library's walls. While there may be fights outside library buildings, however, including some that spill over from nearby schools, there are relatively few such problems inside the building. Library security staff are not empowered to intervene in criminal behavior they may witness outside the building's walls, but should quickly contact police when such behavior is observed.

Besides the difficulties described, the most common problem is vandalism. It appears in two forms: vandalism to the library building, furniture, or equipment, and mutilation of library materials. "Tagging" is the current slang term for the practice of individuals or gang members intentionally marking a wall or other surface to declare their existence or affiliation. Library buildings have many blank walls and other surfaces that attract vandals. Security and custodial staff should be instructed to watch for graffiti, and work as promptly as they can to clean taggers' markings from the building and elevators. They may reappear the following day, of course, but under no circumstances should they be permitted to remain. More seriously than messengers armed with spray paint cans, however, some graffiti practitioners, not content to spray-paint their affiliations on library property, may use pointed objects to "etch" their message into glass or plastic surfaces such as the glass doors at the entrances to the library. Unfortunately, security staff, short of catching perpetrators in the act, have no way of monitoring these activities, although placing a hidden video camera in public areas or the elevators may help to catch vandals. Such a camera would record on a continuous loop, and if graffiti is discovered, the tape could be played in hopes of catching an identifiable miscreant in the act or turned over to police for follow-up action.

More frustrating to librarians and users alike is the constant mutilation of materials, not a problem unique to public libraries, but epidemic within them. Even where and when photocopying is comparatively inexpensive, thoughtless, lazy, egocentric, or cheap people cut articles from reference books, frequently removing entire pages. Librarians discover missing items almost daily. Within a short period of time, recently at one California urban public library staff members noted that maps had been torn from encyclopedias, large reference books, textbooks, atlases, and biographical sources. Complicating matters, such books are often out of print and cannot be replaced.

Few things are more frustrating than coming to the library, finding the book you're looking for, and discovering to your shock that the very page or pages you need to consult have been removed from the volume. Articles on celebrities and states or other popular school assignment topics are favorite topics of fans, idol worshipers, and students, and are taken wholesale out of encyclopedias and biographical sources, while particular poems or short stories get torn or sliced from anthologies. With the assistance and cooperation of colleagues in nearby institutions, the library may be able to salvage mutilated books by copying from another library's materials and replacing missing pages. This does not violate copyright laws so long as the replacement pages are few in number and not designed to stand alone as published works. Often, however, the replacement is too late to meet a student's deadline. The process of tipping in pages is also labor-intensive and may add to the considerable burden of already overworked technical services staffers.

Despite security systems in place, missing items still form a large part of the typical public library's security problem. These fall into three categories: materials that are actually stolen, materials hidden or misshelved deliberately, and items checked out and not returned. Security staff are normally vigilant when they are at their stations at the library exit, but they cannot always catch everyone leaving the library and ask to inspect their bags. Obviously, unless or until libraries can security-tag every page of every item, they will never apprehend all those who vandalize materials.

Items checked out and not returned are what the public finds most difficult to understand. Some libraries have gone to the extreme of employing collection agencies to retrieve materials by calling—or even visiting—delinquent borrowers and demanding that they return the overdue materials. But such moves may backfire: The compensation of the collectors frequently outweighs the value of the missing items, and even if they force a delinquent borrower to pay the cost of the lost items, such items are frequently out of print or otherwise unavailable. Another factor to be considered is the possible public relations backlash attendant upon going after delinquent borrowers in such a rough and determined manner.

There are no inexpensive or easy solutions to these chronic public library problems. Certainly, an expanded and visible security force can act as a deterrent. Private security guards on duty during the afternoon and evening help a great deal, and staff should be vigilant against vandalism, whether by taggers or mutilators of library materials. But it is extremely difficult to catch these individuals in the act, which is the only way to punish them for their infractions and crimes. Furthermore, when dealing with people caught red-handed, one may hear variations of the response "I didn't do it! It was like that when I picked it up!" Then the problem becomes one of credibility—and one of proof, and the burden of proof is on the library.

Many public libraries have attempted to interdict loss of their materials by purchasing and installing Checkpoint or other stop-loss devices to provide materials security. Such systems operate on the principle that magnetized materials will trigger an alarm and lock a turnstile, thus preventing the thief from making off with purloined books. But library administrators and staff should be made aware that it's not all that difficult to defeat such systems (as one example, once you understand how the system works, it's easy to remove the security tags inside the books and other library materials) and, perhaps even more serious a drawback, the turnstiles in use may not be in compliance with the Americans with Disabilities Act (ADA) because they could be locked if a user attempted to leave the library when the alarm sounded.

Summing up, the kinds of problems public libraries may experience are not all that different from those found in academic institutions. Public libraries do not have a campus rules book or academic code to fall back on. However, local statutes that apply to all public places may serve as working guidelines. If necessary, library staff should discuss these issues with local police to find out what behaviors are not allowed in public; what laws exist, apply, and are enforceable; and what recourse we have. This takes time, but it will save aggravation later. It is equally important to educate the public.

Reacting to Security and Safety Violations

Despite any library staff's best efforts, some people are going to perpetrate crimes and misdemeanors within the building, or at least make a serious attempt. It's a fact; deal with it. And when—not if, but when—such incidents occur, swift and competent reaction is called for. Reaction and response to emergency situations includes activities taken immediately before, during, or directly after an emergency that may save lives, minimize property damage, or improve recovery. Among these are emergency plan activation; emergency instructions to patrons in the building at the time; rapid communication with police, firefighting, and medical personnel; and emergency medical assistance if necessary. But reaction to security problems involves much more than acting swiftly, calmly, and decisively during emergencies. It also involves dealing with those who would render the library less than it is intended to be by means of theft, mutilation, and sneakiness. And we cannot ignore the requirement of rapid reaction to any threat to physical safety of the building's occupants as well. These topics are covered in the next two chapters of this book.

Still another form of reaction to problems involves prompt recovery and restoration of services—those activities that restore normal library function, services, and collections in the aftermath of a problem. These involve, for example, removal and clearance of trash and debris, cleaning and rendering serviceable damaged materials where possible, and general facility restoration.

What should a staff member who has just discovered a theft do? At least three types of action must be taken: First, notify appropriate authorities and booksellers about the disappearance of the materials. Second, inventory (a tedious but important task) should be performed on an ongoing or regular basis, to ensure that a reasonably complete picture of what's missing can develop. And third, action must be taken to chronicle events, as far as they are known. Inventory should be done in advance of incidents, and again immediately after each one. Some guidelines are presented in figure 4.3.

There should be no debate over whether to publicize library thefts. The question is no longer a question of whether to notify. The question has shifted, rather, to one of who should do the notifying and who should be notified. The LSO, administration, law enforcement, and public relations staff should plan an appropriate publicity strategy. News releases should be prepared to alert staff and the community to the problems and responses or actions to be taken. The more true-to-life such a statement of resolve sounds, the more respect and assistance the library may expect to receive from the public and from law enforcement. Tell the truth, even if it may cause your library some embarrassment. Staff members, especially, will be inclined to spread rumors if they are not informed honestly. This may demand a delicate balance, as sometimes a lack of information may be perceived as a withholding of information. Too many stories involving real or alleged "cover-ups" have appeared in news stories for people to accept the idea that they're getting the whole story, especially where sensitive matters of security and integrity are concerned. One person—preferably the LSO or the public relations officer—should be the only one to handle inquiries from the news media, and to see to it that everyone has the facts straight. Be sure staff at all levels know to refer inquiries to the designated person.

- *Notification:* All staff members should notify the Library Security Officer (LSO) and appropriate library administrators immediately upon suspicion (certain knowledge is not always possible) that a theft has occurred.
- *Discovery of theft and collection of evidence:* Is there any evidence of intrusion connected with the missing library materials? Any keys unaccounted for? Is there any indication that a patron, staff member, or someone else has stolen books or other materials? Has someone been caught in the act of theft or mutilation? Has a systematic pattern of loss been discovered? Have materials stolen from the library been recovered? Is there any other evidence of a theft?
- *Evaluation:* The LSO must work with the administration, law enforcement personnel, the library security group, and legal counsel, as appropriate, to evaluate evidence and determine a plan of action.
- *Action:* Check the latest inventory printouts and/or take another inventory and compile a list of missing items. Yes, inventory is a boring, difficult job, but only in that way can missing items come to light. Notify appropriate stolen and missing books distribution lists and databases. Notify local booksellers and appropriate specialist dealers. Request action from law enforcement agencies; since they tend to work along hierarchical lines, the most local agency (e.g., local police) should be contacted first. Request action from legal authorities and do whatever you can do to help them. If there are still items in the compromised locations, transfer valuable and vulnerable materials to a more secure location. Check insurance coverage to assure that missing items are covered and begin claims.
- *Publicity:* Historically, libraries and archives have tried to "hush up" or minimize the importance of thefts for fear of ridicule, out of concern that the news would give other potential thieves bad ideas, or for fear of being shunned by donors if the thefts came to light. But there is virtually no institution—big or small, prestigious or not—that has not experienced problems of theft at some time. Law enforcement personnel know from experience that publicity about a case will turn up the heat, which sends a signal to an alert thief not to steal any more items from a particular library, or at least not to do so any time soon.

FIGURE 4.3
Responding to Theft

Action includes a sequence of steps to be followed from the moment the crime is first noticed. Action may involve notifying police, confronting perpetrators, evacuating buildings in an orderly fashion, and knowing what to do when the perpetrator reacts in a variety of ways.

After the security problem or threat, a checklist of things to do would include methods for recovering lost materials, ways and means of increasing security for next time, specific topics in staff training, and learning from the experience.

Crisis Management

Crisis management involves the systematic response to problems that may arise in the library, and requires previous thought concerning possible reactions to a variety of anticipated behaviors. With so many imponderables, it is not surprising that crisis management is a very inexact science. Still, some solutions to specific problems are in order, some of them costing money to implement and some nothing or very little.

Crisis management may entail such measures and procedures as sounding an alarm, notifying the fire department, alerting occupants of the building, remaining calm, and, where necessary, an orderly evacuation.

In high crime areas, there may be a need for silent duress alarms for public service desks (akin to those used in banks) to help staff prepare for trouble and feel safer as they work. Scream alarms in rest rooms might be a workable compromise between the need for bathroom privacy and the availability of signal devices during emergency situations. Surveillance cameras are expensive, and may send just the wrong message ("Big Brother is watching you!"). However, they may make public areas both be safer and appear to be safer.

CHAPTER 5

Emergency and Disaster Management Policies and Procedures

One of the more telling applications of the fundamental values of a society can be found in how that society responds to risk, particularly risk that may result in major losses of human life and/or property. How society prepares for . . . programs to prevent or lessen the effects of such disasters demonstrates the values placed on safety and security . . . and the technical expertise that can be brought to bear on problems. While all risks cannot be eliminated, many can be minimized once they are identified.

—W. L. Waugh Jr. and R. J. Hy, *Handbook of Emergency Management*, 1990

The objectives of this chapter are to:

- introduce and discuss the concepts of a variety of emergency situations in the library—both natural disasters and human actions
- review principles of the Emergency Preparedness Plan
- discuss the expectations, responsibilities, and duties of staff members in emergencies
- provide principles of damage management and control
- detail effective ways for getting the library back up and running after emergencies

Dealing with Emergencies

Like all other public institutions, libraries must occasionally confront emergencies of various types, and, like other public institutions, they need to be ready for trouble when it comes. This chapter deals primarily with natural emergencies and situations, as opposed to those caused by human actions. The last segment covers human-caused emergencies because they also require quick decisions and immediate action.

Emergency considerations all come down to risk—and risk minimization. Everything a library does, in fact, involves risk of one sort or another. But there are levels of risk. Librarians continually deal with crises and emergencies of various types, but the term is often used so loosely as to weaken the true meaning of the term "emergency." Budget cuts, censorship efforts, and sudden threats from difficult patrons may be among the day-to-day challenges of operating a publicly supported, highly visible, heavily used service in a building generally open to the public, but these are not the types of emergencies in which lives or property are immediately threatened.

The primary concern of this chapter is the various aspects of personal safety and effective countermeasures to emergencies. Emergencies are defined as those situations that arise suddenly and need immediate reaction.

By their very nature, emergencies are sudden, so you don't have a lot of time to think things through at the moment they occur. Maybe that's why they're called *emergencies;* if they came with fair warning, reasoned and effective responses would be easier to formulate and effect. Libraries are not immune to emergencies, crises, and disasters, although such incidents are thankfully rare. Different categories of disasters require correspondingly different responses. For definitional purposes, natural disasters are those caused by environmental phenomena, while human disasters are those resulting from human activity, both intentional and unintentional, malevolent and careless. Still, many library administrators fail to acknowledge, understand, or plan for the biggest, most costly, and most serious crises of all: emergencies or disasters that could shut down libraries for weeks, months, or even forever. That's why you need a plan.

Why Your Library Needs an Emergency Preparedness Plan

In February, 1996, an arsonist's fire heavily damaged the Danbury (Connecticut) Public Library, causing at least $4 million in losses and closing the library for at least seven months.

In July, 1996, a suspicious fire caused $10 million in damages to Brooklyn's Pratt Institute and destroyed the school's multimedia center.

These events, and hundreds like them, occur every year, yet many librarians fail to prepare their facilities adequately. In a survey reported by the Regional OCLC Network Directors' Advisory Committee (RONDAC) in 1991, only 19 percent of the libraries surveyed had disaster response plans. Seventeen percent reported that they were "working on them." Sixty-four percent reported that they had no disaster response plans at all.

Having an Emergency Preparedness Plan in place *before* an emergency situation develops allows you to plan and to make decisions about emergency response and recovery.

When disaster strikes, the actions taken in the first minutes or hours can mean a vast difference to the health and safety of staff and patrons. Prompt reaction will also have a positive effect on how much of the library's collection, equipment, and facilities can be salvaged, and how soon (or whether) normal operations can be resumed. All-hazard insurance in force is a must, but frequently insurance does not fully cover the cost of disasters and emergencies. The costs of property damage and business interruption can normally be offset by adequate insurance, but uninsured losses can also occur, such as loss of employees (injury, disability, death, resignations, attrition); cost of temporary equipment and facilities for use during recovery; increased insurance premium costs; and increased costs following recovery and restoration.

Consider, too, the effects of disasters on the community, including your suppliers. Will your library's programs and services be compromised if an essential supplier is knocked out of business by a tornado, hurricane, or other disaster? How long could your library maintain operations without its main suppliers? Do you have a plan for alternative sources? Will your library be able to meet all its commitments?

Creating the Emergency Preparedness Plan

An Emergency Preparedness Plan consists of the development, documentation, testing, evaluation, and implementation of policies, procedures, organizational structure, information, and resources that a library can use to assess potential hazards and develop and prepare appropriate responses to those hazards and strategies for recovery. While Emergency Preparedness Plan objectives may differ substantially from one library to another (e.g., snow emergencies need not be planned for in Florida, while hurricanes are almost unknown in the Midwest), they should always be directed toward the protection of people, protection of property, and preparation for the library to resume normal services as soon as possible.

Each library has special needs that must be fully addressed within its own Emergency Preparedness Plan (EPP). Review your facilities, staff, services, products, and processes carefully to create the best EPP for your library. Creating a comprehensive EPP for your library's specific situation may seem at first to be an overwhelming task. However, according to many insurance underwriters, an EPP is nothing more than a series of documents, tasks, teams, and processes (unified, of course, by the library mission statement, the EPP policy statement, and the guidance and support of upper management). The message is clear and to the point: Don't underestimate the possibility that disaster could strike your library at any time. Be prepared. Start developing an EPP today.

It is, however, probably unlikely that your library need start from scratch in developing its plan. Borrowing liberally from successful emergency planning documents from other libraries—or from other agencies that experience similar conditions and problems—is normally not only permitted but is encouraged. There are few proprietary or protected aspects of emergency planning, and most agencies are more than happy to share their plans with others.

Disaster Management in Libraries

Despite the menace in its name, the term "disaster management" merely emphasizes the need for planning to safeguard people, equipment, materials, and all information created electronically or manually. The literature of disaster planning generally sets out the three salient principles of comprehensive planning (health, safety, and ergonomics) and considers the impact of disasters on human beings and their mental and physical health. Experts agree that there is still much to be learned about planning for quick and effective recovery from disaster. For example, Waugh and Hy (1990) suggest strongly that more research is required about health and safety aspects of such concerns as fire and flood. The need for fire prevention planning, specifically, cannot be overemphasized for libraries, which are filled with combustible material; a safety self-inspection of the premises should address all aspects of the library and can become the basis of defining fire safety concerns.

Specific Aspects of Emergency Management

The following listing (far from exhaustive, but reasonably comprehensive) details some of the principal emergencies that may happen within library buildings or close enough to imperil people, equipment, and materials within. Here is a partial list of situations that may arise that will be dealt with in greater detail. The likelihood of specific problems will vary with geography and climate.

Earthquakes, especially problematic for libraries located in the Pacific states. These may or may not involve volcanic activity, which poses a different problem for libraries.

Structural failures, in particular the collapse of roofing material or walls due to earthquake, flood, snow, or rain

Volcanic activity, centered in the Pacific basin

Hurricanes, which primarily affect library buildings in Gulf Coast and Atlantic states but can cause considerable problems for libraries in inland communities, especially when flooding ensues as a result of torrential rain

Floods, which could imperil any library, anywhere

Tornadoes. For some reason, the United States and Canada experience the huge preponderance of the world's tornadoes and cyclones annually. Nobody knows why. Tornadoes are always accompanied by lightning storms, which can put library operations out of commission for extended periods of time.

Fire. This category of emergency combines wild fires and those started in or near library buildings, both as arson (intentional fires) and accidental events. Both types of library fires are combined here because the results are the same for library buildings and their contents.

Hazardous materials, which vary extensively (e.g., toxins, radiation, asbestos)

It is hoped that you conclude that since there are so many things that may threaten your library, you have a compelling need for an all-hazards emergency management program. Such a plan is recommended for libraries of all sizes and types. Libraries need to have policies in force that cover all these of situations—including those not mentioned above. The purpose of a library's Emergency Operating Plan is to provide a legal framework for the management of emergencies and to give guidance for what to do when an emergency strikes. A well-crafted plan sets out actions in priority order for response to major emergencies involving catastrophic risk, injury, or damage to library personnel, the general public, or library property. The plan should clearly designate who is to do what when an emergency strikes and each staff member's responsibilities in the process of reaction and subsequent recovery. After that, it's a matter of executing the steps in priority order.

Figure 5.1 presents some steps to take in a library building emergency, intentionally generic enough to cover most situations:

- Get on the telephone at once. Call your supervisor, the building's security staff, 911, and local emergency authorities. Call police, fire, ambulance, hospitals, and utility companies. Secure medical aid and other assistance for any injured or ill persons within the library building. Describe the nature of the emergency and give its exact location. Do not be afraid to report the situation to more than one person or agency or to demand rapid, effective action.
- As your first responsibility is to your patrons, stay on the scene and make sure that all persons in the building stand or sit where it is safe. Be prepared to make a statement of the circumstances to responding personnel.
- Protect, secure, and preserve library property, including materials, equipment, furnishings, and vehicles. Security staff may be called to protect vulnerable materials against looting. Curiosity-seekers should be met by persons authorized to send them away.

FIGURE 5.1
Sequential Emergency Procedures

- Assess damage or loss to people, property, materials, equipment, furnishings, and vehicles. Review alternatives (priorities, costs, time frame, emergency and insurance funding) for repairs, replacement, and recovery; consider alternative or interim operating locations. This step will entail a form of triage, such as that used in hospitals in which the most needy cases receive first treatment, while those not in dire or immediate need are assigned lower priorities.
- Public information about the emergency should be furnished to the media so that misstatements, exaggeration, and panic are minimized, as well as to reduce the risk of charges of a "cover-up."
- Set up temporary workstations and locations, if there is any chance of conducting business immediately after the initial crisis has passed.
- Legal and insurance representatives of the library should be contacted early, to prepare a measured response to any lawsuits and to ensure strict compliance with insurance provisions, preventing (or at least drastically reducing) uncompensated loss.
- Obtain authority and funding to initiate cleanup, repairs, replacement, and restoration of damaged property. Someone should immediately be assigned the role of supervisor of recovery, which may entail assessing each library book or other item to determine whether it needs repair, replacement, cleaning, salvage, or discard. This may mean a complete inventory of the collection or assessment of smoke, fire, or water damage. Steps should be taken immediately to protect the collection from further loss or damage due to actions of firefighters or members of the public.
- After the emergency has passed or been resolved, do not hesitate to ask for corrective action, to ensure that the likelihood of recurrence is reduced.
- If your library does not presently have an Emergency Preparedness Plan, urge that one be created at once.

Preparing Staff to Deal with Emergencies

Library staff should be trained to do the following when an emergency breaks out:

- Know when to call 911, when to notify security, and when they, themselves, should act to respond to the crisis.
- Quickly respond to each serious situation of illegal, violent, abusive, or threatening behavior to take reasonable actions to protect life first, and then property and facilities.

- Provide immediate first-aid medical care to injured persons where required.
- Physically segregate and detain any person or persons committing the act and call for police assistance as required.
- Report, keep evidence, and interview those involved.

When the all-clear has sounded and things regain a general semblance of normalcy, the library administration, together with the LSO, should consult with crisis management representatives of local or state government to determine actions to take to prevent these situations from occurring again.

Since many emergencies are much publicized and result in large numbers of human casualties, it makes sense for libraries to attempt to identify risks beforehand, and to work out viable strategies for minimum confusion and maximum protection against hazards. For example, perhaps the best way a library can avoid flooding is for its founders to have decided long ago to build the structure in a high, dry place. And while this may doubtless be excellent advice, it is not always possible to say, "Why don't we just relocate our building to higher ground?" The downtown areas of many large U.S. cities, for example, are built along riverbanks, while others boast ocean or bay frontage but are dangerously close to the water. Saying that those founders shouldn't have built in the locations they chose isn't particularly helpful after the fact. Nor is relocation of the library, in most cases, a viable option unless the administrative entity is willing to spend great sums of money on the project. Ensuring minimum losses when such emergencies do occur is, however, paramount.

Expectations, Roles, and Responsibilities

As this year's hurricane season waxes and wanes, we've been inspired by the stories of how people pull together after a disaster. But for libraries and other cultural institutions, after may be too late. Some items are simply irreplaceable. And even if you think you're fully insured, will your insurance really cover the costs of acquisition and recataloging, which experts estimate to average at least $126 per book, let alone the incalculable cost to your pa-

> trons of being without service? You can't prevent hurricanes or tornadoes or floods or fires from striking libraries. But you can be prepared to protect irreplaceable items. You can prioritize which collections get attention first. You can make sure your patrons and staff know what to do. After all, providing information is your business.
>
> —Christine Watkins, "Chapter Report: Disaster Planning Makes (Dollars and) Sense," *American Libraries* (September 1996): 9.

Given that life entails risk, people still have certain expectations concerning their general safety when they enter public buildings. What do citizens expect in return when they entrust themselves to a library by entering the building? They generally expect—just for openers—that staff members will know what to do in case of an emergency:

- Alert patrons promptly to any emergency or impending emergency.
- Notify the proper authorities (police, fire) immediately when an emergency situation happens.
- Keep those inside the building properly informed of the situation.
- Organize, conduct, and lead an orderly, calm evacuation procedure, when necessary, to relocate citizens away from danger.
- Conduct periodic inspection tours and evaluation of the building with a view to public safety and the removal of hazards or potential hazards.
- Protect, to the extent possible, all human life, equipment, materials, and property.
- Provide for rapid restoration of services.
- Mitigate the impact of future emergencies, having learned from experience.

In simple terms, library patrons have a right to expect library staff to seek to prevent, to respond to, and to manage emergencies effectively, together with assistance from law enforcement agencies, fire control facilities, and civil defense authorities. The library's responsibility for preventing emergencies and handling them smoothly when they do occur includes a number of components (see figure 5.2):

- The library should do all it can to prevent, reduce, and mitigate the risk of an emergency situation occurring.
- If the library is unable to prevent the emergency, it should do everything possible to reduce the severity of the consequences of such an event.
- The director is responsible for all operations of the library and should thus be intimately involved in planning for and handling emergency situations.
- A previously appointed Library Security Officer (LSO), chosen from full-time staff and trained in emergency management, should coordinate all library responses to emergencies.
- The library's chain of command should clearly spell out the names and positions of those to whom each staff member reports and the names and telephone numbers of persons to call in the event of an emergency.
- Background information regarding potential problems should be assembled and compiled into an Emergency Procedures Manual made available to all staff. Librarians should find it easy to search out and gather such information, which is widely available from many sources.
- Employee involvement and practice can best be effected by periodic drills of simulated emergencies, followed by troubleshooting critiques, discussions of procedures, and identification of steps to be taken in time of emergency.
- Information about equipment, communication, first-aid, and safety needs should be discussed with all staff members in periodic workshops. Everyone working in the building should know the location and operation of such items of equipment as fire hoses, first-aid kits, emergency telephones, fire alarms, and smoke detectors.
- Instruction on tactical strategies to be employed during an emergency should be conveyed to all staff in in-service training sessions and by memorandum and should also be part of the orientation procedures for all new staff members.
- Coordination of effort with local police, firefighters, the Red Cross, and other members of the law enforcement and medical communities is helpful and sometimes essential.

FIGURE 5.2
The Library's Responsibility for Preventing Emergencies

Specific Types of Emergencies: Natural Disasters

Let's look at specific classes of emergencies that may face libraries. Naturally, there is bound to be some overlap (e.g., such pairs as fire and structural damage, hurricane and flood). For each emergency situation, a list of precautions is provided that can minimize loss or damage to library buildings and collections. Emphasis is on practical disaster prevention for library buildings and materials, building maintenance, materials storage, and fire and arson. Mention is also made of preventive measures (alarm systems, interior protection), salvage efforts (restoration of the collection), and the library's physical plant and facility.

Earthquakes/Structural Failures

> A little after 5:00 . . . San Franciscans felt the earth rumble beneath their feet. Suddenly the ground vibrated, heaved, and pitched, wobbling in a demonic dance. In two distinct stages lasting a minute and five seconds, the quake stunned the populace. Showering plaster, scattering bric-a-brac, breaking dishes, shifting furniture, toppling walls, and collapsing roofs sent people scurrying. Waterfront houses lurched and fell apart. Streets developed gaping fissures. Many well-built structures survived with minor damage. But fires broke out from severed gas lines and overturned stoves. Wood frame structures were soon ablaze as brave city fire fighters found their work stymied by broken water mains. Ultimately, about 250,000 San Franciscans were made homeless as a result of the quake and its consequences.
>
> —New York Times News Service, April 18, 1996

The above account, published on the ninetieth anniversary of the date when the famous devastating earthquake shook the city of San Francisco, describes the 8.3 Richter scale magnitude earthquake that struck the San Francisco Bay area in 1906. Eighty-three years later, another earthquake—this one rated at 7.1 on the Richter scale—struck the same area again. In the light of these and other data, some scientists predict with chilling confidence that "The Big One" is coming for San Francisco—another earthquake of 8.0 or higher on the Richter scale that will cause devastation unparalleled in this nation's history.

Despite the warnings implicit in so much scientific inquiry, the citizen-taxpayers of that popular city began in 1996 to enjoy the controversial but fully remodeled San Francisco Public Library, boasting hundreds of Internet-accessible computers for public use. Clearly, the smart money in California is betting on a prolonged life for San Francisco and its public library, and, whatever the risk of earthquake, life goes on as though nothing is going to happen. Still, there are things that libraries can do to be *more* prepared than they would be if they were taken completely by surprise by the next major earthquake. Reduction of loss of life and property in earthquakes is a major goal of libraries in areas where earthquakes are known to occur. One way of minimizing personal injury and property loss or damage from earthquakes and related phenomena is strict adherence to the state's or community's building code. A proper code will reduce chances of such hazards as structural collapse, water damage to library contents, and the spreading of fires. Such codes, naturally enough, vary considerably from region to region. In Florida and coastal Louisiana, for example, the major problem is the threat of hurricanes and resultant wind and flood damage. Tornadoes have been reported in every state in the continental United States but tend to group around the nation's midsection. While earthquakes may be of little concern to East Coast states, preparation for that eventuality should be a serious concern for builders and maintainers of library buildings in western states. Preventive steps might include any or all of the following measures:

- Construction of earthquake-resistant library buildings, especially in areas of high seismic risk. Preventing structural collapse is especially desirable. Fire-suppression procedures and methods are equally important.
- Coordination of information about seismic risk with land-use policy decisions and building activity.
- Development of improved methods for controlling risks from earthquakes and planning for reconstruction and redevelopment after an earthquake.
- Education and training of all library staff in earthquake procedures, with two goals: saving lives and avoiding panic.
- Comprehensive earthquake insurance, covering replacement costs of materials, equipment, and structure.

- Building to the specifications and standards of the local or state code.
- Regular and thorough inspections of the structural integrity of the library building, with recommended repairs and strengthening performed immediately.
- Full compliance with code provisions.
- Strict enforcement of the code, with stiff penalties for noncompliance or failure to correct problems in a reasonable length of time.

The importance of adequate insurance coverage for the buildings and contents of libraries cannot be exaggerated or overstressed. Previous lack of recognition of the need for protective and preventive measures against the threat of earthquakes has resulted in additional tragedy for too many libraries.

Volcanoes

Eighty percent of the world's active volcanoes are centered around the Pacific basin. California, Oregon, Washington, Hawaii, and Alaska are states in which volcanic activity is, while not common, enough of a possibility to cause serious concern. In most parts of the United States, volcanic activity is completely unknown. But the eruption of Mount St. Helens in eastern Washington State in 1980 and the subsequent shower of ash on Spokane and other communities provided a warning that volcanoes can and do erupt in our country, and that at-risk libraries ought to prepare responses for such events, in the fervent hope that they will never be needed or implemented.

The results of volcanic eruptions are devastating for human life and property alike. Lava, poison gases, associated earthquakes and other seismic activity, hurricane-force winds, tidal waves, and wind-borne showers of ash are all problems associated with volcanic activity, and all are dangerous to libraries, their occupants, and their collections. It is no coincidence that few libraries are menaced by lava flow during volcanic eruptions; no sensible building plan would recommend building in any proximity to an active volcano. The seismic rippling from volcanoes can cause other problems besides flooding and inundations of ash, even after eruptions subside. Mud slides, moving debris, avalanches, and tidal waves can occur, even quite far from the volcano itself.

The surprise eruption of Mount St. Helens serves as an example of how even planning and preparedness augmented by the latest technology cannot protect life or property against the fury of exploding volcanoes. Scientists knew that something of the sort was likely to occur in the area, but could not pinpoint the exact place, date, and time of the eruption, which made evacuation and protection more difficult. When the crater exploded, parts of Washington and nearby Idaho were quickly covered in a heavy fall of thick, malodorous ash that created problems for everyone, homeowners and librarians, workers and shut-ins, public officials and the homeless. In addition to covering hundreds of square miles of real estate with ash, the volcano killed from fifty-seven to sixty-eight people. Hazard assessment, while not able to prevent eruptions or earthquakes, can go a long way toward heightening awareness of vulnerability and helping plan responses to various problem situations. Ranking volcanoes according to their potential for eruption will also contribute significantly to studying the handling and treatment of volcanic emergencies.

Since no library can get out of the path of flowing lava, no matter how slowly its course flows, the library must take sensible steps to safeguard its building and contents when other problems arise. Among questions to ask yourself are: What is an accumulation of ash on your library's structural outside likely to do to load-bearing components of the roof? What you can do about flooding and wind-borne ash before serious problems begin? In anticipation of an eruption, the library should research the best way to remove the deposited ash before it becomes a hazard and anticipate any health consequences for those responsible for getting rid of it.

Hurricanes and Tornadoes

> Severe tropical cyclones threaten approximately 15 percent of the world's population. With wind speeds of as much as two hundred miles per hour, accompanying tornadoes, heavy rains, and storm surges of up to twenty-five feet, hurricanes (called typhoons in the western Pacific and cyclones in the Indian Ocean) can devastate hundreds of square miles of coastline and cause wind and flood damage far inland.
>
> —W. L. Waugh Jr. and R. J. Hy, *Handbook of Emergency Management,* 1990, p. 61

The distinction between these atmospheric phenomena is principally one of size. Hurricanes may cover entire areas of ocean over 1,000 miles in diameter, while tornadoes may dwindle down at their landfall ends to only a few feet across. Yet both can affect libraries with powerful winds, devastating flooding, and tremendous loss of structure, contents, and even loss of life.

Perhaps most frightening because of their very suddenness and power are tornadoes. They can arise spontaneously in the midst of thunderstorms and follow a meandering route across the landscape, packing winds at more than five hundred miles per hour. Unlike hurricanes, which may be tracked by weather satellites for weeks, tornadoes normally occur quite suddenly and do not normally allow people time to evacuate public buildings. About all people can do when a tornado is apporaching is to seek strong protection from wind. But while a tornado may be relatively small in area of coverage, a wind of more than five hundred miles per hour striking a building is likely to leave nothing standing.

Hurricanes are enormous in size but rarely exceed wind speeds of 150 miles per hour. They can devastate entire states as they come ashore. Even though hurricanes move slowly and so permit authorities to take steps to minimize hazards to human life, there is no way to get buildings out of their path. Given that a library cannot take evasive action, there are still things that can be done to minimize the damage.

Hurricane Andrew is a case in point. The giant storm made landfall in south Florida in August 1992. It totaled thousands of buildings, including dozens of libraries and library branches, as it barreled across populous Dade and Collier counties and then slammed across the Gulf of Mexico and into Louisiana before dissipating in several neighboring states as torrential rains and floods. Could it happen again? The odds are heavily in favor of more—and perhaps more frequent—hurricanes imperiling life and property, due to such factors as ocean currents, global warming, and prevailing winds. The only factor helpful for protecting private homes, libraries, and other public buildings and saving lives is that hurricanes are now tracked by satellite weather systems and plotted as they make their ways across the Atlantic and into the Caribbean. This gives coastal residents and those entrusted with public buildings time to prepare, evacuate if necessary, lay in supplies, and shore up building defenses against wind, rain, high tides, airborne objects, and other hazards.

The amount of damage sustainable by a library in the path of a hurricane, tornado, or windstorm is often a question of building codes. By code, library buildings in high-risk areas should have hardened and reinforced structural components and be elevated out of floodplains. Shatter-resistant windows and doors will help control interior damage. Self-contained power sources and insulated wiring also help. Evacuation procedures are of great importance, and should be practiced before the storm strikes so that staff will be prepared and calm when an actual emergency hits. Fortunately, modern hurricane surveillance methods make it less likely than formerly that anyone will be in the library building when a hurricane or tropical storm actually hits, meaning that the library's principal concern may be for protection of its material contents and equipment.

In contrast to hurricanes, the really nasty thing about tornadoes is that they form suddenly and catch people unprepared. The next worst thing about them is that their paths are extremely difficult to anticipate and impossible to predict with any certainty. A tornado is the most violent storm nature produces, and, in addition, its existence and course are the hardest to predict. The library is not afforded the luxury of days—or even hours—to batten down the hatches in anticipation of a tornado, but it should have some means of minimizing such things as falling trees, shattered windows, and breached doors. A slow, careful walk-through or walkaround of the building and the grounds with an eye to prevention can do much to reduce the damage from tornadoes.

Every community has a disaster preparedness person—they go by different titles—who should be invited to do a building audit to assist library staff in locating the most advantageous part of the building for safe shelter in the event of a tornado. Florida, for example, is virtually a basement-free state, and prior identification of suitable places (e.g., stairwells or interior bathrooms, since they normally do not have glass) will make things go more smoothly when an emergency hits. In tornado-prone areas, there may be someone nearby willing to come to the library and present a program on tornado safety.

Libraries in tornado-prone areas may find that they must get people to safe areas anywhere from two to ten times a year. Staff may also be required to keep people from standing at glass windows and watching the storm. In such cases, it is vital that staff do whatever is required to make sure that rubberneckers and thrill-seekers really do get to shelter and stay there.

After the tornado has passed, an all clear will be broadcast on all radio and television stations, sometimes accompanied by a siren. The Library Security Officer will, however, do well to check visually to make sure it is all clear before letting people return to normality. Sometimes tornadoes embedded in a very severe storm system may linger in an area, and radio warning systems located at some distance from the library building can indicate all clear when that is not the case.

Flood and Water Damage

Flooding, which may or may not be related to hurricanes or earthquakes, is a term referring to any abnormally high water flow that overtops a waterway's confining boundaries. Flooding is generally conceded to be the most destructive and costly natural disaster faced by the United States. Flash floods result from torrential rain and may cause water damage in libraries, but most are accompanied by related problems like mud and debris, snakes, and, later, damaged, mildewed, and otherwise useless books and other materials, if prompt and effective measures are not taken to minimize loss. The unfortunate part is that such remedial methods of book recovery (e.g., freeze-drying, fan-drying) are extremely cost- and labor-intensive. It is therefore much better to prevent destruction of the materials *before* disaster hits than it is to deal with restoration or preservation of those materials after the fact.

The best way to save water-damaged books or those damaged during fire fighting operations is to freeze them as quickly as practicable to prevent mildew, then dry them in a thermal vacuum chamber, thus restoring them to usable condition, even though a slight tang of smoke may be extremely hard to get rid of. A less expensive means of attempting to salvage water-damaged materials is air-drying them with fans continually in operation. In the aftermath of flood, a disaster team should be appointed from among existing staff, with the Library Security Officer as its director and leader, and charged with immediate recovery of as many items as can be saved. Not all our enemies in the aftermath of flooding disaster are natural, however. Looters are always a possibility, although their target is much more likely to be groceries, hardware stores, pharmacies, and private homes. Still, plans and procedures for building security and integrity after the event are wise and prudent precautions.

People and organizations pulling together can often help mitigate the devastating effects of flood damage. The spring flooding of 1997 in the upper Midwest created a disaster of immense proportion for many communities on the Red, the Thief, and the Minnesota rivers in Minnesota and North Dakota. Though it is impossible to give an accurate accounting of how much damage was done to all the libraries in the area and to their collections, at least two such buildings were completely destroyed and had to be razed, while many others sustained very significant damage. In the wake of the flooding, and without assurances that federal aid would be forthcoming any time soon, the Minnesota Library Association Foundation established a Library Disaster Fund to accept contributions for these stricken areas. Any library that sustained flood damage became immediately eligible to apply for assistance from this fund. The goal of such efforts was to help with the restoration of collections and services as quickly as possible, and a gratifying total of cash and contributions in kind came rolling in during the next few months.

In the remote but always possible event of the total destruction of the library building (more likely in cases of tornado than of flood), some prior thought should be given to the feasibility and cost of rebuilding and incorporate preservation and safety concerns in construction, renovation, and routine maintenance.

Fire

> We received reports of smoke, and when we went up there we found that someone had taken volumes off a shelf, fanned them out on the floor, and had ignited them close enough to the shelf so the fire would spread to the spines of other books. Last year, I believe we had two of these incidents.
>
> —Tom R. Arterburn, "Librarians: Caretakers or Crimefighters?" *American Libraries* (August 1996): 32

Library buildings, especially because of the kinds of materials they contain, are far from fireproof, even if their walls and floors are made of materials that cannot burn. Fire prevention is everyone's business, and prudent precautions can reduce the numbers of accidental fires greatly. However, there are many incidents of arson in libraries. Reasons for the commission of library arson vary:

- Arson fires may be set for the intended economic gain of an owner of a nearby building (e.g., insurance fraud), and the flames may spread to the library.
- Fires may be set for the economic gain of the arsonist who receives payment for the deed.
- Arson may also be a form of concealment of some other criminal act (e.g., murder, in which a major fire will render remains unrecognizable).
- The object of setting the fire is sometimes personal satisfaction and gratification (e.g., pyromania, a fairly common mental affliction or illness).
- The fire may be set as revenge for wrongs, real or perceived (e.g., a vengeful former staff member who was fired or downsized).
- Rarely but still occasionally, arson is committed in furtherance of —or publicity for—a political or social cause. A tip-off is when someone telephones a message from a group taking "credit" for the blaze.

Arson is a criminal matter, but the origin of a blaze makes little or no difference in the discussion of what to do to contain a fire that involves or threatens your library. Dealing with fires from a library standpoint demands a two-pronged attack. Fires may be divided for convenience of discussion into two classes: external and internal. Internal fires occur within the building and to property therein. External fires, often accompanied by strong winds, can threaten buildings with total destruction. As there is nothing the library can do to get the building out of harm's way, the best that can be hoped for is to minimize structural damage to the outside of the building, while protecting the building's contents and occupants to the extent possible.

Multilevel libraries can be difficult for good response to fire. A loss of electricity often occurs when fire strikes. This severely limits lighting, and shuts down elevators and computer access, while creating confusion in building occupants and sometimes disabling alarm systems. Building evacuation is, of course, a primary concern, and all persons not required to maintain communications or to assist in evacuation should be removed immediately from the structure and relocated to places of safety. A modern fire alarm system, when triggered by excessive heat or smoke or by human intervention, sounds a loud

Klaxon. More sophisticated models have flashing lights and a recorded voice announcement, which repeats a message like this one:

> Attention! Attention! A fire emergency has been declared. Please leave the building immediately. Do not use the elevators—use the nearest stairway!

At this point, staff should spring into action, urging that everyone remain calm and assisting people in evacuating the building, whether there is tangible evidence of fire or not. Fire stairs should be used to conduct all persons out of the building in an orderly manner within five minutes of the initial alarm, with great care being taken to avoid panic. Once outside, there will be considerable milling about, with evacuees wondering what has happened and when they can re-enter the building, but staff may be of help in keeping patrons who elect to remain in the area well back from firefighters and their work. In cases of fire, electricians should be called early on to check out the damage to the power, lighting, and air-conditioning systems, as well as the emergency power system.

Steps to be followed in the event of fire (drill or actual) include the following:

- Test alarm systems, smoke detectors, and fire extinguishers regularly.
- Always report the alarm or actual fire to firefighters and police first before you are distracted or preoccupied.
- Ensure that everyone takes fire alarms and fire drills seriously as though their lives depended on them—because they do. Even alarms that turn out to be false require full mobilization.
- Sound alarms immediately. Supplement or replace mechanical alarms by shouting a stern but carefully worded warning throughout the building. Direct everyone to leave the building with no exceptions permitted.
- When the alarm sounds, make sure that everyone evacuates the building to a place of safety, no matter what the weather is like outside or what they're doing at the time.
- Regularly inspect fire exits, ensure that signs are present and illuminated, and post diagrams showing the public the location of all emergency exits. Keep windows and doors closed and unlocked when evacuating the building.

- Alert emergency, security, and operations staff who should be prepared in advance concerning evacuation procedures and policies. Prepare institution staff to evacuate themselves. Evacuate the public calmly.
- Respond to the scene of a small fire with extinguishers. Prepare to receive fire trucks and direct firefighters.
- Check security at all exits: Emergencies can cover up looting or theft, especially during an evacuation.

The most serious and obvious danger from fire is human injury or even loss of life. In addition, the loss of property should be considered. Loss of electrical service is another immediate concern. Materials may be harmed not only by the fire itself but also by smoke; the necessary destruction of walls, shelving, and doors by firefighters; and by the water used to extinguish the fire. Soaked or scorched carpeting may prove especially troublesome to restore to its former appearance, odor, and function, and may have to be replaced. Smoke damage may manifest itself in the form of oily soot, and the smell of fire permeating the building may never go away. Worse yet, in the absence of electrical power, the air-conditioning system cannot move air to dissipate the smell of smoke or burned materials. Portable gasoline-powered fans, where available, can be placed strategically to help clear the lingering odor of smoke. Most library equipment is insured, but salvage operations should begin immediately. Electronic equipment protected by surge suppressors may not be harmed by lack of electricity.

In the immediate aftermath of a major fire, all attention should be directed toward damage assessment and quick elimination of smoke. At least one security officer should be stationed as a round-the-clock security guard, to prevent looting or access by the merely curious who could be hurt by damaged building contents subsequent to fire. As soon as practicable, library staff and any volunteers who may come forward should carefully begin picking up the pieces, sorting through the building contents, and doing a form of triage by choosing what needs attention first.

Electrical systems, elevators, and fire alarms should be restored first. Exhaust and ventilation fans should be placed in as many sites as possible around the building to remove the lingering odor of smoke, and should be in operation twenty-four hours a day until the air is comfortably breathable. In the aftermath of fire, a safety assessment of all structural components should be performed as soon as possible, after which the library should begin cleaning up with a view to reopening as soon as practical. The cleanup operation should begin with salvage operations on damaged books and other materials, followed by cleaning and scrubbing surface dirt and soot from walls and ceilings, carpet shampooing and deodorizing, and upholstery and curtain cleaning.

Specific Types of Emergencies: Human Action

Workplace Violence

Over and over again, research into the unpleasant topic of violence in the workplace reveals that a shocking number of homicides reported in the United States occurs in places of business, sometimes robbery-related but not necessarily. In many cases, the victims are people who just happened to be in the wrong place at the wrong time, and who did not know their attackers or give them any cause or provocation for their actions. A 1993 NIOSH Institute's report concludes that "workers most at risk are those who deal with the public, exchange money, and deliver goods and services." Naturally enough, this includes libraries.

This topic was dealt with at some length in chapter 3, but it is mentioned again here as a frequent form of emergency, although it differs from fire, flood, and tornadoes in that it is caused by people. Libraries, whatever you may wish them to be or think they ought to be, are not always tranquil havens of serenity where one can lose oneself in thought, study, contemplation, and peace. They are also workplaces, and, as such, they are vulnerable to a growing concern of people everywhere: workplace violence.

How widespread is workplace violence? Just to provide some idea of the scope and extent of the problem, the following frightening statistics are provided. According to an American Management Association report, "some 2 million violent acts were committed in the workplace" in 1994. In fact, "52 percent of U.S. companies reported at least one act of violence" during that year.

Every library, regardless of size and whether it has a large security force, a small one, or none at all, should consider the merits of forming a violence response team to cope with outbreaks of violence in the library building. The potential for violent behavior on the part of any person is difficult to predict, and relying on a stereotypical image of what the violence-prone person looks like or will do can be extremely hazardous. That's why the library should have a violence response team in place *before* problems occur, prepared to respond quickly, gather facts about a potentially explosive incident, and decide whether to intervene, call the police, or take some other form of action. Prior to forming such a team, the library management should conduct an initial risk assessment. Beyond that, all staff should be trained to report any threat of violence immediately. Individual judgment may be required to determine whether a given incident requires a response. Such judgments should be based on clues such as use of certain words, body language, and tone of voice, and not merely on appearance, hygiene, prejudice, or instincts.

As the LSO or staff member in charge, your first job is to defuse the problematic individual's level of stress and anger by remaining calm and deliberate, not responding to anger in kind, and speaking soothingly while help is being summoned. Remember that you are responsible for the lives and safety of everyone in the building, which should dissuade you from doing anything sudden, precipitous, or heroic to solve the problem or end the confrontation. Actually, the best idea is probably to call the police at the first threat of violence. They normally require some time to respond, and it's best to get the call in to them at the earliest possible moment.

How can a library staff member anticipate violent behavior? No one can do so with absolute precision, but figure 5.3 lists some warning signs. Have any of those events recently occurred in your library building?

How should a staff member or security guard react to a suspicion of impending violent behavior? Just keeping a watchful eye on suspected persons will often deter or dissuade them from antisocial behaviors in the library building. But if you believe that something violent is about to occur, the following guidelines may be useful:

- Call 911 or the equivalent when there is personal injury, intentional destruction of library property, lawbreaking, rule breaking, or even the serious threat of any of the above. Don't delay or rely on others to call. Better to call in a false alarm than to wait too long to summon help.
- When possible, the Library Security Officer should be informed immediately. Such a person will have been briefed in procedures and protocols of smooth handling of problems.

- Threatening statements such as verbal threats to harm or kill others or oneself.
- Raised or angry voices.
- Intimidating behaviors (crossing recognized behavioral boundaries with another person).
- Carrying of weapons. The great majority of libraries have no effective means of detection of weapons or things that could be used as weapons. One problem with weapons detection is that of defining "weapons." They're not all metallic or pointy! Even a library book could serve as a murder weapon if applied to another person's skull hard and repeatedly.
- Strange behaviors reported by others. This doesn't mean that every time a library staff member is told by a member of the public that someone else is "acting weird," it's dangerous; but each such incident should be checked out. This is a judgment call. One person's weird behavior or bizarre actions may be another's harmless eccentricity.
- Obsessive behavior. Anyone preoccupied with another person (a movie star or other celebrity, for example) or with such lurid matters as crime, criminals, concentration camps, morbidity, or expressing a strong desire to hurt others or groups bears watching. What about the First Amendment that guarantees everyone's freedom of expression? True, it's a free country, and people are not necessarily guilty of anything just because they enjoy reading about Auschwitz and its atrocities, but it can't hurt to keep an eye on those who seem fixated on such subjects.
- Serious stress in personal life. In most libraries of any size, it is impossible for staff members to know what stress their patrons are under or what's going on in their lives, unless members of the public choose to share their feelings, beliefs, and experiences (which they sometimes do, unbidden). There are certain key phrases people use, however (for example, "I just can't take it anymore!"), that should act as warnings. Note when such persons are in the building, what they're up to, and where. Of course, when the person uttering that desperate remark is an employee of the library, you may have a potentially more serious problem on your hands (see "Inside Jobs" in chapter 6).

FIGURE 5.3
Warning Signs of Potential Violence in the Library

- Stay calm. Show empathy and humanity to a violent person, but not sympathy with his or her aims or behaviors.
- Do not negotiate, promise, or claim to represent authority (unless, of course, you do). Only persons legally empowered to deal with such emergencies should do so.
- Do not provide compromising or accusatory information.
- Speak only for yourself; do not answer for others.
- Prepare to react and take responsibility to protect yourself and others in the immediate vicinity of the problem. It's part of your job—an important part. Where more than one staff member is on the scene, work as a team.
- After you've called the police and described the nature of the emergency, caution library staff members or security forces not to rush to the scene, overreact, or try to be heroic.
- If your library has an intercom or public-address system, the library staff may find it useful to develop a set of code words or signals like the ones used in airports and department stores. These, if properly chosen, can be used to acquaint other staff members and security personnel with the place, type, and specifics of the emergency without giving undue alarm to other persons within earshot.
- Do not tolerate violent behavior that disrupts work or reflects badly on your institution. Put a stop immediately to horseplay, irrational behaviors, and inappropriate emotional outbursts. Rules should be posted prominently, and all occupants of the building including employees should be covered by their provisions.
- When violence begins, quietly segregate bystanders from the danger. Evacuate or hide people by blocking doors and putting people out of sight of the perpetrator. Firmly request that everyone who is not free to leave the building remain calm and wait patiently for rescue.
- Help staff anticipate and plan to handle potentially violent situations, such as observing members of teenage gangs known to be warring who are observed in the building at the same time. At such times, try to have key staff standing by and unobtrusively ready for anything.

Bombs and Bomb Threats

Let us all fervently hope that your library never has to deal with a bomb or bomb threat. Such events are thankfully rare, but that doesn't mean that you can afford to skip this part of the chapter. Unfortunately, violence often seems, as Malcolm X once said, as American as apple pie. During the 1996 Summer Olympic Games in Atlanta, Georgia, a pipe bomb blew up in a public park during the after-hours revelry of Olympic attendees and others joining in a victory celebration. Anyone who has gone through security gates at airports is now aware that enhanced security precautions are designed to thwart airline bombings by terrorists or deranged passengers.

Terrorists normally choose high-profile places for their bombings because they hope to create the maximum disruption possible and receive the greatest amount of publicity. New York's World Trade Center and Oklahoma City's Federal Building are two chilling examples. In this sense, libraries are fortunate in not being high-profile public buildings, but while libraries are far down the list of sites chosen by terrorist bombers, bomb threats are being phoned into libraries with increasing frequency. Because so many people enter libraries each day, each bomb threat must be taken seriously as a hazard to life, limb, and property, and all staff members should be acquainted with procedures for handling them when they occur.

It is important to remember that not all bomb threat calls are genuine. Not all bomb threats need result in an evacuation, although prudent library officers usually authorize evacuation of the building because there is no way to tell. Because cultural institutions tend to have good reputations, they are rarely the target of serious bomb attempts. But warped or fanatical minds may not distinguish between good and bad institutions, and deranged persons interested in running up a body count may find them ideal targets of opportunity. Libraries, therefore, must occasionally contend with the threat of bombs just like airport terminals, sports complexes, shopping malls, and other public places.

In general, bomb threats must be taken seriously. When someone alerts the library that a bomb has been placed somewhere in the building, there are some guidelines to follow (see figure 5.4).

How should the library respond when confronted by a telephoned bomb threat? The American Management Association urges the administrator to take the following actions in the listed order:

- Preparation for bomb threats should be discussed in advance with local police and bomb disposal teams. Prepare your staff with checklists at each phone number known to the general public.
- Should you receive a bomb threat via telephone, keep the person talking and write down as much information as you can: where, when, how, and why. Pay attention to and note voice characteristics, background noises, repeated emphases, and what the caller knows or doesn't know about you and the library. Frequently, such information will assist law enforcement agencies in catching the criminals later.
- Do not give in to panic. Avoid using frightening words or conversation. Use code words wherever possible to alert others. For example, say "Please tell Rachel she has a telephone call" to refer to alarming conditions when "Rachel" is a prearranged emergency signal.
- Alert the local police immediately. Most police departments have law enforcement officers experienced in evaluating each threat for its seriousness, and larger police forces have bomb squads. Prepare to receive and direct a bomb disposal team without major panic, interference, or negative publicity. The bomb squad will come into the library and make an evaluative determination of how to react and whether or not to evacuate the building. This is not a decision that librarians should attempt to make.
- Prepare regular staff to sweep their building areas visually for items that don't belong or cannot be explained, but ensure that they do not touch or move any such objects. Report anything suspicious and evacuate the area without panic.
- For mail or letter bomb protection, obtain expert advice when there is a perceived threat. These cases are rare but normally difficult to screen.
- In an evacuation, tell members of the public "We are closing early today," and use routine or emergency exits, depending on the evaluation. Check security at exits.
- Check that the emergency is not a ruse or deception to cover a theft, especially during an evacuation.
- A surprising number of bomb threats have proved to be inside jobs, phoned in by disaffected or bored employees to add excitement to their workdays. Should you suspect that such threats are coming from staff members, inform the police immediately.

FIGURE 5.4
Recommended Telephoned Bomb Threat Procedures

1. Take every threat seriously.
2. Tune out all distractions, concentrate, and focus on the caller.
3. Keep the caller on the phone as long as possible so that the call can be traced. Take notes and ask the caller to repeat information. Note any unusual speech patterns and phrases used by the caller. Listen for background noises such as cars or machinery that may help to determine where the caller is. Try to determine whether the call is internal or external. An internal call could signal an employee or patron with a grievance or a warped sense of humor.
4. Collect as much information as possible. Ask where the bomb is, when it is set to explode, what it looks like, who and where the caller is, and why the bomb was planted. You never know; sometimes they'll tell you.
5. Notify a superior and the police and share all information collected with them.

Collateral Damage

Sometimes the library, its contents, and its occupants become vulnerable to events occurring nearby. No one could have prepared the Oklahoma City Metropolitan Library for what happened to the nearby Federal Building on April 19, 1995. The huge blast of the bomb that destroyed the Federal Building caused massive loss of human life just after 9:00 A.M. Less than two blocks away is the downtown library. Fortunately, there were no patrons in the library building at the time, but sixty staff members were on duty. Only two were injured, receiving minor cuts from flying glass as the windows on one side of the building blew in suddenly. The explosion blew out 90 percent of the windows in the building. The director and a staff member were hurled across the room. No one can be prepared for a blast of that size, but the library had a preexisting disaster preparedness plan, and the building was completely evacuated in less than three minutes. Staff had practiced the procedure frequently over the preceding year and were ready to implement the provisions at the time.

The director and the maintenance crew stayed behind to secure the building, but were forced to leave the site about an hour later due to a rumor involving a threat of a second bomb. They returned afterward to cover the windows, putting wood over ground-floor windows and plastic on those on higher floors. Among other steps taken in the aftermath of the bombing, the library bought surveillance cameras and set them to monitor the alley behind the building. A consulting psychologist was brought in to discuss the disaster with staff and to suggest ways to handle reactions of fear, anger, and the like.

In the following week or two, things got more or less back to normal, but staff complained of a generalized "loss of normalcy." This was somewhat ameliorated by swift and expedited repairs, which necessitated replacing lighting fixtures and ceiling tiles. A commercial company was used for cleanup, clearing out debris and cleaning carpets, furniture, and equipment. Each book and every shelf had to be vacuumed to remove dirt and shards of glass. This time-consuming and labor-intensive process involved the use of hand-vacuums to clean library materials.

Still, library officials conceded that the whole problem could have been much worse. For example, in addition to there being no serious casualties, there was no significant structural damage. Almost all of the books stayed on their shelves, which proved a blessing. Anyone who has ever had to reestablish shelf order after a calamity knows what a difficult and time-consuming task it can be. With a little caulking and sealing, the building soon became weather-tight again even if not completely moisture-tight. This problem led inevitably to observable effects of humidity on the library's books and other materials. The library countered the moisture problem by having its ventilation system running on high twenty-four hours a day for several months to circulate air. Finally, staff unable to resume normal duties at the downtown main library were reassigned to branches pending the complete restoration of normalcy in the central building.

Triage and Recovery

Emergency recovery procedures in libraries when a disaster occurs may include such measures as freezing and freeze-drying of waterlogged materials as alternatives to just declaring books a loss and space-drying of rooms damaged. Salvaging books damaged in a major fire necessitates procedures and processes for packing, sorting, drying, and cleaning the books. Removing odors may require air-drying, sprays, solvents, or just a period of time. It is possible for libraries to recover from emergencies, and most of them actually do.

In the aftermath of any emergency, library officials should perform impromptu triage to figure out what can't wait for attention, what can, and what can get along without any immediate consideration.

In the absence of immediate insurance funding, triage will dictate what needs to be done first to get the library ready for a speedy reopening. Based on the assessment of the damage, proposed repairs, and temporary services available, the library administrator or LSO should communicate with the library's community of users, outlining the situation and projecting the restoration of services. The LSO should communicate with all department heads, explaining the scope of the problem, what is being done to fix the damage, and an estimate of the time required for reopening with business as usual.

Public information addressing the concerns of patrons who have borrowed materials and want to know when and where to return them may help to forestall the calls and questions likely to arise. One option, should the circulation desk be closed to the public, is that returns can be continued through the book drops or outside collection boxes. If the building is declared unsafe or unusable after the emergency, a temporary "home" for the library may be established to take care of library services such as reference, circulation, and interlibrary loan.

Hazards and concerns of libraries vary extensively with geographical location, terrain, and prevailing climate. In wet, low-lying areas (and even, as witnessed in September 1996, considerably inland and hundreds of miles from the shore), hurricanes and tropical storms are of seasonal concern, while other regions may have to keep an eye on flooding and water damage, thunderstorms and lightning, tornadoes and wind storms, earthquakes, and dust storms. Bomb threats, fires, floods, chemical spills, power failures, and medical emergencies, all constituting emergency situations, should also be recognized and covered by an emergency plan.

Carpets and curtains may make a library attractive and homey, and help reduce noise in public rooms and heat and sun damage in open spaces, yet the libraries easiest to return to normal have no carpeting or curtains at all. Still, modern libraries have found carpeting and curtains to be both aesthetic and useful in sound suppression. Therefore, every effort should be made to protect carpet during the recovery phase by taping down sheets of plastic in aisles and walkways. Even so, soot from burned equipment and materials may well spread to furniture, walls, and carpeting just from being kicked up by the feet of the rescuers and others.

The object of all these efforts is to get the library ready to reopen to the public as soon as possible, consistent with the safety and comfort of all who enter the building. There's a trade-off at work here: You can have your library back quickly, or you can have it clean—even cleaner than it was before the emergency—but you shouldn't realistically expect to have both at the same time. Money, too, is a factor in the aftermath of emergencies. Once you find out how much is available to commit to recovery activities and how soon funds can be encumbered for the jobs that need to be done, you may be able to project more accurately and realistically the library's date of reopening or restoration of full services.

Most patrons will accept with good cheer less-than-ideal conditions, as, for example, when the main layer of soot has been cleaned or removed, but considerable mess still remains in the building. A few are bound to complain, but a few are always going to complain. The majority of library users will generally be pleased to have access, however, and will gladly overlook or forgive the mess and cooperate by working around (or staying out of) those areas. Cleaning and repainting of scorched or mud-encrusted walls, also a disruption to normal library function, will help greatly with restoring an acceptable level of visual and olfactory tolerance. Fire alarm systems may have to be completely restored and tested before the building can be reopened to the public. And what about the materials themselves? Frequently, it is slow going resorting and reshelving books and other materials that have tumbled from their places in the wake of firefighters' attempts to suppress fires or in the wake of other damage to the structure's interior. Patrons and staff alike will experience a certain amount of inconvenience in the aftermath of a disaster, but signs posted in prominent places that demonstrate awareness of—and offer apologies for—problems help considerably in keeping the public informed, if not necessarily delighted with the speed of recovery.

CHAPTER 6

Legal and Ethical Issues of Security and New Technology

Retail store employees are stealing more than the customers, according to a nationwide survey that also found the industry lost $27 billion because of worker theft, shoplifters, administrative error, and fraud in 1995. A recent National Retail Security Survey conducted by the University of Florida revealed that stealing by employees amounted to an estimated $10.4 billion, while shoplifting losses for the same time period were estimated to be about $9.7 billion.

—Associated Press, November 22, 1996

The objectives of this chapter are to:

- define and differentiate between legal and ethical problems confronting libraries
- discuss the problems of ethical behavior in public buildings and environments involving considerations of invasion of privacy
- explain the problem of "inside jobs" and what can be done to prevent them
- recommend specific remedies for illegal and unethical behaviors in libraries

Legal and Ethical Matters in Libraries

> Honesty may not be the best policy but it is worth trying once in a while.
>
> —Richard M. Nixon (The Watergate tapes transcript)

Supermarkets apprehended more than 276,000 shoplifters last year, an average of about 53 per store, according to the Food Marketing Institute, a trade group (AP Newswire, October 12, 1996). Such a statistic suggests that there is a lot of illegal activity among ordinary citizens, not to mention grave lapses in ethical behavior. Before we attempt to discuss the legal and ethical aspects of human behavior, however, let's distinguish as clearly as possible between legal matters and ethical matters in a library context. Where the law provides clearly for the illegality of certain acts, and provides for appropriate punishment for those committing the acts, we have a legal matter on our hands. Perhaps the most problematic area of difficulty for the library, however, lies in the shadowy realm of ethics, where there are no hard-and-fast rules, and where each person's conscience serves as the only guide. Compliance with the law—whether one thinks the law to be good or bad—is like a true-false examination. Ethical decision making, however, is all essay questions. One of the requirements of ethical decision making is original thought. "Ethics is that process that makes you so uncomfortable that you can only escape from the situation by having to think," explained Fred Friendly, former CBS News president, in speaking to a general session of the American Library Association a few years ago.

Let's begin with a sad affirmation of faith. Whoever said that there's a little larceny in each human soul was only partly right. Experience teaches us that while there may be a little larceny in every soul, there is a lot of larceny in many more. And some of those souls, not surprisingly, focus their eyes on libraries and archival institutions. It may simply be human nature. Witness a recent survey in which high school seniors (tomorrow's leaders and shapers of national destiny, mind you) were asked if they would cheat on a test, falsify a report, misrepresent their income, and so on. A dismaying percentage of them said yes. Obviously, the Ten Commandments are not required reading in this country of separation of church and state, or at least they're not taken as seriously as the writers of the Old Testament once hoped.

These are matters of personal ethics. But how does this translate, except in a general way, into a valid security concern for libraries? For openers, many otherwise honest people, will, in certain situations or citing desperation or lack of time, "borrow" books and other library materials without checking them out. Those who are willing to talk about their crimes and motivations cite a variety of reasons such as "I needed it," "I wanted it," "I just borrowed it for a while," or sometimes, "I didn't want anyone else to get their grubby hands on it."

While there are almost as many reasons for taking library materials without going through authorized procedures as there are actual cases of taking them, each instance is an ethical infraction both of the Golden Rule and library operating procedure.

As was discussed in chapters 1 and 2, which of us has not borrowed (with every intention, of course, of returning it forthwith) a book or other library item for our own use without checking it out? Are you without sin? Good. You may cast the first stone. Who can deny the fact that people have this tendency to remove books from libraries without permission or due procedure?

Perhaps the most frightening manifestation of this is the so-called inside job, whereby a staff member appropriates library materials first. For example, a best-seller is received from the publisher or distributor, and the staff member who unpacks the boxes thinks "I've been waiting for this one. I really want to read it, so maybe I'll just take it home tonight before it gets into the system and goes to all the people waiting on our reserves list." A minor sin, as sins go, perhaps, but against the rules (illegal) and not especially ethical, either. Inside jobs are, understandably, hardest to prevent, because it is the trusted ones who are guilty.

Inside jobs—crimes and misdemeanors committed by library staff rather than by members of the public—are always the most difficult problems to detect and combat. Well over two millennia ago, the Greek philosopher Plato asked a question that remains pertinent to this day: "Who's going to watch the watchers?" Who, indeed?

It is a sad fact that honesty cannot be assumed or presumed in anyone we employ. Some library administrators have developed psychological tests that they administer to prospective employees, hoping to discover and weed out the bad apples, the larcenous, the incorrigible, the malevolent, the mentally unbalanced, and the downright sneaky. The jury is still out on the legality of such tests, however, and besides, it is unlikely that any diagnostic test will ever be devised will distinguish trustworthy people from those less so. We may deplore or even deny the notion that everybody is a prospective or potential thief, but there it is, and we must deal with reality. So since there seems to be no likelihood of perfecting humankind to the point that it refrains voluntarily from lying, cheating, stealing, or tolerating and covering up for, or enabling, those who do, enhanced and improved ongoing efforts in the direction of better library security are in order.

Legal infractions, as contrasted with ethical lapses, are easily defined by consulting the state, local, or campus statutes concerning library property. And the really good thing about legal infractions is that they are spelled out carefully, and appropriate punishment is prescribed by law. It is, therefore, with ethical infractions that we need to be concerned, because such offenses are subjectively defined (one person's shocking crime may appear not to be a big deal at all to another) and there is no consensus on how to respond to them.

Invasion of Privacy

The American Heritage Dictionary of the English Language succinctly defines "privacy" as: "1: the condition of being secluded or isolated from the view of, or from contact with, others. 2: concealment, secrecy." In the age of the Internet and other technological innovations that have found their way into common library use, such a set of definitions is woefully inadequate to the implications of the term. A better definition would include some notion of personal security as well, along with something about the right to be left alone.

New thinkers, scholars, and practitioners are now considering privacy in the sense of the feeling a person has of being secure that personal and private transactions will remain personal and private unless he or she voluntarily chooses to share them with others. And the consensus among these thinkers is that privacy is not just an expected casualty of technology—it is already a victim, dead on arrival. Moreover, unless steps are taken immediately to ensure personal privacy, serious damage can and will be done to our personal freedoms, and to the way we feel about ourselves in regard to the freedom to do as we choose in this democracy.

It is in this context that libraries must also consider the concept, because only when people like library users feel secure in their freedom from prying eyes and unwarranted interference will they maximize their use of libraries and other public utilities. Without privacy, a chilling effect takes over, causing fearful and sensible persons to avoid inquiry into areas that might incur undesired scrutiny, and to fear the use of public channels such as the Internet for their transactions, lest they be called upon to answer for what they want to know and why they want to know it.

It's both amazing and chilling that, using ordinary library records —the kind found in not just government or specialized files but in public libraries almost everywhere—one can, with Internet access and a few hours of intensive work, assemble quite an impressive dossier about another person, consisting of, for example, that person's spending habits, medical history, financial holdings, and political affiliations. And the search is all legal! The information is out there, after all, and just waiting for someone to access it and draw inferences from it, fairly or unfairly. By applying such information, one can even assume the identity of another person, not in appearance, but enough to fool most computers into giving up even more secrets.

Victims complain that it is far too easy for criminals to perpetrate identity thefts in this way. It's really not all that hard to get a new driver's license with your face stuck on the front and someone else's vital statistics typed next to the picture. Critics of state departments of motor vehicles say that the departments don't always question why someone is ordering a new driver's license and having it sent to a new address. Retailers are supposed to ask for other pieces of identification before replacing a "lost" credit card but often do not.

Another problem is that there is a pervasive carelessness in handling personal information. For example, Winn Schwartau (*Information Warfare,* 1996, p. 495) points to the rarity with which automobile dealers shred loan applications before putting them in the trash receptacle or recycler bin, "putting customers at risk because of the ease with which dumpster divers and even dishonest employees can retrieve them and use the detailed information to impersonate loan applicants."

In that context, is it any wonder that unscrupulous parties can get into library records to gain illicit access to private information and to use that information for whatever purposes they see fit? Most people feel that when they signed up for a local library card, they were entering into a tacit contract with the library that their personal information would not be used in any way detrimental to them. But imagine the results if someone with access to the library's records decided to find out who was borrowing books on such topics as bomb making, counterespionage, AIDS treatment, or gay sex. The implications for privacy of individuals targeted by the information thief are frightening.

While it should be obvious that just reading about a subject doesn't accuse anyone of anything (the author, a Jew, has on two occasions, checked Adolf Hitler's *Mein Kampf* out of local libraries, for example), one's enemies or opponents could distort such facts into smoking guns of guilt and shame, and even cause law enforcement authorities to get interested in who's reading what. And with Internet access to library records, there is even the possibility that those library records could be breached, replaced, defaced, or distorted until they contain potentially damaging or compromising information about you and your reading, listening, or viewing habits—at least for those who see such activities as somehow threatening to the state or the public welfare. (Chapter 7 explores technology and the threat of such problems in considerably greater detail.)

Privacy has always been an issue in communication, but now more than ever before—since Internet use became common and convenient—it is among the most discussed problems of library access. Privacy is not only a personal issue, but it is rapidly becoming a national priority as well. The National Information Infrastructure is the result of a forum whose goal was to provide a mechanism for the library community to identify national policy issues, questions, and principles in the areas of telecommunications and information infrastructure. Among the Principles for the Development of the National Information Infrastructure, one may find listed under the heading of "privacy" the following criteria:

- Privacy should be carefully protected and extended.
- Comprehensive policies should be developed to ensure that the privacy of all people is protected.
- Personal data collected to provide specific services should be limited to the minimum necessary.
- Sharing data collected from individuals should only be permitted with their informed consent.
- Individuals should have the right to inspect and correct data files about themselves.
- Transaction data should remain confidential.

These principles are designed to protect the individual's right to be left alone while maximizing public disclosure of public records. Naturally, the more barriers the library community finds it necessary to erect in the way of free and unfettered exchange of information, the more complicated and the slower transactional procedures will become.

For example, detaining and interrogating visitors or surveillance of library areas is inimical to the notion of "freedom." Speaking practically, moreover, they are labor-intensive and thus expensive practices, or more libraries would probably be doing them already. Given library budgets, it is highly unlikely that library security will ever reach the level of airport security, for example. Yet libraries—statistically speaking—are still among the safest places you can be, and news stories about incidents of violence or destruction in libraries (see chapter 3) should be understood in context.

Libraries are not hotbeds of criminal activity or places where people should be afraid to go or to spend time. But a prudent measure of building security seems indicated to ensure that they stay safe. Many methods of enhancing and maintaining security are low-cost, low-maintenance measures that the library can effect immediately. Others will take time and, in most cases, augmented funding to achieve. In the future, security concerns for libraries may be diminished, but a more likely hypothesis is that they will merely change in nature.

Virtual Libraries

It is entirely possible that one of these days the library will cease to exist as merely a large building containing books and other physical materials. For certain library users, that day has already arrived, in fact. For the rest of us, however, the date at which the library will exist only out there in cyberspace is still on its way. At that time, the chances of people being physically at risk in libraries should fall to zero, because they will not enter public buildings to accomplish their informational, educational, or recreational library needs. Everything will be available electronically, and it will be possible for citizens with access to appropriate technology to "visit" the library and make full use of its services without leaving home or even putting on their shoes.

But such a brave new world scenario contains problems of its own if the future library is to be available to all citizens. To begin with, accessing a library from home is impossible for unfortunates who have no homes. And what about people who have homes but lack computers, modems, or even telephones? Such persons would completely lack access to virtual libraries unless there is a public place where they are provided free access to systems and services. This solves the problem of the have-nots, perhaps, but gets us right back to libraries as public places, vulnerable to the ancient security concerns they have had all along.

As security is the entire focus and raison d'être of this book, the ideas and suggestions proffered in the following pages may seem fanciful now, but they are presented as steps toward better security.

A promising new technology deals with the electronic imaging of all documents in collections so that the original need never be displayed, and thus cannot be stolen, lost, or damaged, since the public deals only with cheap copies of inconsequential value. This would deal effectively with the problem of loss of valuable materials, reducing security concerns to the status of nuisances, rather than serious, costly losses.

Borrowing Deterrents from the Private Sector

Present-day library security is not especially effective as a means of either preserving collections or protecting people in library buildings. Certainly, in both regards, there is a need for something better than what we have now. In the area of safeguarding library collections alone, for example, countless times a day, in this nation's more than 9,000 libraries, somebody absentminded but generally innocent exits with an item not properly checked out of the library. Most of the time such an action goes completely undetected. But even if the library has a common detection device in place, triggering its sensors usually results in nothing more than a sheepish "Oops!" followed by a lame, perfunctory apology and a brief, embarrassed wait while the book undergoes proper checking out. The sound of the alarm going off, by the way, is usually a polite ding, a beep, or perhaps a series of sheeplike bleats, just loud enough to alert staff at the check-out or security posts, but not really loud enough to create panic or great embarrassment in the would-be felon, or more than amused curiosity in passersby or those standing in the immediate vicinity.

Coming up with more effective countermeasures to the problem of persistent theft of library materials is worth pondering, so perhaps we should begin with the relative merits of a new technology now being implemented in the retail sector before we call for the pursuit dogs to track down and punish library thieves.

A December 16, 1993, Associated Press article pointed to the beefing up of security in retail stores due to that year's increase in shoplifting across all sectors. In that article, an anonymous man with the title of "Director of Loss Protection" for a major department store chain reported on improved ways of foiling shoplifting in stores, although he admitted that employee crime accounts for as much as 40 percent of total "shrinkage." There have always been shoplifters in stores, of course, just as people have always tried to steal from libraries, but hi-tech shoplifting defense in some retail chains has reached new extremes. The man interviewed for the AP article pointed to shoplifting (he called it "shrinkage") as a $27-billion-a-year industry, amounting to almost 2 percent of total sales, according to the National Retail Federation, and causing retailers to increase their prices to compensate for their losses.

Clearly, shoplifting is a serious problem of alarming proportions. How do retail stores attempt to fight back and protect their property, while permitting free public access to their wares? Figure 6.1 lists a few of the more common ways.

What seems most fascinating, when one ponders the vast losses (*$27 billion* a year!) involved is what is implied by the widespread use in clothing stores of the last item on the list, reportedly the most effective countermeasure available to retail garment outlets. Evidently, a store that chooses that method of security is saying that a stolen garment will be a ruined garment, and it hopes that such a warning will persuade the would-be thief not to take it at all.

The "Director of Loss Protection" quoted in the above article is actually proud, bragging that his clothing store chain now has unobtrusive devices that can be attached to clothes in a way that's hard to remove or disable. When a garment so treated is removed from the store improperly, a capsule of dye erupts in a spray of permanent stain, squirting a considerable quantity of thick, indelible purple or yellow goop all over the item and rendering it unwearable by anyone, whether it's later recovered by the store or not. Besides ruining the item of apparel, the ink falls on everyone in range.

- Electronic cables securing expensive coats or other garments to a rack trigger an alarm if the cord is cut or broken. (Ironically, not much of a leap from the metal chains that kept monastic libraries intact when curses didn't work.)
- Convex mirrors enable a security employee to watch people's activities around corners or in dressing rooms, where the opportunity for shoplifting is greatest.
- Surveillance cameras are used, like those employed by banks.
- Plainclothes store detectives pass themselves off as fellow shoppers but are hired to report or arrest shoplifters.
- Boxes or other containers are designed to make it more difficult for people to make off with cassettes or CDs from record stores.
- Electronic gates trigger an earsplitting alarm when someone attempts to leave the store with merchandise they haven't paid for. This helps security agents apprehend the malefactor with the merchandise and considerable embarrassment.
- Clips or tags are attached to garments and designed to erupt and spray indelible ink on the thief when a garment bearing a security tag leaves the premises.

FIGURE 6.1
Safeguarding Wares in the Commercial Sector

Unlike retail stores, libraries however driven to the ends of their financial tethers by actual losses or statistics on "shrinkage," do not have the luxury of deciding that if they can't keep their unsold merchandise they will personally see to it that nobody else is going to get anything out of it, either. While stores may seem to prefer that the purloined garment be completely unwearable to having it stolen with impunity, libraries cannot risk exploding capsules of ink or dye in their books. But suppose that libraries did (out of desperation and growing really tired of unaccountable losses) adopt their own form of the same countermeasures urged on big stores by the redoubtable National Retail Federation. First, we could forget about tattle-tape and other stop-loss systems that are based on magnetized strips in the spines of books. Experience has shown that these strips are not terribly effective deterrents to library theft, anyway. Actually, it would probably take a clever twelve-year-old only about five minutes of watching to discover how the system works, and only a few more seconds to defeat it.

It is, nonetheless, almost always better to light a candle than to curse the darkness. Such machinery isn't totally useless. A stop-loss checkout system does help prevent thieves from ripping off many items a year, and knowledge of the library's enforcement of penalties can have a strong deterrent value. But is the ink-cartridge idea adaptable to protecting library books? Hardly. It would, if properly deployed, lead to more destruction of library materials and property.

Those electronic cords we spoke of earlier in use in retail stores to protect coats wouldn't be feasible on library books intended for circulation. Record stores make you submit cassettes you wish to purchase to a device that removes the large plastic holder from the small, easily-concealed cassette. Might that work for libraries without making it impossible to browse inside a book? Something like that might conceivably work in libraries, and would no doubt lessen book losses or even negate theft entirely (except for the aforementioned inside jobs —solving that problem is going to take considerably longer).

Inside Jobs: Library Staff as Patron Problems

> A retired employee of the Millar Library at Portland (Ore.) State University was arrested for stealing more than just videos. The former supervisor of the circulation department was arrested in July for stealing money from photocopy machines over a ten-year period. Although the university would not say how much money (the former librarian) is accused of taking, PSU's student newspaper reported the amount to be as much as $200,000. Officials said when copy-machine revenues increased after (the supervisor's) April 1996 retirement, they conducted an internal audit and then turned the results over to police.
>
> —*American Libraries* (September 1997): 26

Turning to another class of problem behaviors in the library, we come to a segment of the population whose actions are the most difficult to control: those on the payroll. Inside jobs, in which library employees misuse their positions to commit theft, are unfortunately ubiquitous, as library staff are in the most advantageous position to leave the building with our possessions. In a recent situation, theft was the issue at the Akron-Summit County (Ohio) Public Library and a security guard was the culprit. When police set up video surveillance inside the library to find out who was stealing videotapes and CDs, they caught the library guard, who was an employee of Ohio Security. Upon investigation, police found seventy-two videocassettes and seven compact discs valued at $1,363.21 in the guard's house and car. Ironically, one of the videos was about home security! (*American Libraries*, September 1997: 26)

What does this indicate to us? It would be very convenient if we could take on an "us-versus-them" position and consider all threats as coming from the public. But too often the greatest threat to our collections (and sometimes even to public safety) comes from those employed by the library. In addition to inside jobs in which materials are purloined by staff members, there are numerous incidents involving threatening or criminal behavior on the part of staff.

It would be folly to pretend that they're not out there—those persons who would damage our libraries by theft, electronic mischief, or sheer negligence with cigarettes or food. What many librarians overlook or discount, however, is that such people aren't just out there—they're in here! And they are drawing paychecks for their negligence or misconduct. There is no evidence to suggest that we have a handle on those who do not work from malice aforethought.

A frequently overlooked aspect of controlling behavior in public buildings is that of managing problem behaviors among workers in those buildings. While we would like to think that threats could never originate on "our" side of the counter or desk, those who work in library buildings are people who experience emotional upsets and domestic disruptions, just as everybody else does. Domestic violence and drunk and disorderly conduct do occur with staff members. In cases where violence by a staff member is a real possibility, other staff members should do whatever seems possible to calm the person down and summon the police immediately. Do not assume that because you know the person, he or she is unlikely to commit violence. Security—not just for staff but from staff—should be a central issue in effective personnel policies and manuals. Most instances of workplace violence come from patrons, not from staff, of course, but it must be recognized that staff may also present a threat to public security.

Inside jobs may be retributive or random, and may be premeditated or without any thought at all. Such acts may be drug- or alcohol-induced or augmented, and the perpetrator may have a history of mental illness, depression, or addiction. A few may even be suicidal or beyond caring what they do or what happens to others. Inside jobs are no doubt the most difficult acts to interdict or prevent because employees are normally spared the careful scrutiny accorded members of the public in their visits to the building.

"One in three employees steals, and it's rising by 5 percent a year," says K. C. Bettencourt, an undercover investigator turned consultant and the author of *Theft and Drugs in the Workplace* (Saratoga, Calif.: R & E Pub., 1990). How can a library hope to thwart employee theft and other employee crimes?

Screening of all employees (especially new hires) helps significantly, but a few staff members may have successfully concealed their addiction to narcotics and may need to steal to support their habits.

Here are some questions to ask yourself concerning the prevention, detection, and punishment of inside jobs:

- Is there a code of clearly stated policies for acceptable employee behavior?
- Do all staff members recognize that being caught pilfering library materials will lead at minimum to immediate dismissal and may result in criminal prosecution?
- Does the library prosecute staff members found to be committing pilferage or other theft?
- Does the library's personnel officer conduct thorough background and reference checks for all new hires?
- Is there a way to limit access to telephone long-distance calling and supplies only to essential staff?

Only if the answer to each of the above questions is yes is the library's interest in building, materials, and personal security at an adequate level of preparedness.

What should the library do when it discovers that a staff member has been stealing? Guidelines may suggest what should be done, depending on the motive for the theft, what the rule book says, the personality of the administrator, and the importance to the library of the culprit. For first offenses, where the motive is clearly not related to substance abuse, the range of penalties is considerable and can be any of the following, singly or in combination:

- a stern warning and the requirement of a promise never to do it again
- a requirement that psychological counseling be sought immediately
- being placed on probation for a specified time period
- immediate transfer to a position that does not involve handling valuable items
- demotion with reduction in salary
- widespread publicity so that all staff and the outside world are made aware of the situation
- being fired on the spot
- the summoning of police and the pressing of criminal charges

The first step, however, is not to be surprised when employee crime occurs. We must acknowledge that many of our thefts are inside jobs carried out by library employees who often work with little supervision and who have access to expensive collections. There are ways to lessen the risk of such crimes, however. References on applications must be thoroughly checked. The use of a "weighted application form" produced by security consultants might be a start, but may be illegal in your area.

There are inexpensive predictive tests available whose proponents claim can identify the potential for thievery, but many security experts challenge the effectiveness of such tests. By ascribing a score to applicants' responses to certain test questions, security agents claim to be able to predict those more prone to steal, based on certain factors descriptive of those previously caught stealing. Recently, the American Psychological Association concluded that professionally developed integrity tests are valid predictors of dishonest and counterproductive behavior in the workplace and are more scientifically acceptable than other predictors of theft.

Should your library be unwilling or unable to acquire and administer such tests of prospective honesty, the question becomes how else to discourage dishonest staff members. Obviously, the best way to keep workers from stealing is to refrain from hiring thieves in the first place. Better background checks would help a good deal. But many library managers prefer to trust their instincts in hiring, figuring that they are keen and perceptive judges of human nature.

Hiring people by "gut instincts" or "chemistry" is too risky. It is too easy to make a mistake based only on appearances or what the applicant says about himself. Certain danger signs may point to crime-prone employees, or at least the ones to watch:

- violation of company policies on a regular basis
- record of frequent tardiness or absenteeism
- display of a poor attitude, erratic behavior, or constant complaints
- frequent patron complaints about the employee
- unexplained shrinkage of materials or supplies inventory
- products found concealed in areas accessible only to employees
- discrepancies in accounts
- unexplained losses from petty cash

FIGURE 6.2
Danger Signs to Watch For in Employees

Other loss-prevention rules include locking the safe, verifying cash deposits with a second signature, and having all employees sign a pledge or code of conduct. This "honor system" works surprisingly well in many cases. What about lie detector tests? In 1987, the U.S. House of Representatives passed a bill banning lie detector tests in private industry, with the notable exceptions of drug companies and nuclear regulatory agencies. Government workers (most librarians) are exempted. An expert on hiring cautions that 25 percent of all résumés and employment applications are shown to contain at least one major fabrication. What implication does this have for you and your security program? What steps are you taking to strengthen your background checks and security clearances?

At the minimum, every library should dedicate itself to following such basic steps as the following:

- Investigate all applicants by means of preemployment background checks.
- Be suspicious. Don't rely on what prospective employees tell you about themselves.
- A clearly written policy covering appropriate staff conduct in dealing with the public—including both verbal and physical ha-

rassment or intimidation—should be circulated to all employees for their signatures.

- The library should attempt to create as humane a termination policy as possible to lessen negative feelings among those fired.
- Tighten security by posting loss-prevention rules in conspicuous places.
- Verify petty cash totals daily and lock the safe at night.
- Consider random drug testing of all staff.
- Conduct workshops and discussions on dishonesty and consequences.
- Enforce strict lock and key access.
- Promulgate a systemwide honor system. The honor system frequently doesn't prevent larceny, but it's always worth a try, especially when those found to be in breach of the code know that they will be summarily fired.
- Prosecute staff members who commit crimes.

One persistent problem among staff members is the emotional disinclination to tell on a fellow employee, colleague, or friend. "Whistleblowing," while not universally applauded, should be encouraged so that staff feel willing to report theft, substance abuse, or emotional instability. Employees should be encouraged to report any suspicious activity immediately. They should also be encouraged to overcome their fear of making a mistake or getting involved.

Other Inside Crimes

I can resist everything except temptation.
—Oscar Wilde

A major form of "inside job" is employee misappropriation of library funds or materials. *Library Journal's Library Hotline* in 1988 reported that a California city had charged its head librarian of eleven years with embezzlement. It seems the library director had bought textbooks for his wife's private use with library funds. The amount in question was just over $500 in city funds. Not much of a crime? Perhaps not, but the principle is the same as much larger crimes and indicative of the risk institutions take when they trust their employees.

As an example of a larger crime, *American Libraries* for April 1996 reported that a former library employee at the University of California at Los Angeles had been sentenced to three years and four months in state prison for the theft of more than $1 million of library materials. The man was a student assistant in the library for almost two years, which gave him access to rare manuscripts, first editions, motion picture and television scripts, photographs, and other archival materials from the library's special collections. Fortunately, many of the missing items were recovered. This is another example of the vulnerability of libraries to inside jobs, especially when a library is large and complex enough to own irreplaceable items. Staff are accountable for 75 percent of all library theft!

Trinkaus-Randall (1989) suggests that some extra precautions be taken when dealing with special materials. These include background checks on employees and limiting the number of master and vault keys. Researchers should be interviewed. They should not bring anything into the reading area except pencil and paper or electronic devices. Material should be carefully checked upon return. Marking manuscripts may help protect them, although this is a time-consuming process and may harm the items.

In the private sector, corporations assert an absolute right to protect their property however they can. When employees log on to corporate computer systems, they get a stern reminder that the data they are accessing are "confidential and proprietary," and that misuse or malfeasance could get them fired and possibly prosecuted. Libraries, too, are moving to protect themselves similarly from their own employees. Much attention has been given to outside hackers who electronically break into sensitive computer files, but many administrators will attest that dishonest and incompetent employees do the most damage.

Libraries, of course, are not normally in possession of competitive or proprietary information. However, more and more libraries are writing and enforcing strict policies for computer use by employees, sometimes even installing expensive electronic gear to detect violations. Violators are often fired. But employees and security consultants acknowledge that just having a policy helps keep people honest. Some enforcement measures may come close to invading worker privacy. And a staff that feels its privacy is invaded suffers a drop in morale and an increase in turnover.

It is impossible to tell just how big a problem computer abuse is for two reasons. First, victims of computer abuse are rarely willing to talk about it for fear of looking stupid or careless. Second, it is in the nature of computer abuse that the victims are not always aware their materials have been stolen until long after the event. One library staff member told the author that his superior, a well-paid middle-management department head, spends her days playing endless video games and conducting Internet explorations instead of performing her assigned duties. Is this a form of employee theft? Many would say that it is, because the employee is doing little within her job description. Because she works for a public university library system, she is in many respects cheating her employers and the taxpaying public just as much as is a person who takes home notepads, sticky notes, pencils, pens, and staples.

Worse yet, it is estimated that less than 2 percent of incidents of employee theft are reported to authorities, according to a survey by the Data Processing Management Association. Employee abuse—including fraud, software copyright infringement, and loss or theft of information—clearly costs companies and libraries hundreds of millions of dollars a year. Whom to trust with sensitive information and data is among a manager's worst nightmares. There is no sure way to guarantee that employees will be honest and ethical, despite all manner of psychological tests.

Here is another example. A library contracts with a major commercial online database supplier for unlimited searches for an annual fee. This means that anyone in possession of a user identification and current password can search hundreds of online databases free and do as they like with the information. An employee happens to mention this capability to his uncle, who owns a small information-for-pay company. The uncle concocts a scheme. He will pay his nephew $25 per hour for online searching of topics he will supply. The nephew figures the library's none the worse off, since a year's usage is paid. (Note: There is a licensing agreement, but few ever bother to read it or even mention it.) He's not cheating anyone by using the system, he thinks. The licensing agreement maintains that the search system is for pedagogical and research purposes only, but who cares? So the nephew earns $25 per hour, vastly superior to the wage he earns as a library clerk. And this is in addition to his salary. The uncle reaps the benefits of this arrangement because he peddles the information to his clients at rates from $150 per hour. And the library is none the worse off because it has prepaid for search time, and making use of it is only good sense. So who loses? Is it a true win-win situation?

Never mind the morality of this: Is there a legal problem here? When the library authorities discover the arrangement, what should they do with the nephew? The real loser, of course, is the database supplier. If enough such abuse is carried out, the supplier will probably either discontinue the arrangement, or will merely factor the loss into future rates and charges, meaning that the service will cost more.

To combat this problem, libraries attempt to restrict access to certain categories of information, notably patron records and technical data. In addition, policies generally discourage workers from using library computers for private business matters. A *Wall Street Journal* article for 1985 reports that an employee used company computers and related supplies and equipment over a two-year period to make $64,000 by operating a private mail-order business.

Duplication of software, in contravention of licensing agreements between the supplier and the library, goes on all the time. Some employees caught in the act claim that they didn't even know it was wrong. It is one of the unique properties of information—unlike beef or timber or aluminum siding—that one can give it away limitless times and still have it. This is at once the best and worst feature of information, and the one that proves the trickiest for libraries to control.

Of course, the true value of a policy that expressly lists prohibitions is that it helps make penalties stick. It is important to impress all employees with computer access that breaking into other people's files and personal records is improper behavior—unethical, at least, and illegal in many cases. With a policy in force, the library has a strong basis for taking action against offenders. Another way to enforce the policy is to require all new employees to sign forms saying that they have read the library's computer and confidentiality policies and agree to abide by their terms.

The problem with purchasing sophisticated monitoring systems—even if the library can afford the price—is that the capability of employers to monitor who is using computers and what is being entered into them looks like "Big Brotherism." Many staff find such monitoring unwarranted, an unpleasant intrusion into their privacy, and a tacit statement that library managers trust no one to behave responsibly and ethically. Another problem is "Who's going to watch the watchers?" This is only an admission that, human nature being what it is, no one is above suspicion, and managers are as likely to be transgressors as line staff.

Unauthorized telephone calls are another problem. Forcing employees to pay for calls not related to the library's business seems only appropriate; firing those so apprehended may seem extreme. Yet making personal calls on company time and over company lines is another form of theft and should be dealt with in the same way as the library deals with those who steal books or mutilate magazines.

The bottom line may be that libraries must accept a certain amount of unauthorized use of its resources but may conclude that overt prosecution of those who are caught may be counterproductive. Smarter and happier people work in places that allow them to be innovative, which may mean looser rules. Violating the privacy of others with computers, however, is a serious matter, and should be dealt with seriously.

Lie detector tests might help weed out dishonest or devious employees, but they are not always reliable. The use of such tests was banned by the U.S. House of Representatives in 1987 as unwarranted intrusions on the privacy of persons not charged with any crimes.

Newsweek for April 22, 1996, reports that a Net Access Manager software is now available that allows companies to monitor and regulate their employees' computer activities and Internet behavior. The program lets managers read employee e-mail and selectively block access for individual users. It can also generate reports that detail everything a user has done on the Internet. Whatever your views on the privacy issues involved are, this will at least help to keep employees honest.

Employers expect and need honest, trustworthy employees. There is also the very real threat of lawsuits, as libraries are vulnerable to suit by injured patrons. Screening services are available, and they are good at finding things out about potential employees.

Codes of Conduct and Security

Vexing legal questions of security in libraries remain to be considered. Many libraries do not enjoy the financial luxury of having security guards on duty in the building during hours of operation. Sometimes all staff are charged with responsibility for building security, with predictably varying results. For those libraries with security guards, however, a policy manual is required, charging them with being the eyes and ears of the police and the library staff. The security guard should be well acquainted with the library's approved code of conduct. Each one should have a clear idea of what is acceptable conduct for all persons in the building and what is unacceptable and requires action. It is the duty of the security guard to be alert at all times for suspicious behavior and to report it to superiors and to the police if necessary.

Libraries differ, and they may vary widely as to their codes of conduct for patrons. Just as one example, consider the treatment of sleepers in library buildings. Should the guard be empowered to awaken sleepers? How should this be achieved? Is the guard permitted to touch a person in an effort to shake him or her awake? Should repeated instances of catching a sleeper result in that person's being required to leave the library? And if so, should that eviction be for that day or for a longer period of time?

Another question is that of offensive odors. Must the guard wait until a member of the public complains of a foul-smelling patron, or may he act on his own to solve the problem? When a malodorous person is required to leave the building, is such an eviction for the rest of the day or may it extend until the problem is solved? Another question arises when the source of the offending smell is not personal body odor or simple lack of hygiene but strong perfume, cologne, deodorant, or hair spray. Should the rules apply equally to all strong odors about which members of the public complain, or only to those concerning body odor? And on what criteria should a guard decide that action is necessary or desirable? As reported in chapter 3, an arbitrary rule such as "If I can smell him from six feet away, out he goes!" will not stand up to legal scrutiny for a number of good and sufficient reasons.

Library cleanup crews often remark with surprise about the number of soda cans and food wrappers they find in reading rooms when policy clearly forbids their use. If there is such a policy, what should a security guard do upon witnessing eating and drinking in a library? Many visitors to libraries bring food even when signs specifically prohibit such things. An increasing number of libraries actually offer food and beverages for sale, frequently constituting a valuable financial supplement for the library. If your library has a policy forbidding patrons to eat or drink in the library, the policy must be uniformly applied with no exceptions.

Catching people committing crimes and misdemeanors in the library building is still rare. Suspicion, on the other hand, is common, as alert security guards and staff members watch those who visit the library. When a guard accosts people because he or she feels that they are acting suspiciously, where is the dividing line between prudent enforcement of library rules and unwarranted threatening? When may "probable cause" be construed as harassment?

Is it generally permissible, for example, for a guard to follow a "suspicious" person through the library to see where he goes and to deter him from inappropriate behavior? Or is that something that could be construed as harassment? Herein lies the most significant (and possibly unfortunate) difference between academic and public library security regulations. Academic library security personnel are normally given permission to stop loiterers and other "suspicious" persons, or those who don't look like they belong in their buildings. They can demand to see student or other identification, with the assumptive right to eject persons who do not produce valid reasons for being there. Public library patrons, however, are not required to belong to anything, or even to reside in the jurisdictional area of the library, giving the guards much less latitude as to what they can ask and of whom.

At the University of Georgia, a library staff member and part-time security guard was linked to the theft of hundreds of rare books, prints, and maps from the university library. The university's loss was estimated at over $1 million. Information about the thefts was released to *AB Bookman's Weekly* and others who might help locate the stolen items. When law enforcement agents caught the thief, they discovered him not to be a skulking or shabby person, but a gentleman, a churchgoer, and a respected member of the community. How did they catch him? He tried to sell property belonging to the university to private collectors. And how was he punished? The university merely accepted his resignation, declined to prosecute, and police closed the case.

Pressing Charges

Let's assume that a staff member or a patron has been apprehended by security personnel and charged with a crime or misdemeanor. Let's further say that we can persuade police to appear and arrest him or her. How far should the library go toward prosecution? Remember that under our legal system, witnesses must testify against those accused, who are always given the presumption of innocence.

Let's say we decide to go to court in an effort to deter others. Courtroom trials take time and money. Money is entailed when the library must hire legal representation to defend itself against harassment suits. And don't forget the dollars in lost employee time while they appear in court. In short, we have to be willing to go all the way with our charges or they become meaningless, and the library will have lost, in addition to time and money, the threat of deterrence.

Then there are potential public relations problems. How does the library appear to the general public when people learn that someone has been arrested for committing a crime within its walls? Frequently such a story serves to reduce the number of visitors to the building, out of fear that the library has become a dangerous place. Another factor is how the story reads: A creative reporter on a slow news day may write a story either making the library look like the guardian of public safety against criminal, depraved, or perverted malefactors, or a bunch of bluenoses out to harass and punish people for non-threatening behaviors. There are no easy answers, but the questions must still be considered.

CHAPTER 7

Electronic Security Issues

In any given year, U.S. government systems are illegally, though not necessarily maliciously, accessed at least 300,000 times.

—Robert Ayers, Chief, Information Warfare Division
U.S. Department of Defense
Division of Information Security Analysis

The objectives of this chapter are to:

- describe and discuss some problems specific to the protection of electronic library files
- identify hackers and others who seek to penetrate our defense
- detail methods of electronic intrusion into the library's information resources
- list and discuss effective countermeasures to various forms of electronic trespass
- provide a checklist for the library to use in assessing its electronic security and deciding how to defend against intrusion

Electronic Security: The Attack

Trouble in Cyberspace

Less than five percent of intrusions are detected, and no more than ten percent of those detected are successfully plugged.

—Winn Schwartau, *Information Warfare,* 1996

Cyberspace is a term coined by a science fiction writer back in 1982. It is coming into common usage as the Internet continues to evolve into something everyone can access and exploit. It has many properties of a physical place in that people go there, meet, and exchange information. But unlike Italy or San Antonio, it is at once a place and not a place. Where is it? It's out there somewhere between our phones and computers; it's where telephone conversations occur. It's the place between phones, the place where two human beings, or a human being and a computer, or two computers actually meet and communicate. In one sense, however, cyberspace is becoming an actual place because many people seem to live in it now. People have met there, disagreed there, conducted their business, and been married there. It is, in many senses, a real community: People plot and plan and dream there. Gossip is exchanged, along with valuable data and malicious viruses. The problem is that we don't really understand how to live in cyberspace yet. We are feeling our way into it, blundering about. It's like the real world, though: We take both our advantages and our troubles with us when we enter. "Cyberspace is a new place to live, and one way or another, we're all moving in," wrote Clifford Stoll in *The Cuckoo's Egg* (1989), and it's even truer now than it was then.

Among the troubles in this brave new world made possible by technology is the potential for people to commit crimes and misdemeanors against other people and their systems by the manipulation of computer programs and equipment. The difficulty is that crimes against libraries and other institutions are increasingly being committed not in the physical world, but in cyberspace. This is a sort of wide-open frontier town of a place, where pretty much anything goes because there are few rules and even fewer laws. And while cyberspace may not exactly be "real" in the physical sense, things happen there with genuine consequences. Sometimes the consequences are extremely dire, in fact. Perhaps worst of all, people may not be aware that they are victims until much later, if at all.

The territory of cyberspace demands a new set of definitions, metaphors, rules, and behaviors, and we've only begun to work out what to do about problems there and how we're going to achieve our goals. "I think we're going to see a lot more computer fraud on the Internet," said Janet Reno, attorney general of the United States, in an interview appearing in the *AARP Bulletin* for December 1997 (pp. 3–5). "And it's going to be on the rise because we're going to have perpetrators from around the world. The Internet, a global computer network that allows messages to be transmitted at the speed of light, is opening up a whole new frontier for crime. The Justice Department has beefed up its efforts to curb all types of computer fraud by creating a special Computer Cybercrime Section to combat fraud on the Internet." In addition, the FBI notes that every form of scam already operating over the telephone is now appearing on the Internet.

A few popular movies that included Internet access as part of their story lines have acted as the proverbial double-edged swords: They have not only served as wake-up calls to people with electronic files to protect, but they also may have put dangerous ideas into a few heads. Here are only two examples:

In *War Games* (1983), a young computer whiz, more or less as a lark, makes his school computer change a few flunking grades to better ones. Then he manages to hack into a high-security military installation's computer. After innocently challenging it to a strategy game, he realizes that the "game" entails the launching of global thermonuclear warfare.

In *The Net* (1995), a reclusive computer systems analyst accidentally stumbles across a mysterious Internet program that can access highly classified databases. It becomes apparent that someone knows that she knows. Those mysterious people, thinking she knows too much, first delete her electronic identity by removing all record of her existence from various computers. Then they decide that she herself must be deleted.

Such films may be fiction, but they have implications for security, both offensively and defensively. Dozens of times each day, computer systems in America are penetrated by hackers, crackers, cybercriminals, and other electronic information warriors. These penetrators are free to do as they choose with the information they find. And despite reams of anecdotal evidence that this ongoing crime wave continues and grows day by day, comparatively little about information security is to be found in the literature. Why is this so? One explanation is that there is a massive attempt to cover up the frightening range and scope of such crimes, participated in freely by libraries, computer companies, and software vendors, working in concert. And exactly why has the extent and scope of various types of computer fraud been so diligently covered up? There are many reasons, among them:

- At its best, computer theft is undetectable.
- Routine procedures that could detect intrusion or theft are not installed or run.

- People suffer embarrassment and fear of ridicule or loss of confidence.
- People have a tendency to blame the other guy.
- People blame bad luck.
- People believe that after a first intrusion lightning never strikes twice in the same place.
- There is too much compartmentalization in large organizations or systems.
- People suffer from incredulity and denial.
- There is misplaced trust and naïveté.
- There is technological ignorance.
- Vendors fear hindering sales by telling potential customers the truth about how they could become victims.

In order to study and discuss information security, the propositions in figure 7.1 are presented as background.

1. Every library—no matter what size or what kind—must be concerned with predators of various descriptions who are waiting for opportunities.
2. The Internet, which has changed everything in society and had a vast impact on libraries, has created an entirely new class of criminal —the electronic thief.
3. Security for library records stored electronically is not essentially different from physical security for library books and other materials. Without security measures in place, your library's records are vulnerable to predators. Any library with a disaster plan covering such hazards as fire, flood, earthquakes, or storms must consider electronic penetration a form of disaster as well.
4. The unique properties of information held electronically (e.g., you can have it and give it away at the same time) make it particularly vulnerable to attack.
5. Those who attack our information or information systems are a very real threat to library systems and service.

FIGURE 7.1
Some Axioms concerning Electronic Security for Libraries

6. Whether predators prey out of malevolence, principle, greed, or curiosity, the result for the library system is the same: loss.
7. Employees want to be trusted, but trusting too many people with keys, passwords, access numbers, and so on is asking for trouble.
8. You're not paranoid if they're really out to get you. Trust is a luxury you probably can't afford.
9. An organizational code of ethics is nice to have but cannot be relied upon to keep everybody honest.
10. In the absence of operational electronic security measures, people are free to do what they want, and that cannot be tolerated.
11. Proactive electronic security countermeasures against hackers, crackers, and other data thieves aren't just nice—they're essential.
12. It doesn't take a genius-level IQ to figure out how to rip a library off electronically. Just about anyone can do it.
13. Electronic theft, tampering, and destruction of library records is a problem of tremendous financial consequences, not to mention privacy and recovery considerations.
14. Unfortunately, there is an inverse ratio and inevitable trade-off between a high level of library security and a high level of personal privacy. You can't keep both at the highest level at the same time.
15. Crackers and hackers who achieve illegal entry into library files are criminals, and they should be prosecuted to the fullest extent of the law.
16. Inside jobs (employee theft or sabotage) go on all the time and constitute a very real security problem.
17. Security is a borderless problem. Stringent law enforcement is required, and that requires international cooperation.
18. Despite all the daunting problems mentioned, there are effective measures that a library can take to safeguard its electronic security most of the time.
19. Like conventional thieves, electronic thieves choose to commit the easiest or safest theft, and they will always select the one with the least chance of getting caught.
20. In electronic security, it's frequently a case of "spy-versus-spy," as improved deterrence begets improved weapons of attack.
21. To catch a thief, one must learn to think like a thief.

(Continued)

FIGURE 7.1 *(Continued)*

22. One of the principal problems of electronic library security is the complacency syndrome.
23. In security matters, the best offense is often a strong defense.
24. Without an uninterruptable power source, your library's electronic information is inaccessible and your most sophisticated computer is little more than a series of paperweights.
25. The first step in addressing your library's security problem is to admit that there is a problem.
26. Good security is imperative, but expensive.
27. Really good security is really expensive.
28. Perfect security (electronic or physical) is impossible.
29. Security should be thought of as a journey and not a destination. You're always en route but you never really "arrive."

A New Definition of Theft

Most dictionaries define the term *theft* as "an act or instance of stealing or larceny." Simply put, however, theft refers to taking something that doesn't belong to you. Electronic theft is somewhat harder to define or classify. Why? Because the act of stealing information electronically may result in taking something that doesn't belong to the thief, but that remains with the owner of the information, who may actually be unaware it has been taken. Information theft, therefore, differs radically from the theft of commodities like pencils, lumber, or prime steaks. In those cases, once the item is stolen, it is no longer with the owner but with the thief; it cannot be in two places at the same time.

Information, however, whether a single password or an entire manuscript, cannot only be stolen from its owner, but it can also be disseminated throughout a network without causing the owner to notice its loss. Once the information has been stolen, however, the consequences for the owner are unknowable but unlikely to be pleasant. This new form of crime—information theft—creates entirely new aspects of being a criminal or a victim—and our codes of sanctions and laws are going to have to adapt.

Assaulting Camelot: An Exercise

Since human time began, people have attempted to secure their homes and their lives against a variety of threats and enemies. Some of our ancestors chose to dwell in caves high up on hillsides, where marauders or intruders could be detected early and dealt with easily before they could enter homes to rob or slaughter the occupants. Others built walls designed to serve as defensive fortifications against intrusion and death. Arguably the best security concept of the Dark Ages came about when someone first had the cleverness to choose an island completely surrounded by water for his residence and equipped his home with a drawbridge that could be raised and lowered from within as the sole access point. For the most part, such early technology did a pretty good job of keeping the good guys safe inside and the bad guys out.

But that doesn't mean that the castle dwellers were completely safe against intrusion, however wide or deep the moat or strong their walls. Then, as now, there was no such thing as perfect security, and there never will be. As the Trojans discovered to their everlasting sorrow during their war with the Greeks over 2,000 years ago, there is nothing more damaging, stupid, and wrong than the conceited notion that you are completely safe behind your walls and need have no fear of being defeated by an outside enemy. As the previous chapters of this book have demonstrated, determined people continually attempt to steal physical materials from libraries. But what about the library's other assets? What about assets that exist physically only as magnetized spots on tape, but which constitute much of the information that makes the library valuable? And what about proprietary and sensitive electronic files held in the library's computer systems? Are they sufficiently protected against intrusion, vandalism, theft, and destruction?

Today, with modern high-tech computer equipment and telecommunication capabilities, it's been said that you can cause more devastating and long-range damage to a library with an electronic assault than with a handgun. The analogy of misplaced confidence in stone walls to libraries feeling secure that their system is invulnerable should be clear. But to drive home the point, the following exercise is designed to open your eyes.

> King Arthur lives in Camelot, a strong-walled castle surrounded by a wide and deep moat. He earnestly seeks to preserve and defend the lives, safety, and property of all within, and he knows that their lives and his own depend on that security. Behind Camelot's

stout walls, Arthur employs reliable guards and deadly archers to watch all traffic heading across the drawbridge by day and all possible approaches to the moat by night. The result is supposed to ensure that only people who belong can enter the castle. Yet the king and his extended family cannot remain inside forever. Because all within must eat, they need vast nearby fields under cultivation and dairy herds beyond the drawbridge. Every day, therefore, agricultural workers leave the security of the castle walls and go to work growing food, under the vigilant guard of the castle's field security team. Upon their return at the end of the workday, those employed in the fields and dairies must identify themselves by sight or acquaintance to the guards before they are permitted to cross the lowered drawbridge. The only legitimate way to get into the castle, therefore, is to enter via the drawbridge in plain sight of the guards. Only authorized persons can safely enter and avail themselves of food, shelter, and safety. At night, the bridge is raised and everybody inside is as safe as can be. That's the way it's supposed to work. Good guys inside, bad guys outside.

But now imagine yourself as one of Arthur's determined enemies, standing across the moat from the castle after the drawbridge is secured and seeking unauthorized admission. You have no moral compunctions about wholesale slaughter, but you can't kill men you can't reach. Your strongest archers can't shoot their arrows across the moat and through the castle's ports and windows. So your problem is how to get inside, kill those within, loot Camelot's fabled possessions, and take possession of this prime piece of real estate for yourself.

As Arthur's wiliest enemy, consider your options, given the state of technology a thousand years ago. How might you go about penetrating Camelot, given that it lies across a deep moat, its people are heavily armed, and they are strongly predisposed to keep you out? With a little thought, you might try one or more of the ideas in figure 7.2 to achieve penetration by hook or by crook, by stealth or by force.

Assaulting the Library Computer

In more than eighty percent of the computer crimes investigated by the FBI, unauthorized access was gained through the Internet.

—Winn Schwartau, *Information Warfare,* 1996

- Have your best swimmers swim across the moat under cover of darkness, climb the wall, and cut the drawbridge ropes.
- Sue for "peace." Under the flag of safe parole ostensibly to talk about the terms of peaceful coexistence, whip out your sword and kill Arthur and everyone else you can reach.
- Have one of your band hire on as a credentialed king's employee, entitled to access to Camelot as a member of its crew.
- Grab a hostage—someone of importance—and deal from strength.
- Hurl catapulted balls of flaming pitch over Camelot's walls in hopes of starting fires that will consume everyone inside or drive them out where you can get at them.
- Attempt to fool the guards on the drawbridge by assuming the identity of one of those who belongs.
- Lay siege via a war of attrition, in which you attempt to starve the castle's inhabitants out by denying anyone inside the ability to leave.
- Attempt to bribe a trusted member of the Camelot gatekeeping force into lowering the bridge.
- Build a large "gift" statue for Arthur, fill it with troops, and leave it at the place where the drawbridge falls.
- Watch, wait, and hope that somebody careless will leave the bridge down a bit too long.
- After assessing the situation, determine that penetration is too difficult, risky, or time-consuming; go assault someone else's castle.

FIGURE 7.2
Arthur's Enemies' Options for Assaulting and Sacking Camelot

Now let's fast-forward to the present day, and substitute for strong-walled Camelot the totality of the defenses around your library's electronic files and records. The analogy of defending Camelot a millennium ago to protecting today's electronic library assets doesn't really require much of a stretch of imagination. Just substitute the protection and preservation of proprietary information for King Arthur and his court and you can see the way things line up. This time, assume that Arthur is the administrator of the computer network, and you are one of the "bad guys," an information warrior intent upon breaking into and entering his computer system and seeking to move around within it at will. What are your options?

- Cut the power lines, rendering the computing power useless.
- Impersonate a credentialed user via identity theft or misuse.
- Bribe a system employee into giving up the needed access codes.
- Become a credentialed system employee, entitled to access proprietary files by means of an authorized account and password.
- Attempt to eavesdrop electronically on private conversations.
- Hack into the system and, once inside, shut it down, temporarily or permanently, from a remote location.
- Insert a virus into the mainframe via remote access, which will, when triggered, shut down the system.
- Destroy the system's electronic files by means of a high-energy particle weapon beamed through the library's walls.
- Snoop around casually by looking over shoulders in the library's computer center until you find someone who is not careful about password change or protection or access code use.
- Root around in dumpsters, trash containers, and office wastebaskets until you find something that you can use.
- Shoot your way into the computer center and compel employees to give up what you need to know by threatening their lives.
- Build and execute an electronic "Trojan horse" program that will, following its programming, execute a destructive sequence into the system.
- Befriend or bribe an employee privy to high-security information and get him or her to talk about the job by using guile, romance, alcohol, or other inducements.
- After assessing the situation, determine that penetration is just too difficult, risky, and time-consuming; go assault someone else's system.

The task of protecting electronic assets is much more difficult than hunkering down in a castle across a moat from your enemies for a very simple reason: It is customary, in the case of libraries' information, for the "drawbridge" to be down during normal business hours, entitling—and even encouraging—bad guys and good guys alike to mingle, enter, and partake. Anyone who imagines his system to be invulnerable behind stout and unyielding castle walls has another think coming.

> All you have to do is walk into any university computer lab, log on the Internet as guest—they have no concept of physical security—and off you go. It's the easiest thing in the world. If I wanted to send a death threat to the President (a clear federal infraction), I could do it with impunity, and there is no way my true identity could be captured. Most sites have amazingly poor audit trails, and if you can't see who's coming at you, there's no way you can catch him.
>
> —An anonymous hacker quoted by David H. Freedman and Charles C. Mann, @ *Large* (1997)

In the world of information security, there are three basic tenets requisite to keeping information secure:

Confidentiality (everything you have to do to keep secrets secret)

Integrity (maintaining accuracy of data)

Availability (making sure that systems and data are always available for use)

All three of these facets must be obtained and preserved in order for your system to do its job. Technological aspects of electronic security have serious consequences, as theft of intellectual property has potentially costly implications. It is estimated that billions of dollars are lost each year worldwide to various forms of electronic piracy. And as much as librarians and other information providers may wish that there were no barriers to the free flow of information, most would acknowledge that "fair use" copyright laws should provide for authors and publishers to receive just compensation for their efforts and products. The honor system demonstrably doesn't work. In an attempt to remedy or at least slow the problem of thievery, various innovative measures are currently being considered to control the flow of proprietary electronic information.

Hackers: Their Objectives and Tactics

> Internet hackers infiltrated the Justice Department's home page Saturday, altering the official web site to include swastikas, obscene pictures, and lots of criticism of the Communications Decency Act. The official web site, which was disabled by government technicians when it was discovered Saturday morning, was

> changed to read "United States Department of Injustice," next to a red, black and white flag bearing a swastika. . . . Hackers used the majority of the web site to criticize the Communications Decency Act. . . . The doctored page also had links to other web sites, all unflattering, about (President) Clinton, Republican presidential nominee Bob Dole and conservative commentator Pat Buchanan.
>
> —Associated Press newswire, October 3, 1996

So who are the bad guys? It is important that we understand both the hackers—our enemies—and ourselves, and how we make it so easy for them to have their way with us. A hacker or cyberthief, operating inside and outside legal boundaries, can assemble a very thorough electronic dossier on anyone he or she chooses or merely break into a high-security government or commercial file and snoop around at his or her own discretion. It is already possible, using existing Web sites with names like Dig Dirt and SpyForU, to purchase complete reports on individuals, including their net worth, salary, private telephone records, credit card bills, airline travel records, and even medical histories. Obviously this can be employed subsequently to do mischief against adversaries, real or imagined. Everything you want to know about someone else is for sale, and almost everything you may not wish others to know about you and your business is available to others. The only brakes on such unwarranted intrusions are:

- How much you can afford to spend.
- How much risk you want to take.
- What your personal morals or ethics are.

> Why is hacking harmful? It's like my house. If I don't invite you in, don't come in, or it's called breaking and entering and I'll call the police.
>
> —Winn Schwartau, *Information Warfare,* 1996

There is general consensus around a neat distinction between "hackers" and "crackers," terms often confused. The hacker tries to figure out how any code of data operates and normally drops it at that. The cracker not only discovers how a database operates, but "cracks" into it, sometimes for nefarious purposes. Hackers are thus the self-styled ladies and gentlemen of the information highway, while the crackers are the crooks and thieves. This is not to suggest that all hackers are harmless, but many do what they do as an exercise in curiosity and are careful not to disturb anything once inside someone else's computer. Crackers act out of malicious motives and will do what they can to screw up your system, if you let them.

All hackers may not be villains, but they employ the very same techniques as villains do: They seek to access and take possession of what is not lawfully theirs by whatever means are available or necessary to get the job done. What kinds of people would seek to penetrate our electronic security, even if they don't plan to cripple our system or steal our secrets? The answer is never simple and can actually be extremely complicated. Hackers and crackers can be as unalike as snowflakes or fingerprints in their physical descriptions, their motives and intentions, and their tactics and strategies. However, forensic science has over the years worked up a generalized psychological profile of the typical hacker. But beware: Like all profiles, it may not fit a specific case. A stereotypical hacker matches many of the following characteristics:

- Male between twelve and twenty-eight years of age.
- Very likely from the middle to upper socioeconomic classes.
- Smart and perhaps brilliant, but did poorly in school because he couldn't accept the established rules.
- Possessed of boundless curiosity.
- A loner, a misfit, and misunderstood. From a dysfunctional family. Few if any friends and not much of a social or sex life.
- A tendency to view himself as a freewheeling intellectual explorer of the highest and deepest potential of computer systems, the postmodern electronic equivalent of the cowboy and the mountain explorer.
- An earnest desire to make access to computers as free and open as possible.
- A strong belief that fine aesthetic beauty can be found in writing the perfect program, and that the resulting rush can liberate the mind and spirit.
- A grandiose sense of self-importance, and a belief that one day soon the world will recognize him for what he is.
- A preoccupation with fantasies of unlimited success.

- A general sense of having been overlooked, underestimated, or misunderstood.
- A tendency to react strongly and negatively to perceived slights or threats to his self-esteem, which could lead him to an act of revenge through sabotage.
- Strong feelings of entitlement, which justify what he is doing to himself.
- A goal of control over others. Suffers from a lack of empathy with others.
- A principal objective of disruption of service by any means possible or necessary.
- A definition of property and privacy markedly different from conventional ones.
- Doesn't see it as a big deal if he breaks into your computer without your permission to use its computational power or to look around inside without hurting or taking anything.
- Resentment of and resistance to the idea that he is a voyeur, snoop, invader of privacy, trespasser, perpetrator of fraud, or any kind of spy.
- An active and resourceful imagination.
- No regard for the law, or a feeling that the law is unjust or doesn't apply.
- May have convinced himself that intrusion into proprietary files is a moral duty because "information wants to be free."
- A sense of outrage against governments, authority, and rules.
- A feeling of smug superiority as one of the information elite.
- A perception of hacking as a game.
- A deep compulsion to keep hacking, even when caught red-handed and punished.
- A belief that stealing from institutions is not like breaking and entering private homes with the motive of theft.

Rather a daunting list, isn't it? Perhaps the kindest thing that can be said about most hackers, from the standpoint of the victimized library, is that in many cases greed and financial gain are not the principal goals. If he fits the profile, he tends to prefer to sit back and laugh as he watches from a vantage point of safety while your helpless programmers and systems engineers try to figure out just what went terribly wrong and what, if anything, they are going to be able to do about it.

Of course it is possible and perhaps even justifiable to differentiate hacking into small hacking (say, poking around in the library's unauthorized files) and big hacking or cracking out of malice, revenge, or for profit. Breaking into a computer system, cracking its password scheme, or learning how to beat down the front door is often referred to as hacking in distinction to cracking. The difference? Cracking frequently provides income. Hacking can be done just out of curiosity, to improve system performance, to impress your friends, or just for the hell of it. Clifford Stoll (*The Cuckoo's Egg*, 1989) says there is a big and obvious difference: He sees it as the difference between finding a cockroach in your kitchen (hacking) and finding your bedroom teeming with big, hungry sewer rats (cracking).

Motivations of Hackers

> Imagine that somebody steps into your house though an open window. They find your house keys, make copies of them, toss some of their stuff into one of your closets, and walk out the front door. What have you lost, exactly? Nothing but your peace of mind. . . . Library computers are like houses. You can make them difficult and inconvenient to break into, but there's always a way around the best safeguards.
>
> —James Large, "Hacked!" *American Libraries* (August 1996)

Hackers only rarely enter library computers to rob them of money. Libraries, after all, don't generally have a lot of money at their disposal. Most hackers do what they do for a variety of reasons that have little or nothing to do with financial gain. When reporters asked Sir Edmund Hillary to tell them why he had gone to all the trouble and expense of being the first European to scale Mount Everest, he is reported to have answered, "Because it was there." So assuming that greed and the acquisition of wealth is not paramount in his intentions, exactly what does the hacker seek to do by intruding into the library's electronic system? He may seek to:

- listen to conversations between the computers on the network.
- gain illicit entry into the computers and look around for valuable data.

- gain illicit entry into the network for the purposes of shutting it down or rendering it scrambled.
- learn passwords and access codes that will give him unlimited access to the network any time he chooses.
- listen to "private" electronic mail between users on the network.
- indulge his idle curiosity.

Now that we've described and profiled the hacker, let's try to understand how he selects a victim. When police authorities asked Willie ("The Actor") Sutton why he robbed banks, he answered, "Because that's where they keep the money." Since government agencies and banks have very high levels of information security, however, the hacker will normally search out easier prey. What he needs is a target that relies heavily on communication and computers to do business or operate, yet one that does not have a firewall or other good system of electronic security. A library, for example.

Targets of Hackers' Intrusions

Hackers are not all alike, and thus different people may target different aspects of your security system. Here, however, are some of the most attractive (and most easily penetrated) electronic facilities to electronic thieves:

- Network management systems
- Privileged accounts and passwords
- Dial-in modem access numbers and networks
- Data communication network connectivity
- Source and destination addresses
- Trust relationships
- Partitions and firewalls
- Electronic communication (e.g., e-mail)

Unwitting Accomplices: How Libraries Assist the Hacker

To assist in his nefarious deeds and the achievement of his objectives, the modern-day cyberthief has at his disposal an impressive array of weapons, strategies, and tactics. Regrettably, however, the best help the villain can hope to get is not from technology but from you, the well-intentioned but overconfident or careless castle gatekeeper who just forgot to raise the drawbridge for the night. If someone has carelessly left the drawbridge down, penetration of the castle's defenses becomes a piece of cake.

There is no perfect security. If you accept this premise, you will not be surprised to learn that every library—even one reasonably up to code on security procedures—suffers from a myriad of system vulnerabilities to electronic trespass. These holes, lapses, and Achilles' heels in the library's security perimeter can make it almost ludicrously easy for the bad guys to breach the walls, get in, move around, and do whatever the hell they please. Your system is likely to have, unless you protect and monitor it thoroughly and regularly, a daunting number of Achilles' heels by which unauthorized persons can tap in, access accounts, and create general mayhem in your files. Among these potential holes are:

- The user.
- The memory inside the keyboard.
- The terminal emulator.
- The LAN or network driver software.
- The LAN connection card.
- The network cabling or server.
- The peer or other user's nodes.
- The gateway, router, or bridge to other networks.
- The WAN or wide area network interface.
- The mainframe front-end processor.
- The channel to the mainframe.
- The mainframe application.
- Antiquated or faulty wiring.
- No encryption (or poor encryption).
- Naïveté or apathy about the problem.
- Overconfidence or ignorance (the "Maginot Line" syndrome).
- No accountability or responsibility for security.
- Overconfidence in security measures already in place.

- Out-of-date security or no security at all.
- Procrastination.
- Budget constraints that ignore or slight security precautions.
- Lacking the will or time to follow through in punishing criminals.
- Lack of networking and information sharing.
- Untrained staff.
- No security policy or standards in place.
- No or inadequate firewalls.
- Unsafe computing.
- Poor password protection and authentication mechanisms.
- Poor paper-handling procedure (e.g., no shredding).
- Failure to indoctrinate users of the system properly.
- Lack of vigilance.
- Poor screening of employees, especially new hires.
- Behaving passively or reactively instead of proactively.

How Hackers Attack

The selection of weapons used in any attack on your library's system will depend on the desired aims and objectives of the perpetrator. Most electronic intrusion is achieved via the Internet, that vast and amorphous electronic apparatus that seemingly grows every day and that has changed the world of communication forever. The Supreme Court of the United States has recently declared that the Internet constitutes a vast public forum, whereby a person with a phone line can become a town crier with a voice that resonates far beyond any soapbox. True enough, but keep in mind that, using the Internet, a single person, armed with determination, some modestly priced equipment, and utter ruthlessness, can bring a library's electronic files down in a heartbeat.

Other, much simpler systems know how to protect themselves rather well. Security precautions found in the simplest and most ubiquitous electronic equipment are intended to preserve the integrity of the shielding of the contents. A modern pay phone, for example, has been carefully designed to resist coin slugs, zaps of electricity, chunks of coin-shaped ice, prybars, magnets, lock picks, blasting caps, and mistreatment by furious or careless people. Can your library's electronic security do that? There is, in addition, a perceived difference between someone taking a crowbar to your pay phone and hacking into your computer. Police may not see the difference; they think a crime's a crime. Do you? The police call it theft and theft is a crime. In the world of the police, everything is good or bad, black or white. In the computer world, where there are few laws and only emerging rules and guidelines, everything is shades of gray.

Thus far, our discussion has centered around library vulnerability to electronic intrusion. But hackers seeking to access your account and impersonate you so that your account gets charged for someone else's merchandise can attack you not just at work but in your own private transactions as well. It's now possible for anyone with a credit card and home dial-up access to a Web browser to do much of their shopping without leaving their homes. Nearly everything from flowers and candy to the latest best-seller can now be purchased online at the touch of a button. But while many consumers are attracted by the convenience that online shopping offers, many remain uncomfortable with sharing credit card numbers and other information over the Web. Security continues to be the main issue stopping massive use of the Internet for buying and selling. Here are some ways you can protect yourself:

- Use common sense. Research companies that you're unfamiliar with.
- Always keep track of your monthly credit card bill, and contact your credit card company immediately should you discover any false or unauthorized transactions on your account.
- Look for security icons. Netscape and Microsoft Web browsers now include protection that prevents your online connection from being tapped, or at least warns you when it is. Look for a solid key icon in Netscape's Navigator browser or a padlock icon in Microsoft's Internet explorer.
- Seek certification. Legitimate sites usually display a digital certificate —a window that asks for confirmation before proceeding with your transaction—to verify that you've reached the proper Web site.
- Wait for next year (or possibly the one after that). Software developers are designing programs that use Secure Electronic Transaction (SET) protocols, enabling secure payment transactions. Experts predict that the industry standard will provide sites labeled as compliant with the SET standard by the turn of the century.

Weapons of Choice

The cybercrook's weapons of choice are dictated by his technological sophistication, the funds he has at his disposal, the time he is willing to put into his scheme, and several personal variables. Above all, however, while he seeks ultimate recognition for his genius, he is normally smart enough to take strong evasive action and trail-covering actions to avoid getting caught. That means that his weapons of choice are

- invisible
- passive
- insidious
- triggered by remote control or time delay
- deniable
- untraceable
- likely to cause maximum damage to your system
- at their best when they cause collateral damage (e.g., lengthy service disruptions, loss of money)
- likely to cause long-term fallout in the system (e.g., confusion, suspicion, finger-pointing, blame and recriminations, firings)

Winn Schwartau (*Information Warfare,* 1996) refers to those who hack or crack into our files and snoop around or do damage as "information warriors," which may be a more complimentary term than what many others would use. Information warriors, Schwartau warns, are capable of using both existing and innovative technology to access our information. While it may be a game for the hacker or cracker, it can have deadly serious consequences for libraries and other institutions that maintain large amounts of sensitive information in their electronic files. The choice of the weapons used against your system will vary with the intentions of the hacker or cybercriminal: Is he just having a good time snooping around, or does he have a much more serious and damaging intention when he enters your files? Schwartau says that to defend against such intrusions into our private data, we must become information warriors in our own right to counter the attacks of those who come against us and even, on occasion, to ensure that our enemies are no longer effective in the struggle to compromise our information and defeat our mission.

The weapons already residing in the arsenal of today's information warrior are given in figure 7.3:

- "Bag jobs" or physical entry into the target, replacing or adding a chip to the computer or printer, or placing a "bug" in the telephone connector.
- Dumpster diving and wastebasket prowling.
- Standing behind people and watching their keyboard entries.
- Offensive software, which can alter or destroy files.
- Sniffing communications software, which can detect and penetrate supposedly secure communication wires and, once inside, "sniff" out valuable data (e.g., personal passwords, network protocols, trade secrets, privileged communication).
- Electronic eavesdropping equipment, which can easily intercept private conversations, listen in, and capture what is said.
- A Daemon dialer—a common piece of underground software that scans thousands of phone numbers to determine which ones connect to a telephone and which ones connect to a computer. The software automatically lists the numbers that have computers at the other end, while other software attempts to break into each computer network by cracking passwords. This information, and the software to obtain it, is often shared by various types of cyberpunks who populate the computer underground. The hackers then go after their ultimate target: the computers and networks.
- Chipping programs (AKA "time bombs," Trojan horses)—malicious programs which, once installed, can lie silently and patiently within a system or program until commanded to act, and then create complete havoc in the system while the installer is thousands of miles away with an airtight alibi.
- Directed energy weapons such as HERF guns that can fire bolts of concentrated energy through walls and shields without detection or harm to living creatures, but can completely destroy all data in the system.
- Inside helpers employed by the system, privy to passwords and protocols, and secretly working for the hacker.
- "Psyops" (psychological operations), used by spies in all theaters of warfare, and intended to demoralize an enemy or cause them to suffer a crisis of confidence in their system.

FIGURE 7.3
Weapons Available to the Well-Equipped Hacker in Attacks on the Library's Computer

Frightening list, isn't it? And such hackers and crackers may work their evildoing against library computers for motives ranging from idle curiosity to furious revenge. But just as it doesn't really matter to the frog why the boy has thrown a rock at it, the results of being hit are exactly the same.

The Loss of Privacy

> If privacy is outlawed, only outlaws will have privacy. Intelligence agencies have access to good cryptographic technology. So do the big arms and drug traffickers. So do defense contractors, oil companies, and other corporate giants. But ordinary people and grassroots political organizations mostly have not had access to affordable "military grade" public-key cryptographic technology.
>
> —Phil Zimmerman, "Why Do You Need PGP?" in Peter Ludlow, *High Noon on the Electronic Frontier,* 1996

All libraries should be aware that hackers are after your data, and in many cases, they'll come away with their prizes without your knowledge. This is the Internet age. The Internet provides an unprecedented and previously unimaginable freedom of access to information. That's good, but a serious potential shortcoming of the Internet may be the loss of privacy to all Internet users. You may not be aware of it, but as your e-mail travels over the Internet, it gets relayed via numerous transfer points, and is thus subject to interception by hackers intent on mischief.

Just as it is entirely possible to receive someone else's mail in the regular post, it is equally possible to get into someone else's e-mail, past the password protection, and into the content of those messages. In this way, an unscrupulous hacker can go on to access your telephone number, credit card numbers, and the same data on everyone you contact or who contacts you. Hackers sometimes go on electronic fishing expeditions, in fact, just randomly trolling for something they can use. Even more alarming are recent reports of attempts by business concerns to gain access to a wide variety of personal data on people, ranging from financial records to health records, arrest records, and the like, with the intent of selling that information to others or using it for their own purposes.

How shall we librarians, the underpaid but noble custodians of the record of human experience, seek to defeat those who would steal from us electronically, now that they can tap in from home, without even having to put on their shoes?

We know better what we can't do. We can't shoot them. We can't ban them for life from the library. We might even have trouble with the law if we demand that they leave the system when we catch them in the act. No comprehensive solutions have presented themselves to date. And there are limits to privacy, for the sake of everyone else . . . or are there?

Figure 7.4 offers a few privacy-oriented guidelines that will protect users to the extent possible in a limited budget situation.

Computer Viruses

> You can tell people that they have crummy locks, but you can't make them change them.
>
> —Clifford Stoll, on the failure of many users to heed Internet warnings that could have prevented virus spread. *The Cuckoo's Egg,* 1989

Computer viruses are human-created programs usually designed—with malice aforethought—to replicate themselves infinitely, taking over or crowding out all other information on a disk or drive. A fast-acting and malevolent virus can turn your library's hard drive or core storage into a paperweight faster than you can do anything but watch and wail. All possible steps must be taken to protect library computers from viruses, which can turn a hard drive full of important data into a useless slate, wiped clean and unrecoverable.

Most computer systems are now equipped with some form of virus protection, as a form of vaccine against these programs. They work to a certain extent, but new viruses are coming along faster than barriers and shields can be erected against them. The best way to guard against having malevolent viruses engulf your system is to make all staff aware of the potential consequences of placing bad diskettes in the library's drives. When such a thing happens, and the miscreant can be identified regardless of motive, prescribed penalties must be on the books and enforced.

This is not intended to alarm you unduly, but you should know that in certain cases your library's entire computer system can be felled permanently by a computer virus. The Michelangelo virus struck on March 6, 1992 (commemorating the five hundredth birthday of the Renaissance artist and sculptor Michelangelo Buonarroti), erasing many hard drives so thoroughly that there was no way to recover the information that had been stored on them.

- Have a well-thought-out and legally sound information policy in place.
- Check with appropriate legal authorities to make sure that you're on the right side of the law in your defensive safeguards.
- Stay alert and be suspicious. It is far better to be thought paranoid than to be too naive or trusting.
- Perform a comprehensive electronic risk analysis on a regular basis.
- Try to think like a crook to catch a crook.
- Don't expect any privacy on the Internet unless you use encryption.
- Don't say anything on the telephone that you wouldn't want read in the newspaper.
- Don't write anything over the Internet that you wouldn't want persons other than the intended recipient to read.
- Do what you can to put obstacles such as electronic moats, air locks, and alarms at strategic points in your system to detect unauthorized intrusion or attack. Trip-wire software programs act as the electronic equivalent of those caged canaries that coal miners used to carry down into the mines to warn them of pockets of methane gas. Any or all of these defenses in the path of would-be hackers are intended to make their job so difficult and time-consuming that they may throw up their hands in exasperation and leave your system alone.
- Encourage all employees and users to guard their passwords carefully.
- Require that all employees and users change their passwords regularly.
- In choosing passwords, users should be dissuaded from picking default or easily guessable passwords, or those consisting of a first initial and their last names.
- Passwords should neither be requested nor given out over the telephone or the computer system, and all users should understand that they will never be asked to provide them by anyone via telephone or e-mail.

FIGURE 7.4
Guidelines for Maximizing User Privacy in Computer Systems

Computer viruses are small hidden programs that alter the way your computer operates without your permission or knowledge. They may be created by people for various reasons ranging from malevolence to curiosity and may have various effects. Who creates and sets viruses in motion? Some viruses, it is true, are the innocent results of ghastly accidents and other unintentional transmissions. But assuming that virus transmissions are the intentional work of deliberate people, what kind of person would deliberately and maliciously seek to destroy the computer files of everyone who uses them? The motivations of all virus creators cannot be understood or explained, and the perpetrators are hard to catch. Still, a few informed guesses are in order:

Computer enthusiasts with way too much time on their hands seek to make the library the victim of a practical joke.

Curious programmers accept the implicit challenge in other users' security precautions. They seek to hack into your program just because it's there and to destroy it just because they can.

Persons with low self-esteem relish the feeling of power they receive from bringing the computer system of others to a screeching halt.

Malicious individual computer users or conspiracy theorists see enemies everywhere and seek to hurt those enemies.

Former employees or other persons with motives of payback or revenge for real or imagined slights or insults from the library, its staff members, or administrators.

Neo-Luddites and other enemies of technology, seeking to destroy computers and thus defeat their users. Such "flat-earthers" may feel that there is something ungodly or merely economically menacing about computer networks, and thus experience a special secret pleasure in using technological methods to defeat technology.

Insiders or staff members may stand to gain from destroying or otherwise irretrievably altering the library's files.

Computer viruses can hitchhike on a program that you download from the Internet or be acquired from swapping diskettes with someone whose computer is infected. In very rare cases, you can even get a virus from a brand new (and shrink-wrap-protected) program you bought in a store. You cannot acquire a virus using text-only electronic mail, although one can be part of a text file. What is the best way to ensure that no virus fells your system? A good rule of thumb is to adopt a realistic mixture of common sense and paranoia: Be very wary of downloads and attachments from anyone you do not know.

Libraries, of course, are not helpless in the face of such assaults on their systems. But there are decided limits to security, all the same. Virus detectors and vaccines can offer protection, but they're proven effective only against certain known viruses. Unfortunately, however, new ones come along all the time. When the library manages to defeat one threat, a hacker often redoubles his efforts to work his will with the library's system. The game's afoot.

But be advised that every time your library's computer staff figures out how to harden your system against a virus, the perpetrator is likely to devise a new, even more virulent strain of virus. If he is successful, this will cause you to attempt to defeat the new threat, and so on. New viruses appear continually. Antivirus products cannot recognize and defeat them all. Antivirus research teams report that they see 150 to 200 new viruses each month. The only solution is to be aware of viruses and try to be vigilant without resorting to measures that will reduce the library's utility to the community.

Trojan Horses

The Greek storyteller Homer wrote, millennia ago, of a Trojan horse that helped Greece bring down the strong walls of Troy by trickery. Over recent years, similar methodology has been developed for bringing computers down, and it uses much the same technique. The term *Trojan horse* is likely to evoke images of antiquity, but can be a present-day nightmare for managers entrusted with security for library records. In 1988, in Fort Worth, Texas, a former programmer was convicted of planting a computer virus in his employer's system that wiped out 168,000 records and was activated like a time bomb, doing its sabotage two days after he was fired. A person in Texas can be convicted of "harmful access to a computer," a third-degree felony with penalties of up to ten years in prison and $5,000 in fines. But, as always, the burden of proof lies with the complainant. Since many libraries don't wish to appear as victims (lest the news deter others from coming to the library, voting for its upkeep, or donating their collections) the library in Fort Worth didn't want to let anyone know there had been a breach of security. Consequently, the charge was reduced to the lesser crime of computer sabotage, which carries with it a much less severe penalty.

A Trojan horse is not exactly a virus in that it doesn't replicate itself. However, when awakened from dormancy and triggered, it can silently scramble, garble, or erase other data stored in a computer's memory, totally or selectively. The original computerized Trojan horse was a political thrust aimed at AIDS activists and intended to create trouble for their network out of doctrinaire reasons of distaste for its members. Another well-known early Trojan horse carried in its fine-print "license agreement" a warning of ominous side effects if the user didn't send $378 to a post office box in Panama.

It is no accident that the term *Trojan horse* is applied to electronic breaching of the other side's fortified walls. After years of dispiriting battle, the Greeks discovered that they could not successfully manage to storm the gates of Troy. They accomplished the same purpose by getting men inside those walls under the guise of a gift. With commonsense Trojan precautions, the war might have turned out differently for all concerned.

Spoofing Authentication

Imagine this chilling scenario. Let's say that your interface to a commercial database system runs through your university's mainframe computer. As a legitimate user, you have been issued an account number and password, which entitle you to discount access to a system that costs up to $5 per minute for commercial users. You've never had any problems with your password, and you pride yourself in practicing safe computing (never giving your password out, never letting anyone else see it, and so on).

Yesterday, however, an unscrupulous but highly skilled hacker gained access to the computer's highest level of security by persuading its authentication program that he was a "root" or Class-A user, entitled to enter and read all parts of the vast network of computers that run through the mainframe. Using these virtually unlimited powers, he inserted a few lines of code into the university's DIALOG interface, installing his own "greeting" or welcome screen just ahead of DIALOG's.

Today you log on to the mainframe. As you request entry to the online service, you find a familiar screen saying:

WELCOME TO DIALOG INFORMATION SERVICES

PLEASE LOG IN NOW:

LOG IN:

Your terminal will now wait until you enter your account name and send it by hitting the return key. The next screen you see is also very ho-hum:

ENTER YOUR PASSWORD:
XXXXXXXX

As always, you type in your password, which you have long ago memorized and never divulged to anyone else. This time, however, the hacker's program stashes your name and password into a secret file, as it politely tells you:

SORRY. TRY AGAIN. PLEASE RETYPE PASSWORD

and then disappears. Thinking you've mistyped your password, which has certainly happened before, you try to log in again. This time you're successful, and so you put the incident out of your mind as you access the expensive online database. But by this time, your access number and private identity have already been stolen. And as soon as you log off, the wily hacker can log on, posing as you, providing proof of identity that the system cannot suspect or refute. And neither you nor your employer discovers all the fraudulent and illicit searching, printing, and downloading that goes on in your name until the end-of-the-month bill for service comes in, showing that you or your university are responsible for what could come to thousands of dollars.

Identity theft is a large, growing, and extremely serious problem throughout the nation, and it's only getting more prevalent since the advent of the Internet. The intentional electronic masquerading of oneself as another person is a powerful way to infect a victim's electronic life with misery. Firewalls are good defenses, but it is possible to breach electronic firewalls if the attack allows someone to illicitly impersonate another user by using his IP network password or address. When successful, such an attack causes the firewall to permit penetration, because its instructions for identifying a "friend" have been satisfied. The best defense against such IP spoofing is a continual change of passwords, coupled with encryption of data. Even if the enemy illegally accesses a system, then that system's content is rendered meaningless to hostile or prying eyes, while "friends" can still read it plainly.

Electronic Inside Jobs

Just as libraries and all commercial establishments are highly vulnerable to employee theft, internal security is especially difficult or even impossible to ensure when it is a library's own workers who pose security risks. The library has both the responsibility and the right to protect its property however it can. Much media attention is given to outside hackers who electronically break into sensitive computer files. But in many cases it is dishonest and incompetent employees who do the most damage. Hiring decisions for sensitive jobs working with computer systems should be made with extreme care. A strict policy should be promulgated, understood by all employees, and enforced by management. Violators should be fired immediately, and, in some cases, prosecuted. Still, there is little evidence that having such a policy helps keep people honest. If they aren't honest to begin with, and are resourceful and malevolent, they are unlikely to be deterred by whatever safeguards the library places in their way. Also, there are privacy issues here: for example, if management reads employees' e-mail or monitors their telephone calls or conversations. When you consider the expense of enforcing a policy together with possible damage to employee morale, the whole idea frequently becomes counterproductive.

Crimes committed by persons authorized to be in the area and use the equipment are the hardest to detect, and equally difficult—if not impossible—to guard against. It is more important for the library to analyze this situation and consider such matters as the following:

- What if anything could have been done beforehand to prevent such an event or to make it impossible to execute?
- How best can the library help the staff and system "pick up the pieces" when such an event does occur?
- How can the library make the system safer against the next time someone inside the organization seeks to bring it crashing down?
- How can an organization select employees in such a way that no one in a position of access and trust would attempt to commit such a crime against an employer?

If the library had chosen more carefully in its hiring decisions, a person as unethical as a Trojan horse perpetrator could never have been hired and thus wouldn't need to be fired or prosecuted later. But hindsight, while a very good teacher, is not especially useful in prevention of crime. What can be done to prevent recurrent episodes of computer crime? In future job interviews, a thorough background check should be performed on all applicants, and a personnel specialist should be watching carefully for any tell-tale signs that a prospective employee is not honest, ethical, or a good security risk.

Electronic Security: Defensive Strategies and Tactics

> The best defense against the damage caused by any type of bombs is to prevent their delivery in the first place.
>
> —Winn Schwartau, *Information Warfare,* 1996

Sadly, shockingly little computer abuse (including fraud, software copyright infringement, and loss or theft of materials or information) gets reported to the authorities. In the private sector, it is estimated that such abuses cost U.S. companies hundreds of millions of dollars a year, and there is no reason to believe libraries are immune to such incursions. Furthermore, librarians have in the past tended to be reluctant to discuss their incidents publicly.

Electronic trespass is, in addition to being a potential financial problem, a privacy issue of enormous and growing proportions. Information disseminated through hacker publications and bulletin boards has frequently been used to commit serious crimes, with losses sometimes reaching millions of dollars. Hackers do not acknowledge the value of their information to those who produce it, even while jealously guarding access to some of their own files.

All corporations and most public facilities such as libraries normally take elaborate precautions to protect themselves against the statistical probability that a tornado will blow away their operations centers. The possibility that a flood will sweep through your building requires that you be insured and plan for a natural disaster. What the great majority of companies and libraries have not prepared themselves for, however, is a well-organized offensive assault against their information systems and their information. It makes little sense to assume that you have secure information just because your library's computer sits in a dry room in the basement of your building. In fact, such a naive assumption may be the first step in the destruction of what your library is all about: its ability to render service to its community of users.

Naturally, no single method of defense is going to solve the problem of electronic intrusion for all libraries. There are different approaches to the dilemma. What we can do is erect better walls and put up more difficult barriers to defeat. But, as with preventing theft of books and other library materials, the problem keeps coming back to the same thorny questions:

- How tough are we prepared to get when dealing with persons we catch stealing or mutilating our materials?
- In the same vein, how tough and how serious are we willing to get with those people who steal or distort our records?
- How much money are we willing or able to allocate to our goal of protecting our resources?
- What special solutions can we devise to protect electronic libraries from electronic methods of theft, fraud, and vandalism?
- When it comes to implementing programs of library security and thus protecting our resources, can we or should we say that the end justifies the means, or are we bound by some ethical code that doesn't apply to our antagonists?
- If we are successful in hardening our defenses against unlawful electronic intrusion, what will we have lost in the process?

In order to do what it can to ensure the maximum security for its electronic information, a library should consider the list of sensible precautions given in figure 7.5.

- Users have to learn not to leave their computers on, and to guard their passwords and access codes the way they would their wallets or money.
- Users must train themselves to notice when something suspicious is going on in the computer center and report it promptly.
- People in charge of computer systems need to secure data with firewalls, encryption, and other means of keeping private files private.
- Security at the server level, so that only authorized persons have electronic access to the systems containing proprietary information, is essential. All others should receive some version of the familiar "Access Denied" message upon seeking access. They should be instructed to what data their clearance affords them and how they can gain access to the desired information, such as by subscribing or

(Continued)

FIGURE 7.5
Commonsense Precautions Designed to Enhance and Preserve Information Security

FIGURE 7.5 *(Continued)*

belonging to a company or group. Restricted file access means that, while librarians will make a sincere effort to render as much information as possible available without charge or password to all users, some files are simply "off limits."

- Encryption—the conversion of words, characters, numbers, and other electronic information signals to code unintelligible to those lacking the "key"—is among the safest means of protecting information. But encryption is both labor-intensive and potentially vulnerable to hackers and crackers, who like nothing better than a challenge to break and decipher codes.
- Digital signatures (also known as authenticators or cybernotaries) are express written authorization for users to enter proprietary and/or sensitive areas of information, which bear the notarized approval stamp of the proprietor.
- In the future, libraries may be able to afford biometric passwords, which uniquely identify a body part of each user and prevent all others from masquerading as that person. For the time being, however, such systems are prohibitively expensive for all but the largest library networks.
- There should be classes of users who have varying degrees of need-to-know access to sensitive information in the library's computer system. Limiting exposure by restricting access to certain categories of information is not only a good idea—it is essential to information security. Only those with the need to know should have access to proprietary, confidential, or sensitive data. Proceeding from the basic assumption that all data held in library files belongs to the library—even when the library is a public institution, or part of one—unauthorized access to records can be viewed as theft. Theft is always a crime, meriting prosecution to the fullest extent of the law.
- Shred all waste. Since a resourceful information thief can find out a good deal just by browsing wastepaper baskets and dumpsters, shredders should be used to turn all discarded paper into harmless confetti. But "shredding" applies not just to physical documents but to electronically stored information as well. Remnants of deleted files can lurk on your hard drive. Just because you don't see them or can't call them up onto your screen, there's no guarantee that a determined hacker can't access them. It's the electronic equivalent of dumpster diving. Some of your ostensibly best-kept secrets may be just waiting to be discovered by prying eyes. That's why corporate America and the United States Department of Defense are testing "Shredder," a software program designed to destroy all lingering evidence of deleted files from your hard drive by immediately overwriting text up to twelve times. In case of emergency, a programmable panic system can obliterate a designated directory in milliseconds, preventing anyone you don't want to find it from ever discovering it.

Staff Selection and Supervision

While you may be legally or administratively prevented from interrogating all present employees of your library or system, you can (and certainly should) exercise extra care in all new hires. Among recommended steps to reduce the risk of hiring an untrustworthy new employee are the following:

- Screen all prospective employees carefully and check their references.
- The higher the position of responsibility, the more carefully you should screen staff.
- Access to more sensitive files and information should be granted only on a need-to-know basis.
- All personnel should be made aware of the organization's ethical guidelines and the penalties for non-compliance.
- System administrators should subscribe to existing Internet security networks so that they can network with their peers in other institutions.
- All staff should be required to adhere to all copyright restrictions on all company software and applications.
- Make security training, awareness, and education an ongoing part of employee programs.

Virus Protection

High on the list of remedies for computer visuses is a form of avoiding or "curing" them by testing disks. Backup disks, especially where there is only one original diskette, are also highly recommended. Computer programmers are urged not to trade programs promiscuously and to use protective software at all times.

Punishment of those caught with plenty of publicity would also be helpful, as with the notorious prosecutions of copyright infringers. We need vaccines to keep up with new or improved viruses and new laws with stiffer penalties. What kinds of penalties?

What may be needed to keep hackers and crackers from destroying library records is some mix of penalties for the guilty and wake-up calls for unaware staff. Stiff fines would help, perhaps with community service obligations, or, in some cases, imprisonment. Keep in mind that viruses and Trojan horses themselves are not the enemies. They're just doing their jobs, quickly making copies of themselves or scrambling or deleting the files they encounter. It's the perpetrators we need to work to put out of business. Since the entire problem of viruses and how to protect against them shows how vulnerable the nation's electronic systems are, a campaign of public awareness is strongly urged.

Erecting Firewalls

> All incoming software was searched for viruses, but most of the ones they found were nonmalicious—like the one that flashed "Sunday" on the screen to tell workaholics to get away from the keyboard, or "Taipei" that created a clicking sound with every keystroke, or "Talos" that froze computers on June 29 until the phrase "Happy Birthday, Talos" was typed in. A few, like "Michelangelo," which erased all data on March 6, the artist's birthday, were more malevolent.
>
> —Tom Clancy and Steve Pieczenik, *Op-Center,* 1995

Perhaps even more reliable than making sure that your library hires no bad guys inadvertently, however, is a series of measures that can serve to harden the library's defenses against incursions into records. Think of information security as part of a war in which your enemies seek to defeat you by breaching your security and diminishing both your will and ability to fight. There are normally two ways to breach the other side's security. The traditional method is to win the battle by the force of superior numbers of troops or weapons. The other method, à la the Trojan horse, is to seek to breach the walls of your enemy's defenses by using various forms of spies, subterfuge, stealth, trickery, and sabotage. One defense is a firewall, or coded access by which the only persons granted entry to vital and important areas are trusted and dependable.

Firewalls are designed to reduce to zero the possibility of DOS, which in the security context stands for "Denial of Service," something the hacker seeks to perpetrate against you and something you wish to prevent. Perhaps the best way to prevent the hacker from succeeding in his DOS quest is to keep him out of the system entirely. The firewall is designed to be a choke point and impenetrable barrier that keeps what you want guarded safe inside, while denying electronic admission or intrusion to all outsiders.

The term *firewall* refers to a barrier used to stop the spread of a fire. A familiar example of a firewall is the reinforced metal wall in your automobile designed to prevent, in the event of a front-end collision, the hot engine from penetrating to the passenger compartment. In a computer context, firewall is used in an analogous sense to refer to a system that enforces access control between two networks or between a network and the Internet. Here are the uses of firewalls:

- to require that all traffic between inside and outside pass through it, without exception;
- to admit only authorized traffic, as defined by the local security police, and allow such communication to pass through;
- to employ built-in software that detects when your system is under a DOS attack and sends an immediate message to the primary ISP, advising its software to cut off all traffic from a certain address; or detects when your system behaves in certain ways, such as messages of considerable length repeated constantly;
- to ensure that the system itself is immune to penetration;
- to be capable of filtering the source of potential disruption and putting it in the electronic trash;
- to collect and retain unauthorized and bogus messages and other attempts at intrusion for later forensic use;
- to contain a "data mirror" leading back to the source for easier identification of intruders.

Expressed in simple language, the purpose of a firewall is to protect a trusted internal network from an untrusted external network. Typically, the untrusted network refers to the Internet. However, remember that the unauthorized access can as easily come from within and behind the firewall as from outside the walls.

Internal firewalls are also necessary and desirable, especially in large companies or systems in which there are separate networks for sales, marketing, payroll, accounting, production, and product development. Access normally is on a strict need-to-know basis, with firewalls in place between networks as prudent security measures. Firewalls have been shown to reduce inside jobs and the threat of internal hacking (unauthorized access by otherwise authorized users), a problem that consistently outranks external hacking in all information security surveys.

Access to records and electronic files is granted to library employees as necessary and as a privilege. When a computer user performs an action that he or she is not permitted, that constitutes an abuse of privilege. The ideal deployment of firewall technology makes it impossible for such impermissible actions to occur. Each employee requiring access is provided with a specified level of privilege and cannot exceed that level of authorization. The operative problems connected with such a plan are authentication of each user (proving that they are who they say they are), the use of a password known only to the employee, and perimeter-based security by which a network is hardened by controlling access to all entry and exit points through gateways. The most secure type of password, by the way, is a one-use-only temporary password that disappears at the end of the day. Users would complain bitterly if they had to reapply daily, but such a plan would prevent all manner of unauthorized intrusions.

Many methods have been tried to prevent unauthorized access, but the best antidote against unlawful system abuse is an overall hardening of the system so that it can better resist data-driven attack. Sometimes such attacks on the system are encoded in innocuous-seeming data strings, camouflaging an attack in innocent commands or data. The essential purpose of a firewall is to detect such trapdoor attacks before they can attack the essential data. And while hardening systems is an expensive, labor-intensive process, the result—a high level of data security—is worth the cost in most situations.

One final note of caution: While the use of firewalls can protect and preserve the library's records from outside attack, it may well be attack from inside that we need to fear most. Inside jobs—attacks on our records from those we trust most—represent a problem we can never hope to defeat entirely. That's why levels of access with few if any employees given carte blanche to move about inside the system is only sensible, even if it ruffles some feathers when people find out that the level of trust granted them is less than that of colleagues or superiors. As with so many other things, it's a matter of trade-off: In order to have high security for its data, the library may need to restrict access to sensitive and essential information to those who absolutely need it and to employees who are entirely trusted by those in power. While such a scheme may smack of both elitism and of paranoid suspicion, to do anything less is an invitation to disaster. Eternal vigilance is the price of security, especially in the age of electronic information exchange when tapping into mines of data is very easy and potentially destructive.

Several problems with firewalls, however, can be identified immediately:

- inconvenience of extra steps and attendant delays in service
- misplaced trust
- desire for barrier-free communication
- security an afterthought rather than built in
- lack of understanding
- linked computers
- insider attacks
- no intrusion detection

Encryption

In this less-than-perfect world, there are people who seek to disrupt the information systems of libraries for political aims, for personal gratification, for revenge, for competitive purposes, or merely because they can. In an information society, protection of electronically held information is vital. The consensus of the best way to do this revolves around encryption, which is the encoding of data and information in such a way that only authorized users can access and understand it. Currently, U.S. policy aims at encouraging widespread use of cryptography for the protection of the information of individuals, businesses, government agencies (including libraries), and the nation as a whole. But here's the dilemma: At the same time as we protect our files through encryption, we must respect the legitimate needs of law enforcement and keep as much information as possible open to those who need it. How best for the library to accomplish both purposes and keep them in some sort of balance? It's not going to be easy. It may not even be possible. But government at various levels is working on the problem every day.

We must acknowledge two basic points at the outset: First, there is going to be a trade-off between hack-proof security through encryption and the legitimate right of people to information. Second, a high degree of information security is vital to the protection of both library resources and confidential personal records. Some readers may take a dim view of the idea of government, the private sector, and libraries working together for some sort of coherent policy at the national level to protect all stakeholders in the struggle for information access versus information security. More than a few may doubt that such a policy—protecting everybody's interest—is even possible. But the only alternative may be the continued, gradual erosion of accessible library collections, especially to members of society who lack the financial wherewithal to purchase their information at the going rates.

Information may well be the most valuable possession of future society, and access to that information may well become the most divisive issue for future lawmakers. It is obvious that a high degree of electronic security is important at present. It should be even more obvious that a higher degree of security will be important as time goes on. What is needed is an awareness that you can't be too careful about your files, your messages, and your authorized users. One problem with encryption schemes is the risk of having a cypher so bulletproof that not even legitimate government agencies can penetrate it. Such a device in the hands of organized crime or drug-running operations would be devastating. Encryption is designed to protect secrets, yet the government correctly insists that security of this sort must meet the legitimate needs of law enforcement.

Fixing Other Problems

Among other problems connected with electronic information security that may require remedial action are those connected with employees not doing their jobs. They may be:

- using library computers for personal enterprises or private business matters;
- spending library time engaged in personal e-mailings;
- playing solitaire or other computer games on company time;
- performing online searches in commercial databases for personal use;
- duplicating licensed software for personal or prohibited means;
- selling or even giving away private or proprietary information.

This type of malfeasance, unfortunately, goes on with impunity all the time in libraries. In fact, the average employee may not even know it's wrong. After all, it is a unique property of electronically stored information that it is possible to give it away and still retain it. That's why suppliers of proprietary programs go to great lengths to protect their software by shrink-wrap barriers, written license agreements, threats, warnings, and other ploys. But there is little they can do to interdict computer theft completely. With present technology, there is no real way to keep unethical or even unaware persons from opening the shrink-wrap, sticking the disk into a computer, and running off an infinite number of copies for prohibited uses. In essence, they are placed on their honor not to commit crimes and are merely warned of vague adverse consequences should they violate the terms of the licensing agreement. Library management must make it very clear that duplicating licensed programs, breaking into public records, or getting into other people's files is highly improper behavior, and that destroying or altering public files is a crime!

Security guards are employed in most larger libraries to keep an eye on patrons as they move about the library building, but today such personnel may find their roles expanded. Security staff should be trained not only to deal with problem patrons but also to watch for fraudulent or dangerous practices on the library's computers—not just the public computers, but the staff computers as well. How to balance the need for computer security with the understandable desire of employees to be left alone and free of surveillance is one of the difficulties of running a secure, responsible public institution.

Many libraries have resorted for financial and copyright reasons to coded photocopy machines on which only persons with access codes can make copies. Others need cash or copying cards. Similarly, in today's electronic environment, it is necessary either to scan all computers electronically for unauthorized use or to rig those machines so that only authorized persons may use them.

Methods that will defeat unauthorized entry and access are being improved all the time. A new field known as steganography offers promise. It is the electronic equivalent of a watermark on paper, an authentication of information. Only those intended to read proprietary information are able to do so, and only those with permission can capture and download protected files and information. The downloaded information would be "watermarked," showing the permission of owners.

Cyberspace either needs some sort of Web police or a more effective security system—or both. According to a recent *Wall Street Journal* article, Internet vandals have in recent years scrawled messages across or completely demolished home pages on the World Wide Web. Among recent victims are the Nation of Islam, the British government, and the American Psychoanalytic Association. Hackers have apparently been able to break security codes, scrawl electronic graffiti, or eliminate pages or whole Web segments entirely.

The Computer Security Institute, an association of security consultants in San Francisco, says that reported incidents of computer fraud are on the increase nationwide, although exact numbers are unknown because of a pervasive reluctance to talk about the problem. Vandals' motives vary, but some of the younger ones apprehended have admitted that they did their deeds in the attempt to impress people or vandalized home pages as a personal challenge. Their actions, however, are serious and can be very costly for the victims. They should be warned that they may be prosecuted under the federal Computer Fraud and Abuse Act. Meanwhile, it is important for libraries and other institutions and individuals who develop Web sites to take sensible precautions to secure their pages and sites while cybertechnologists attempt to develop better security procedures.

Lest you think of the Internet only as the enemy of security and file integrity, be aware that the Internet has been used occasionally for catching criminals. For example, a fugitive listed for six years by the Federal Bureau of Investigation as one of its ten most wanted criminals surrendered to authorities in Guatemala after his picture appeared on the Internet. The FBI has a home page that is accessible beyond the U.S. borders. It featured a photograph of the fugitive, who had escaped from federal custody in 1985 following a conviction for armed robbery and a number of lesser charges. As its use continues to grow, the Internet may become a new tool of law enforcement to help locate criminals around the world and catch them in the web of criminal justice. In that connection, librarians should think through their responsibilities should they discover (or even suspect) that their users or cardholders are wanted criminals. This is merely a high-tech extension of the longtime problem of patron confidentiality versus the public safety.

Good, tough security, unfortunately, often entails issues regarding the privacy of information contained in patron databases that have resulted from online circulation systems. A certain amount of trade-off is inevitable: The greater the degree of access, the more the threat to information security, while the greater the threat to security, the more incursions into personal privacy may follow. Every library needs to acknowledge the importance of information security right alongside the other two vital concerns of materials security and personal security. The manual of library policies should therefore contain strong language concerning:

- protection of information in patron records
- ensuring compliance with all information policies
- limiting the data collected

- security authorizations
- creating and modifying patron records

Fighting Back: Electronic Countermeasures

Even the heralded totally electronic libraries of the future will probably not have the extensive computer security problems they do today because they will have built-in safeguards in their access components. But there may well be new problems unimagined by the present-day designers of computer networks. Vandals, hackers, crackers, and assorted thieves may still attempt to destroy equipment, alter programs, gain entry to subsystems or distant brokers, illegally download data, or physically remove both hardware and software from the library. It is therefore incumbent on administrators and staff to be aware not just of present problems but of potential dangers, and to take all prudent and necessary precautions. It is important to remember that it isn't just the hacker who has offensive weapons at his disposal. The library can fight back in many ways. If you believe that sometimes you have to fight fire with fire, here are some tried and occasionally effective ways of getting even.

One low-cost quick fix is simplicity itself. Many computer-related security problems can be eliminated simply by using carefully selected passwords and changing them frequently. The enemy, however, is both clever and resourceful. Clifford Stoll (*The Cuckoo's Egg,* 1989) notes that one wily hacker managed to infiltrate systems without actual knowledge of any proprietary access codes simply by using logical account names such as "root," "guest," "system," "field," "default," and common names as passwords. Employing this primitive method, the hacker gained access to about 5 percent of the invaded computers, sometimes even gaining system manager privileges such as the ability to alter or delete accounts and records! Lawrence Berkeley Laboratories, where Stoll worked at the time, instituted the following changes after the hacker incident: password expiration at regular intervals, expired account deletion, elimination of shared accounts, incoming traffic monitoring, alarm setting, and workshops for user education and awareness.

Not all threats to a library's files, however, are generated by malevolent human intruders. There are many areas of vulnerability caused by exposure to such things as heat, light, moisture, and mold, including potential damage to tapes, disks, and computers, which are sensitive to many physical threats; common circuits and electrical surges; and damage during physical transportation. Diskettes and hard drives, for example, are sensitive to magnetic fields, heat, extreme cold, dust, and even insects (the phrase "bugs in the system" may sometimes be taken literally). To minimize the problem of sudden electrical catastrophe, surge protectors should be installed on all computers. This will save both money and data in case of power line problems or lightning strikes.

It is frustrating to contemplate that no matter what we do to guarantee the integrity and security of electronic systems, somebody will find a way to break into them. But there is no such thing as absolute computer security! There are, unfortunately, only various degrees of insecurity. The goal, therefore, is to reach the lowest degree of insecurity by making it as difficult as possible for those who interfere with the library's computers. In that connection, here are some logical recommendations:

- Passwords should be given only to users with authorization or a need to access the system.
- Passwords should be carefully selected by users (i.e., uncommon and unguessable combinations of alphanumeric characters) and changed frequently.
- Equipment that is not meant to be used by patrons should not be accessible to them. It should be located in a secure area.
- Public access terminals, monitors, printers, and the software necessary to run them should all be physically protected when not in use to prevent vandalism and theft.
- Encryption devices should be acquired and installed—especially where sensitive or proprietary information is to be protected—scrambling documents, information, and data for anyone who does not have authorized passwords or translation capability for decoding files.
- Security staff may want to build dossiers on known or suspected hackers and their tactics.
- Network with other libraries, archives, and museums that may have similar problems. Subscribe to and regularly visit Internet bulletin boards concerning security matters.

- Audit the trails of users who visit a specified electronic site so that you can know who is consulting what.
- Attempt to turn any hacker you've caught by offering not to press charges in exchange for cooperation in catching others.
- When you catch somebody, prosecute.

A Defensive Information Warfare Plan

Here is a starter outline to use in evolving a comprehensive plan to keep electronically held records and files as safe as possible.

STEP 1: Assess the Current Environment

a. Conduct electronic sweeps.
b. Perform vulnerability assessment.
c. Configure systems for protection.
d. Perform periodic intentional intrusions to test your own defenses. (Try hacking into your own system.)

STEP 2: Close Exploitable Holes

a. Engage in information exchanges with other libraries about their problems with electronic intrusions.
b. Install "trip wires," vulnerability sensors, and other alert systems.
c. Consider cookie-dropping programs to identify users who visit your electronic site frequently.
d. Train all staff in the elements of data security.

STEP 3: Redesign for Bolstered Security

a. Write a crisis planning and sequence policy document.
b. Follow strategic plans for mobilization when intruders are detected.
c. Outline the requirements of an appropriate level of security.
d. Install encryption systems for the transmission of sensitive information and be extremely careful about who gets the key.
e. Estimate costs of the items on your security wish list.

STEP 4: Strategic Deployment of Technology

a. Implement token-based one-time passwords.
b. Inaugurate encryption of sensitive records.
c. Require digital signatures of all trusted personnel.
d. Build and maintain electronic firewalls.
e. Acquire security administration tools.

A few additional considerations to ensure a high degree of security in your electronically held documentation are shown in figure 7.6.

In the past, since it was often not economically feasible to prevent intrusions, most service providers like libraries focused their efforts on controlling losses through reactive deterrent and control measures.

- Practice safe disposal of sensitive documents.
- Back up your system continuously.
- Have a redundant arrangement so that all data are in at least two places.
- Plan for disaster—both natural and human.
- If your organization handles or generates sensitive reports or information, consider establishing a data-classification system for your library (e.g., secret, classified, general).
- Coordinate physical and electronic security efforts.
- Test your security frequently, probing for holes.
- Take advantage of one of the existing commercial technical security solutions.
- Continually make higher-ups aware of the need for a high level of security and security funding.
- Publicize breaches of security so that your community of users will understand the problem and the importance of practicing safe computing. There is some trade-off here, however, as there's always the possibility that persons who have never thought of hacking will be inspired to begin.
- Strongly resist pressure from higher-ups to keep intrusions a secret.
- Remember that there's always room for improvement in your system's security.

FIGURE 7.6
Steps to Ensure Security in Electronic Documentation

What is needed today is a coordinated and proactive security posture that's up and running at all times, with the clear and unequivocal goal of making the would-be thief's job of penetrating your system so difficult and fraught with risk that he says "To hell with it!" and goes and bothers someone else. Since absolute and perfect security is only a fantasy, what we should strive toward is security so stringent that our clever enemy sees the task of penetration of our system as not worth his trouble and the risk of getting caught and punished as unacceptable.

Human beings are almost always the weakest links in computer security. Hackers quickly learn that the simplest way to learn things they are not meant to know is simply to exploit the knowledgeable people. Bits of specialized knowledge you already have can serve as a key to manipulating people into believing that you are legitimate. You can then coax, flatter, or frighten them into revealing almost anything you want to know. Deceiving people especially over the phone or via Internet turns out to be easy. Exploiting their gullibility is very gratifying; it makes a hacker feel very superior. And most techniques require little high-tech expertise.

Security against Electronic Intrusion, Passive and Proactive

Security for electronically held information has two salient aspects: passive (always in place) and proactive (springing into action when an intrusion is detected). Following are lists that summarize the steps to be followed in improving and maintaining the library's security, both before and after experiencing an electronic attack.

Passive

Designate. Assign someone who can be trusted the responsibility for being the Library Security Officer.

Deter. Since there is no such thing as perfect security, all appropriate measures should be taken to ensure that hacking into the library's computer is difficult, time-consuming, and has a very good chance of being discovered.

Warn. Prominently placed notices in the library itself and on all library Web pages and welcome screens should warn those contemplating unauthorized entry into the system of adverse consequences.

Read-only. Designate as many files and documents as possible as read-only, meaning that that they are readable and downloadable but cannot be altered by any user not cleared for system-level access.

Restrict access. Design a coding system so that persons who need to access files and records may do so, while all others are kept out of the system. Sensitive, personal, and proprietary information should not be accessible to anyone not intended to read it.

Password-protect. Ensure that access to the library's computer files is by authorized password only, and that each user's password is commensurate with his or her security clearance level.

Firewall. Install electronic choke points so that outside users can only access inside computers after passing through a screening of identity.

Virus-protect. Install and maintain the latest version of virus protection software on all computers, so that no virus can enter the system uncaught and undetected.

Encrypt. All proprietary, personal, or sensitive information should be encrypted before transfer from one computer to another, using one of a variety of commercially available software programs.

Authenticate. Establish procedures and protocols that reduce the possibility of identity theft or fooling the computer into allowing an unauthorized person access.

Change. Require all users to change passwords regularly. Encourage them to select passwords not easily guessable, such as the user's first initial and last name.

Anticipate. Expect intrusions to the system, guard against complacency, and anticipate what steps will be taken—and in what sequence—when intrusion is detected.

Proactive

Monitor. Monitor electronic system traffic activity continuously so that there are ongoing logs of who logged in, when, what they did in the system, and when they left.

Trip wire. Install trip-wire programs that will alert system-level staff immediately when an unauthorized individual seeks to access protected files.

Mobilize. Your library's emergency response procedures should be implemented immediately, and all staff should know their jobs and do whatever they can to catch the intruder in the act.

Isolate. As soon as an attempted intrusion has been detected, the system should immediately isolate that person and every terminal his or her probe has touched, with the objective of containment.

Trap. The isolation process should trap the hacker, identify him, and provide a means of locating him physically by accessing his terminal ID and providing system personnel with his location.

Damage control. Assessment of the intrusion should begin immediately to ascertain what if any information was stolen, damaged, compromised, or lost, and how the hacker obtained uninvited access to the system.

Patch. It is now important to "patch" the access point by electronically sealing it against further intrusion or against the hacker's escape by a trapdoor program. System integrity can best be prevented by patching the leak immediately and preventing further loss or damage.

Prosecute. If the trapping of an intruder leads to the identity of the hacker, the library administration should regard him as a criminal, and thus do whatever it takes to have him arrested, charged, and prosecuted to the fullest extent of the law.

Publicize. Once a successful prosecution of criminal activity has been achieved, the library should spread the word to the local and campus news media so that potential hackers will know that your facility is unafraid to punish those caught illegally entering the system.

Network. All persons charged with maintaining the library's security should read widely in appropriate publications, regularly consult security Web sites, attend conferences dealing with electronic security for libraries, and talk to other libraries facing similar problems.

Learn. There are lessons to be learned from every incident involving attempted intrusion into your library's electronic files. Similarly, there are lessons to be shared by other libraries that can save your system much loss, aggravation, and service interruption. Learn those lessons well.

Improve. Upgrade and improve your library's security posture continually as funding permits. Ensure that funders understand the relationship between money spent on security and the level of effectiveness of the library in carrying out its primary mission and responsibilities. New security hardware and software is being introduced continually, and it doesn't hurt to make a wish list of desired security items, in the event of an unexpected windfall.

This discussion of electronic security is not intended to provide you with all the answers. It is, however, designed to get you to ask the right questions. Additionally, it is designed to bring home the message, worth repeating again and again, that security is a journey and not a destination. And it is meant just to reinforce a sense of where the ultimate responsibility for electronic library security lies: Next time you're in the rest room, take a good, long, hard look at yourself in the mirror.

CHAPTER 8

The Future of Library Security

> Create a culture of security. People have to learn not to leave their computers on, to notice when things are going on, and to be willing to report what they have observed, without fear of "whistle-blowing." People in charge of computer systems need to secure data with "firewalls" and other means. As for law enforcement, we need international cooperation. This is a borderless problem.
>
> —Dan Gelber, counsel to the U.S. Senate Subcommittee on Investigations, reported by Winn Schwartau in *Information Warfare,* 1996

The objectives of this chapter are to:

- review some advances and emergent technology with implications for the improvement of library security
- imagine alternative futures for library security and the problems and opportunities they may offer
- summarize the future of library security

"The times, they are a changin'." As previous chapters in this book have discussed, there are many threats to the security of libraries, some ancient and some the result of advances in technology. Modern technology does not merely promise to create or improve better sensors and alarms to protect library collections. Emergent technology may actually slam the door on potential criminals, rendering them incapable of achieving their goals while helping publicize thefts and alerting other libraries. One thing on which book thieves have normally relied is that libraries do not talk to one another or exchange information about missing materials, thieves caught in the act, and methodologies used by those who steal. Communications networks like Bookline Alert, Missing Books and Manuscripts (BAMBAM) tell rare book dealers if a book they are about to buy was stolen and from whom it was stolen. A responsible and ethical dealer will not engage in any transactions if the item has been reported stolen.

Sadly, however, nothing will eliminate crime in libraries altogether. The urge to possess what they cannot come by honorably is just too strong in some people. John Maxwell Hamilton ("Is There a Klepto in the Stacks?" 1990) reported that the New York Public Library found one man caught stealing books was renting two apartments, one to live in and another for his stolen books, which reached from the floor to the ceiling even in the bathroom. The peculiar thing was that he didn't have any particular speciality. "He didn't even read them. He just liked to be around books," reported a NYPL security officer.

Libraries have faced security problems and varying degrees of personal and professional risk since their earliest beginnings, and they probably always will. One could even look at attempts for security as an exercise in futility because all attempts to make any library completely crime-proof have met with failure. Some security experts variably estimate losses of book stock in libraries at anywhere between 10 and 30 percent annually. But will the same security problems that libraries have faced all along persist into the future? Maybe they will and maybe they won't. Advances in technology may actually serve to make both theft and mutilation of materials and violence in library buildings things of the past by the simple expedient of removing the building from the equation. But even if we can never hope for perfect library security in existing buildings, we can at least work conscientiously toward that goal.

As virtually all of the information in the preceding chapters was intended to demonstrate, those entrusted with security and safety in libraries are engaged in an ongoing war with criminals and caretakers embroiled in a ceaseless struggle for the possession of materials. There is no clear winner in view. In the coming age of virtual libraries, the era of the smash-and-grab thief will be over for libraries, and the day of the clever, resourceful electronic thief will be upon us, supplanting one problem with a potentially greater one.

But even in this imperfect age of library vulnerability, we're getting better at catching crooks, or at least making their nefarious tasks far more difficult. The trouble is that as better security measures are implemented the crooks get smarter, too, inventing new and even more ingenious methods of ripping us off. Still, in the foreseeable future, libraries might just have a few tricks up their sleeves to help them in this struggle against theft and pilferage.

Subliminal programming, understandably a highly controversial issue, is based on the theory that the unconscious mind can absorb information that is imperceptible to the conscious mind. This effect can supposedly be achieved by flashing messages so fast that the eye cannot catch them or by playing soft audio messages that the conscious mind does not hear. Such messages are intended to communicate directly with the subconscious. A subliminal message interrupts the television program at random intervals just long enough to flash its text on the screen for one-thirtieth of a second. At that speed, the conscious human mind is numb to the intrusion.

That speed may be too fast for the human eye to register, but, apparently, not so fast that the mind doesn't register its presence. The only presupposition is that the viewer is watching intently and concentrating. Looking down or away will, of course, defeat the whole purpose of the subliminal exercise. In one case, a Michigan couple interested in losing weight reported that one hour of combined exercise and subliminal messaging a day had a dramatic and noticeable effect within a three-month time span. Would such messaging—assuming that it were cleared for public consumption—work as a deterrent to theft and other bad behavior in a library building? Perhaps, but the flaw is that people may watch television every day, but they do not normally visit the library to be exposed to messages on a daily basis. This means that the one-time or occasional library visitor may not get a sufficient dose of message to be able to alter behavior.

Is subliminal conditioning a good idea or a bad one? Are there potentially adverse consequences to its use? The developers of the subliminal weight-loss home system claim without hesitation that their programs do not pose any serious psychological danger to most people, since TV viewers naturally filter out painful or unpleasant messages. Detractors, however, view this new technology with alarm. Who knows whether, in some subjects, the ostensibly harmless message could trigger involuntary reactions causing serious psychological repercussions of unknowable intensity and eventual impact?

But let's put aside our qualms for a moment and consider the potential benefits of such technology for a library striving to hold onto its books and other property. Suppose a library administration, fed up with the continual shrinkage of the collection of materials, decided to give a variation of this idea a try. It would be interesting to see whether the rate of book theft and other unexplained losses would drop and by how much after the institution of such programming. But there is a serious privacy issue involved here, since subliminal messages are invasive, and no one likes finding out that someone else has programmed such a message. One would hope that if a library began pumping subliminal messages into the heads of unsuspecting patrons, it would only be implemented consistent with certain safeguards, for example:

- The message and delivery system would both be approved only after a long period of testing on human subjects.
- The only message(s) permitted to be used would be specific deterrents, concerned with dissuading people from stealing or mutilating library materials.
- There would be an array of governmental safeguards and prohibitions in place and daunting penalties for proof of misuse.

Biometrics: The Body as Password

> Biometric smart cards. At the 1998 Winter Olympics in Nagano, Japan, some athletes won't be able to pick up their equipment unless a machine recognizes the iris patterns in their eyes. The latest technology is intended to remove completely the threat of persons with forged or false identity having access to such things as target-shooting guns.
>
> —*Sarasota Herald-Tribune,* December 16, 1997

Since the problem of authentication of users is paramount in virtually all security problems, science has been trying to find new ways to ensure that people are who they say they are. Emerging technology is providing some very interesting ways of identifying people by using factors as diverse as voice recognition, heartbeat, retinal structure, and even body odor.

In the past, authentication of identity relied on such methods as personal signatures, driver's license photographs, credit cards, and office keys. But all of these have been shown to be unreliable, granting unscrupulous persons access to untold proprietary collections and similar electronic mines of guarded information. It is relatively simple for an ambitious felon to duplicate keys, forge driver's licenses, or reproduce credit cards. To get into your most private and personal files, for example, all a thief requires is knowledge of the password you use to access your account, or, in some cases, the PIN you use to complete your financial transactions.

Clearly, new and more reliable means of identifying ourselves to systems are called for. It's beginning to look as though the age of the biometric body-part password is here. Using biometric technology, your unique biological characteristics—such as your voiceprint, hand geometry, eye structure, fingerprints, and personal odors—can be mapped, digitized, and retained for comparison with persons claiming to be you. And because in each of those respects we are as unalike as snowflakes, fraudulent impersonation will become impossible and library crime will be greatly reduced.

Body parts already are being used as passwords in various systems, public and private. Inmates in some prisons must submit to retinal scanning as they come and go to court appearances, as the iris is the most unique feature of the human body, according to IriScan, an optical technology vendor. Digitized fingerprints are being used in some states to match welfare records with recipients, to prevent and detect attempted fraud. Frequent travelers crossing into Canada from Montana can now zip through an automated voice verification system run by the U.S. Immigration and Naturalization Service. Lotus employees pass through a hand-geometry scanner in order to pick up their children from in-house day care, while Coca-Cola is using hand geometry at the time clock to prevent workers from punching in late colleagues' time cards.

In the near future, cameralike eyes will sit atop personal computers in the workplace, checking at preset intervals to see whether the person at your keyboard is indeed wearing your unique iris signatures or general facial contours. Voice verification machines are incapable of being fooled by even the most skilled impersonators. They offer highly secure ways of authenticating users, simply by comparing their reading of a line or two of English prose or poetry of their choice with a previously stored version.

DNA, the body's unique genetic code, may also be pressed into service as a foolproof means of identifying individuals and rendering attempts at impersonation either foolish or impossible. As we come to rely more and more on silicon-based electronic systems, we should not forget the information processing potential of carbon-based systems like our bodies. In the future, an individual's unique DNA "signature" might replace credit cards, driver's licenses, photographs, passwords, social security numbers, and other personal identifiers. Already, U.S. service personnel are required to have specimens of their DNA on file to assist in casualty identification. In the past, however, the matching of samples was slow, demanding work, and DNA analysis took several weeks of thorough testing, which would make such a means of personal identity authentication in libraries infeasible. Today that process has been streamlined to about fifteen minutes, but it still requires blood testing. Tomorrow, we are promised, however, DNA testing is expected to be as simple and non-invasive as scraping off a minuscule amount of human skin, passing it under an analyzer called a flow cytometer, and matching it by computer to previously stored bits of one's personal DNA with virtually 100 percent reliability. Should such testing devices become both cheap and ubiquitous, there is no reason why libraries cannot have access to this foolproof technology for establishing and authenticating each patron's identity.

All of the above innovations offer extremely effective new means of authenticating identity, and all of them are eventually going to be adaptable to library admission or access. The only problem, aside from invasion-of-privacy qualms, is going to be the cost. Machines that perform those various electronic tricks presently cost thousands of dollars each, putting them well beyond the affordability of most libraries. About all that security-minded libraries can do for now is to keep their eye on progress in such emergent security technology, and hope that the price drops, as it almost always does. A little over a quarter century ago, one of Texas Instruments' first four-function pocket calculators sold for $295. Today, such calculators, boasting numerous additional functions and greatly improved speed, are credit-card size, and so inexpensive to manufacture that banks and other businesses give them away like mint candies. There is no reason not to believe that scanners and authenticators will become much cheaper in the future until they are found in every library security checkpoint.

The objective of all attempts at authenticating identity by the use of biometrics is to make the possibility of identity theft or impersonation less likely, but such fraud may never become impossible. Sad experience has shown that no matter what triumphs in security are invented, someone very clever and determined goes immediately to work to figure out a way around that obstacle.

Virtual Libraries: Questions of Safety and Personal Privacy

How safe are electronic library holdings, now that virtual libraries may soon make books seem as archaic as stone or clay tablets? The advent of the virtual library may be the most significant change in the nature of the library since Gutenberg's printing press. Libraries without walls, containing books without pages, are now broadly available on the Internet, and more paperless books are coming all the time. Such a capability makes it possible for users to consult a library's catalog and use or purchase books without ever setting foot in the building or even traveling to the host city. But this brave new world, in which a modem serves in lieu of a library card, may be fraught with problems of security that, in some cases, outweigh the benefits.

Digital books in virtual libraries, in fact, may be vulnerable to destruction or alteration—intentional or accidental—from a power surge, a lightning strike, or acts of sabotage. The fragility of digital files, in fact, is of great concern to libraries, since more and more of them rely on silicon storage to hold and archive their materials and to make them more accessible without the risk of loss. Loss and the problem of paper deterioration make computer storage attractive as a medium of retention and distribution.

The promise of electronic libraries is alluring and seductive for librarians up to their necks in crumbling print and hard copy information. But one positive thing can be said for paper storage: In the event of power failure, it is still there, and accessible. A power failure in an electronic library renders even the most powerful computers into mere paperweights, and even the largest store of information inaccessible. Then there's technological obsolescence. Today's state-of-the-art computer program is very likely to be tomorrow's unusable document, what with the rapid and accelerating pace of technological progress. Information itself is becoming more fragile: Ordinary type can withstand everything but destruction of the page on which it is printed, but it takes only a stray magnetic field or power surge to kill an electronic file forever. To this end, some malevolent people spend an inordinate amount of their time working up viruses that will spoil or erase other people's files.

For example, the Library of Congress boasts an estimated 107 million items, ranging from the papers of twenty-three U.S. presidents to one of only three existing perfect copies of the original Gutenberg Bible. Complicating the problem, the collections of this superlibrary grow by more than 5 million items a year. Electronic storage media offer such libraries enormous opportunities to reduce ponderous and vulnerable print collections, while making their collections available to scholars and students without necessitating either personal travel to Washington, D.C., or interlibrary loan. Sounds wonderful, doesn't it?

But even a completely digital library can have serious problems. Experts say that digital archives will last only as long as the physical matter (e.g., silicon magnetized dots on mylar) on which they are stored. After all, a conventional text can still be recognizable as written text, even when the language is unknown, as in the ancient Rosetta stone. But once a document is converted to silicon storage, its meaning is submerged in a bit stream of electronic digital zeros and ones. The resulting digital file is meaningful only to the software that created it. Anyone who has ever discovered that a document that is perfectly valid on one system cannot be read by another knows the truth of that assertion. Thus, reliance on electronic libraries and archives may make knowledge more vulnerable than even paper pages ever were or could be. A large segment of the U.S. population, moreover, still considers books their only interest in libraries and views automated services with varying degrees of alarm, suspicion, incomprehension, and mistrust.

In the southeastern and south central United States, meteorologists continually keep an eye on hurricanes during the six-month-long annual season. Some of these can cause, in addition to loss of life and property, days or even weeks of electrical disruption. The consequences of such disruption are many and varied, but whereas life goes on without such luxuries as refrigeration and air-conditioning, without electronic access to information all high-tech libraries and their computers are useless. Whatever the cause of the disruption, every library has to address the question of converting to electronic storage and delivery and solve the problem of what to do when the power goes off. This is not to be construed as an indictment of the rush of those libraries that can afford it to automate their holdings. It is only a warning that not all change is progress, and that not all progress is forward. Still, the dilemma of how to preserve and protect electronic documents while carefully observing all provisions of the copyright law continues, and will continue into the discernible future.

Keeping their heads up and their eyes open may well, in fact, be the best way librarians can keep a reasonable level of security in library buildings. Security forces help, too, especially trained professionals who know their jobs well. And developing technology has provided and will continue to provide ways that we can safeguard our collections and assure the safety of people in our library buildings. Unfortunately, however, that same modern electronic technology, while it provides a wealth of solutions to library problems, frequently becomes a two-edged sword, inviting new and different problems as well.

Imaging the Library

> If the Emancipation Proclamation had only been digitized before it was destroyed in the Chicago Fire in 1871, perfect reproductions of the original document could still be generated at will. . . . Digitize George Washington's reports to the Continental Congress, and those reports can be enhanced to look exactly as they did when they were written.
>
> —Kenneth A. Cory and David W. Hessler, "Imaging the Archives," 1993

Despite all the ominous aspects of the technology revolution that have overtaken libraries, one extremely hopeful and favorable aspect of technology deserves to be recognized. Imagine a virtual library in which the library's holdings are electronic, consisting of magnetized documents available to users by means of telecommunications and computer equipment. The risk of losing materials in the customary way—things lost to mildew, wear, vandalism, or walking out the door concealed on the persons or in the belongings of patrons—becomes a non-factor. This means that the archival (principal) copy of each document could be held in a secure, remote location, unvisited and untouchable by users, and preferably backed up by additional copies held in other sites, safe against the possibility of fire, sabotage, lightning strikes, or other catastrophes.

Under these circumstances, the matter of library theft becomes a non-issue because users never really hold original copies in their hands. That removes both the desire and the possibility of theft. Imaging means that access to information is widely available and that there is literally nothing to steal. Nothing we would know or recognize as books, periodical issues, or works of art would have to be entrusted to users, which would protect the materials against loss or damage due to casual neglect or intentional malfeasance.

For definitional purposes, imaging is the application of digital (i.e., computer) technology to the management and manipulation of information in non-digital formats such as paper, photographs, microforms, or voice. By scanning or frame-grabbing (in the case of video stills acquired from motion video), images of correspondence, maps, charts, or drawings are converted into digital files which are sent to a computer's central processing unit. Scanned images appear on the computer's monitor. Although high-resolution monitors are desirable for viewing and acting upon one or two complete page images at a time, low-cost monitors can be used effectively to view partial pages.

Libraries exist both to provide access to information and to preserve information, but these two goals have in the past often been at cross-purposes. Previously, libraries favored tight security for their rare and irreplaceable documents, requiring that they be used only with stringent restrictions, the most user-unfriendly being that they did not circulate. This did nothing to promote scholarly investigation or resultant publication and caused libraries to severely restrict the people who could have access to an item and the place where that item could be viewed or read.

Today, with imaging technology, it is possible to hold in your hands a copy of the most unique and fragile archival document, without causing anyone the slightest anxiety about how you treat it or where it eventually ends up. A document preserved in digital format can be reproduced endlessly, and even laser-printed and made available to patrons for a nominal charge. This eliminates the demand for photocopies, which must usually be refused because of the potential for damage. Allowing patrons to take home copies of previously restricted documents will eliminate at least one motivation to steal materials. Moreover, digitization makes possible sending copies to scholars and users continents away. High-quality imaging can create copies nearly indistinguishable from the originals of rare, expensive, and fragile materials that otherwise would not circulate.

Thanks to digitization, there is no need for patrons to see or hold the original documents, which can be kept under safe and optimal conditions in archival storage. Therefore, and paradoxically, even while it permits librarylike usage, imaging will eventually eliminate the need for security for library materials because scholars will work with high-quality facsimiles instead of originals.

Another real advantage of imaging is automatically generated backup copies of each archived document. For security purposes, duplicate copies of each disk can be made and stored off-site. At this point, the library may actually discard digitized paper documents. It is astonishing that, with imaging, reproductive fidelity is sometimes even better than the original documents, because scanners are not sensitive to wrinkles or tears in paper, and faint images are vastly improved by scanning. Even glossy photographs can be replicated with acceptable fidelity through laser and video printing. This is a major advantage of imaging over microfilm.

Not everything connected with information provision would be completely secure, however, even if imaging became cheap, reliable, and pervasive. Still vulnerable to theft would be the computer equipment and software used by the system. But even these things would be unstealable in the physical sense if the system were truly virtual and everyone accessed libraries from home. So as libraries move slowly but probably inexorably in the direction of virtuality and home access, the good news is that theft is likely to become a non-issue.

The best news for all concerned, however, is that librarians who convert their holdings to electronic format will be able, by using imaging technology, to secure the safety of their data and original documents while at the same time creating substantially greater opportunities for using the information contained therein. Document imaging technology boasts several advantages for use in libraries and archives as well. But as with every new development in the technological sphere, there is the inevitable trade-off to consider. There is, of course, a corresponding list of common drawbacks and objections to imaging a library's collection—which must be addressed in all fairness (see figure 8.1).

The good news is that—whatever the merits and drawbacks of imaging collections—as Cory and Hessler ("Imaging the Archives," 1993) remind us, "it is highly likely that the availability of images of archival documents will generate substantially greater usage of archive centers while the original documents will be secure from theft or damage resulting from that usage."

- *Preservation.* Archivists caution that an optical disk is not a long-term storage medium, and data reliability for a WORM optical disk cannot be guaranteed beyond ten to fifteen years. Nevertheless, images can be transferred from an old disk to a new disk at any time without data loss.
- *Potential damage during scanning.* While imaging eliminates the need for photocopies, scanners, like photocopiers, can damage pages.
- *Obsolescence.* Because of the rapid advances in information technology, some libraries are reluctant to invest in optical disk technology out of fear that new developments will render it obsolete.
- *Costs.* The present hardware cost of an imaging system is considerable, ranging from under $10,000 to well over $40,000.
- *Vocabulary control.* Imaging software allows each document to be assigned dozens of descriptors. However, when a large quantity of descriptors is locally created, the problems of vocabulary control are increased. Also, documents in pictorial format require voluminous quantities of information to transmit a picture.
- *Lack of standardization.* Imaging technology at present requires that the indexing be done by knowledge engineers, i.e., classification specialists. Employing such personnel is expensive.
- *Disruptions.* Preparing documents for conversion and scanning or frame-grabbing, keystroking in descriptors, putting the original documents back together, and reshelving converted documents is time-consuming and can be messy, disruptive, and expensive.

FIGURE 8.1
Drawbacks in Imaging

The Twenty-First Century

The twenty-first century is almost here, and with it a whole spectrum of new challenges to libraries. Clearly, something beyond what is happening now in the area of security has to be done to protect both people and materials in libraries. The precise form of such measures is speculative and open to debate, and it may actually take us by surprise. Just as one example of ways libraries could adapt the new technology to their security interests, however, the *San Jose Mercury News* in 1997 reported that the United States Defense Department had rolled out some working models of tiny flying machines ("micro air vehicles") said to be no larger than birds (and potentially much smaller), which could greatly assist law enforcement with surveillance, aside from military uses. One prototype mini-helicopter is said to be able to fit inside a peanut shell. Such tiny surveillance craft are described as "suited for tasks such as locating hostages in occupied buildings, sniffing out poisonous chemicals, and finding enemy snipers." Each micro air vehicle carries cameras, sensors, transmitters, and antennae.

Another story, making its appearance in the same year, revealed that live cockroaches can now be fitted out with cameras, microphones, and sensors. Since they scuttle about in dark, remote places, they may as well be put to use as surveillance ancillaries. Such developments as these could greatly aid in the cause of library security, once they became mass-produced and sensibly priced. Awareness of such mini-devices and their presence in the stacks and reading rooms of libraries might help deter or dissuade prospective thieves or other criminals from their intended deeds. On the other hand, cockroaches in libraries—whether equipped with surveillance cameras or not—are probably unlikely ever to be welcomed.

Are such applications for security purposes in libraries unlikely? Perhaps. But impossible? Don't bet on it. "When a distinguished but elderly statesman says that something is possible, he is almost certainly right," said noted author Arthur C. Clarke. "But when he states that something is impossible, he is very probably wrong."

> If we don't solve our own problems, other people will—and the world of tomorrow belongs to the people who will solve them.
>
> —Pierre Elliott Trudeau, former prime minister of Canada

Some of the ideas and suggestions introduced in this chapter admittedly appear far-fetched. But it should be kept in mind that many other ideas, when first put forward, were considered either impossible to implement or met with open derision. In the future, library security will become a field ripe for experimentation. Assuming that the goal of library provision will still be access to information, it makes sense to seek to improve security at the same time as we strive to enhance and maintain free access. Do you have an idea for holding onto what we have better than we can today? As long as it's legal and within the boundaries of ethical practice, give it a spin. Why not? You have, after all, nothing to lose but your books.

This book on library security concludes with a recapitulation and restatement of the objectives of all library security measures: Security measures are intended to preserve our materials and their value to our users, while at the same time to protect the library building's occupants. Anything that furthers those ends—or is likely to do so—is worth considering, at least in the light of costs, ethics, and practical factors. Keeping an open mind about library security is equally important to your determination to hold onto the heritage of civilization represented by library collections. To lose such a battle, after all, would be to concede defeat in an extremely important war for access to the cultural record of mankind.

Glossary

Achilles' heel. *See* Hole, Security.

Antivirus software. Commercially available software that installs on the user interface where it detects and destroys virus programs, thus preventing them from being acquired by computers. An up-to-date virus detector/destroyer will greatly reduce the chances of being hit with a virus by permitting only screened and approved word processing to enter a computer system.

Attack. An electronic intrusion designed to acquire unauthorized, sensitive, or proprietary information, or otherwise forbidden knowledge, by tapping into files or databases thought secure by their proprietors.

Audit, Security. The electronic equivalent of a building security walkaround in which a group of security-minded and technologically proficient employees conducts a comprehensive inspection of all internal and external system access points, looking for holes in security.

Audit trail. The "footprints" left by an intruder who attempts to access a computer system without permission, which can be discovered through systematic auditing of network traffic. Well-constructed audit trails create a summary of the activities connected with a particular user or account, and may prove useful in tracking down intruders.

Authentication. The process by which a computer verifies the identification of a user and permits that person to pass unchallenged into proprietary information and files.

Authorization. The express permission of a database proprietor for the user to enter and make use of files and databases, usually by means of a password or PIN.

Back door. In computer security terms, a secret password known only to the agency or individual who sets up the password security system. Unscrupulous or disgruntled former employees, whose authorized access is canceled upon termination, have been known to use a back door to access the employer's computer for personal gain, sabotage, or revenge.

Bag job. Unauthorized physical entry into the target computer, replacing or adding a chip to the computer or printer, or placing a "bug" in the telephone connector.

Biometrics. The encoding of biological information (e.g., fingerprint, retinal scan, voiceprint, DNA) onto a machine-readable card, virtually eliminating identity theft.

Bulletproofing, System. *See* Hardening, System.

Chipping program. (Also called Time bomb.) A malicious program that can lie silently within a system or program until commanded to act, and then activate itself and create havoc. So called because it is programmed to remain passively in place until certain conditions are met.

Choke Point. (Also called checkpoint.) The interface between a user seeking to access a computer system and the system itself, where the user's identity and legitimacy are queried.

Clipper chip. An integrated circuit that contains government-approved encryption software for privacy.

Computer security. All methods used to prevent fraud and theft in electronic commerce and to assure the validity of financial transactions. It can keep vandals from altering a Web page and prevent unauthorized persons from reading confidential documents and mail.

Cracker. A hacker whose goal is to gain unauthorized access to computers and networks, usually for personal gain or revenge. Some crackers do it for the challenge presented by computer security systems. Others do it to obtain private information, plant bogus information, infect systems with damaging computer viruses, or commit other malicious acts.

Cryptography. *See* Encryption.

Cybercops. Police or other authorities privileged to monitor and eavesdrop on data networks, searching for incriminating evidence of intrusion.

Cyberpunk. *See* Cracker; Hacker.

Cyberspace. The virtually unmappable web of interlinked computers and networks, including public areas such as the Internet and commercial services.

Daemon dialer. A common piece of underground software that scans thousands of phone numbers to determine which connect to a telephone and which to a computer. The software automatically lists the numbers that have computers at the other end, while other software attempts to break into each computer network by cracking passwords. This information, and the software used to obtain it, are frequently shared by various types of cyberpunks who populate the computer underground.

Data. Raw streams of information bits that flow through a conduit or are stored in computers. When converted to human/readable/audible/viewable form, data becomes information.

Data mirror. The process of bouncing an attacker's pathway of attack back to him, revealing both his identity and access point within the system.

Defensive computing. (Also called Safe computing.) Commonsense rules for checking software before installing, along with guarding account numbers, passwords, and PINs, and changing them regularly.

Denial-of-service. Frequently the goal of an intruder, denial-of-service is the temporary or permanent shutting down of the library's computer, thus denying legitimate users the ability to access and make use of information.

Deterrence. The combined effect of security, defensive computing, cryptography, and vigilance that causes targeted attacks to fail because perpetrators perceive that it is easier to get information some other way or to target someone else's computer.

Directed energy weapon. An electronic device that can fire bolts of concentrated energy through walls and shields, completely destroying all data in the system without detection by or harm to living creatures. *See also* HERF gun.

Dumpster diving. Information collection by means of collecting and examining waste paper in wastebaskets, lab bins, and recycling facilities. Especially effective where shredding of waste paper is not standard operating procedure.

Electronic eavesdropping. Gaining access to information by stealth, using electronic equipment to intercept private conversations, listen in, and capture what is said.

Emergency response. A planned sequence of steps that should be understood and easily accessible by all system personnel, whereby once an intrusion is detected or an attack has been carried out, the procedure for restoration of service and repair gets under way immediately.

Encryption. Defensive program that encodes sensitive information, turning captured data streams into arrays of characters meaningless to those who do not have the code.

Ethics. Specific moral choices made by an individual in dealing with others. Ethics refers to the ability of the human mind to distinguish right from wrong, and to choose the right, at least most of the time. Not to be confused with legality, which defines actions punishable by law.

Firewall. Since the best way to prevent the hacker from succeeding in his quest is to keep him out of the system entirely, a firewall is a hardware device or software program designed to reduce to zero the possibility of denial-of-service due to intrusion, by requiring each user to identify and authenticate his or her identity.

Footprint(s). Any telltale trace of intrusion on an electronic network, providing cybercops a starting point for an attempt to apprehend a cybercriminal and put him out of business.

Gateway. The point of interface at which a user encounters a system and seeks entry past the choke point and into the files beyond. Also refers to any connection from one computer network to another, allowing users of one electronic mail network to exchange with other users on a different network.

Hacker. A dedicated computer user who enjoys digging deeply into how the various parts of a computer network operate. Although the term carries a negative connotation—and is often confused with cracker—a hacker may actually be motivated to make improvements to hardware and software systems without resorting to illegal or unethical means.

Hardening, System. Various remedial measures—both physical and electronic—intended to harden and strengthen a computer system against intrusion or attack from outside users or from inside jobs. *See also* Firewall.

HERF gun. High Energy Radio Frequency weapon used by information warriors to target only computers (as opposed to people). A HERF gun shoots a streamed high-energy radio signal into a computer in order to overload all its circuits and put it out of commission. *See also* Directed energy weapon.

Hole, Security. (Also called Achilles' heel.) A weak or vulnerable point in an otherwise secure computer system; an unguarded access point or trapdoor, which, once discovered, permits an intruder to enter, exploit, or manipulate information to his own ends.

Identity theft. Impersonation of another system user in an attempt to gain access to files to which one is not authorized or to avoid paying for service. When identity theft is successful, the computer permits the user past the choke point because it believes him to be an entitled user.

Information warfare. The totality of methods, tactics, and procedures used by an outsider to attack a computer to gain access to private, privileged, classified, or sensitive information, and frequently to use that information as a weapon.

Inside job. The most difficult type of information theft to prevent, an inside job occurs when a trusted employee inside the system, privy to account information, passwords, and protocols, is secretly recruited by, and works for, an intruder.

Internet. The worldwide connection of computers and networks used as a messaging and information-sharing network through shared protocols. Unlike a commercial online service, the Internet does not have any governing organization.

Intruder. *See* Attack.

Legality. Viewing security matters not on whether they are ethical but on whether they are statutorily legal or punishable by law.

Level of security. The degree to which information owners regard a specified piece of information or an individual user, which determines the accessibility of that information. *See also* Trust.

Library Security Officer. A designated employee, empowered by the director or the library board, with chief responsibility for the coordination of all security efforts.

Loophole. *See* Hole, Security.

Malicious software. A software program deliberately intended to create damage, destruction, or undesired alteration to information within the system.

Network analyzer. A monitoring program designed to assist in network repairs, whereby a system keeps track of usage and can detect both authorized use and unauthorized intrusion. A powerful tool for the network administration, it is also a fine weapon for a hacker or cracker. *See also* Sniffer.

Offensive software. *See* Malicious software.

Passive security. Measures in place on a secure system that are passive until an intrusion is detected, when they go into action to trap and trace the intruder.

Password. A sequence of letters, numbers, or punctuation symbols used as a key to allow a user to access a computer or network. A password should be kept secret to prevent anyone else from accessing the computer by impersonating the authorized user.

Patch, Software. First aid at the scene of an intrusion—a temporary electronic stopper for a discovered computer security hole.

PIN. Personal identification number. An additional security password, which ideally is known only to the user and to the system, and thus prevents unauthorized use.

Policy, Security. A document clearly stating the library's posture with regard to the security and preservation of its materials—including information held electronically—and specifying the procedures to be followed to that end.

Privacy. The right to protect oneself against intrusion by the outside world. In the electronic context, it refers to the right of the user to secure transactions on a system network.

Proactive security. Actions taken by the library or computer system to interdict or reduce criminal activity or to apprehend criminals (as opposed to passive security, which consists of preventive measures already in place at the time of an incident).

Property. A term having special meaning in the area of electronic security, due to the unique characteristic of information held electronically: that it can be given away, sold, bartered, transferred, or stolen and yet still retained.

Protocol(s). A set of rules governing the format and transmission of information among computers. A protocol can turn into a standard protocol either by industry agreement or by common usage.

Psyops. Psychological operations. A type of attack on a system's computer security designed to demoralize staff or users and sow suspicion, paranoia, mistrust, and discontent among system users. Chiefly intended to cause users to suffer a crisis of confidence in the system's integrity, safety, and security.

Read-only file. An electronic file that permits free access to information to system documents but no ability to modify, add, delete, or alter those documents.

Restricted access. Placing certain information off limits to an individual user or certain classes of users, either because of the information's sensitive or personal nature or because the user's account access code does not permit access to such files.

Server. A computer-controlled device (usually a computer itself) that acts as a centralized information warehouse or switching center to which other smaller computers (clients) connect.

Sniffer. A communications software program that can detect and penetrate supposedly secure communication wires and, once inside, "sniff" out valuable data (e.g., personal passwords, network protocols, trade secrets, privileged communication). Can also be used defensively to sniff out an unauthorized user, who can then be trapped and traced.

Spoof. The act of fooling a computer's security program into recognizing a user as entitled to gain access to system-level files (i.e., having ability to make changes in information). This can be achieved by various means, but usually entails identity theft of a valid user's account or personal password.

Superuser. Anyone authorized to move around freely in an electronic information system at the system level, so called because no data files, account information, or personal passwords are hidden from view. Usually refers to the network administrator and/or system supervisor, from whose access codes nothing is concealed. If an intruder can persuade system security that he is a superuser, he can do whatever he likes.

Theft, Information. The unauthorized accessing, reproducing, or downloading of proprietary electronic information. Such an act is theft, and theft is a crime punishable by law.

Time bomb. *See* Chipping program.

Trade-off. The inevitable equation that results when a system is hardened against intrusion. In electronic terms, it refers to the sometimes cumbersome procedures users must go through in order to assure themselves that their transactions are secure.

Traffic analyzer. An electronic monitoring program that continually monitors traffic on a network and is capable of revealing who is accessing (or has accessed) what at any given time. *See also* Sniffer.

Trap and trace. A defensive strategy by which unauthorized intruders are detected, isolated from doing any further harm to the system, and, ideally, traced back to their access points so that they can be prevented from getting away with their theft.

Trapdoor. An escape hatch left in a malicious software program that enables the intruder to leave the system quickly if he feels that he is being monitored, trapped, or traced, and to return just as quickly when the danger has passed.

Trash research. *See* Dumpster diving.

Trip wire. A defensive program by which a system network analyzer is alerted immediately whenever unauthorized access to proprietary files is attempted, successful or not.

Trojan horse. Program that permits the unauthorized breaching of the target system's barriers by masquerading as a few lines of innocent code. A Trojan horse is not exactly a virus in that it normally doesn't replicate itself, but when triggered or executed, it activates and silently garbles or erases other data stored in a computer's memory.

Trust. In electronic networks, trust refers to the degree to which a user is granted access to files. The higher the trust factor, the more levels of the library's electronic information to which the user is granted access. The greatest damage to electronic files occurs when a trusted attacker gains access to files that permit modification or deletion. *See also* Level of security.

User interface. The point at which a human and a computer meet. In personal computers, the user interface is the computer's on-screen persona, which determines how the human user controls the computer and responds to its actions.

Virus. A computer program designed to propagate clones of itself. A virus will make copies of itself without restraint, spreading from one computer to another over time until all vulnerable and infected computers are overrun with it.

Vulnerability. The degree to which an electronic system is attackable from the outside due to exploitable security holes.

WORM. A computer program that, through rapid replication, eats up the memory of a computer or system, overloading it until it brings the system to a grinding halt. *See also* Virus.

Bibliography

Ader, Elizabeth R. "Violence in the Workplace: An Issue for Librarians." *Show-Me Librarian* (fall 1995): 12–14.

——, and J. Pinnell. "Security and Safety of People in Urban Academic Libraries." In *Academic Libraries in Urban and Metropolitan Areas: A Management Handbook*. G. B. McCabe, ed. New York: Greenwood Press, 1991, 159–72.

"Agencies Study Workplace Violence." *Library Personnel Newsletter* (May-June 1994): 2–3.

"ALA Conference: Judge Sarokin Speaks." *Newsletter on Intellectual Freedom* (September 1992): 134–36.

Allcorn, Seth. *Anger in the Workplace: Understanding the Causes of Aggression and Violence*. Westport, Conn.: Quorum Books, 1994.

Allen, Susan M. "Guidelines Regarding Thefts in Libraries." *College & Research Libraries News* 55 (November 1994): 641–46.

——. "Preventing Theft in Academic Libraries and Special Collections." *Library & Archival Security* 14:1 (1996): 29–43.

Allred, C. B. "Negligence Law for Libraries." *Law Library Journal* 77 (1984/85): 199–222.

Anderson, A. J. "The Trouble with Larry." *Library Journal* 111 (June 15, 1983): 45–46.

Anderson, Barbara. "Ordeal at San Francisco State College." In *Social Responsibilities and Libraries*. Patricia Glass Schuman, ed. New York: Bowker, 1976, 290–97.

"Arson Strikes CT's Danbury Public Library after Hours." *Library Journal* (April 1, 1996): 14.

"Arsonists Destroy High School Library." *School Library Journal* 35 (July 1989): 11.

Arterburn, Tom R. "Librarians: Caretakers or Crimefighters?" *American Libraries* (August 1996): 32.

Atkins, Derek, and others. *Internet Security: Professional Reference*. Indianapolis: New Riders Press, 1997.

Atwood, Thomas, and Carol Wall. "A Case Study of Periodical Mutilation in a University Serials Collection." *Library & Archival Security* 10:1 (1990): 35–42.

Bahr, Alice Harrison. "Electronic Collection Security Systems Today: Changes and Choices." *Library & Archival Security* 11:1 (1991): 3–11.

———. "Library Security Training: Sources." *Library & Archival Security* 9:1 (1989): 37–43.

———. "Security Technology: Information Sources." *Library & Archival Security* 9:2 (1989): 55–58.

———. "The Thief in Our Midst." *Library & Archival Security* 9:3–4 (1989): 77–81.

"Barred from Library, Patron Sues to Regain Access." *American Libraries* (April 1993): 291.

Bean, P. "An Overview of Crime in Libraries and Information Services." In *Security and Crime Prevention in Libraries*. M. Chaney and A. F. MacDougall, eds. Brookfield, Vt.: Ashgate, 1992, 13–31.

Becker, Karlyn. "Letter-Theft Suspect's Serene Self-Portrait." *Washington Post* (August 21, 1987): A1–A4.

———, and Nancy Lewis. "D.C. Author Arrested Second Time." *Washington Post* (August 19, 1987): C1–C6.

Becklund, Laurie. "Man Writes Novel Chapter in Annals of Library Theft." *Los Angeles Times* (April 28, 1991): A1.

Beisler, Lynn. "Emerson College Library Security Guidelines: November, 1989." *Library & Archival Security* 10 (1990): 43–53.

Berner, Richard C. "Manuscript Collections, Archives, and Special Collections: Their Relationships." *Library & Archival Security* 5:4 (1983): 9–17.

Blommenstein, Z. V. "Coping with Losses the Electronic Way." *Cape Librarian* 39 (October 1995): 12–13.

"Bomber Holds Librarian and Patrons Hostage at Utah PL." *Library Journal* (April 1, 1994): 17.

"Book 'Slicer' Hits Over 20 California Poetry Collections." *American Libraries* (May 1995): 391.

"Book-Mutilation Suspect Surrenders to Authorities." *American Libraries* (February 1996): 10–11.

Boss, Richard W. "Practicing Librarian: The Library Security Myth." *Library Journal* 107 (March 15, 1980): 683.

Brady, Eileen E., and John F. Guido. "When Is a Disaster Not a Disaster?" *Library & Archival Security* 8:3–4 (1988): 11–23.

Brand, Marvine. "Security of Academic Library Buildings." *Library & Archival Security* 3 (1980): 39–47.

———, ed. *Security for Libraries: People, Buildings, Collections.* Chicago: American Library Association, 1984.

Brawner, Lee B. "Insurance and Risk Management for Libraries." *Public Library Quarterly* 13:1 and 13:2 (1983): 5–15, 29–34.

———, and Norman Nelson. "Improving Security and Safety for Libraries." *Public Library Quarterly* 5:1 (spring 1984): 41–58.

Brookes, Paul. *Electronic Surveillance Devices.* London: Butterworths, 1996.

Bruce, Lisa. "Never Mind the Sex; What about the Violence?" *Library Association Record* 92 (January 1990): 55.

Bruske, Ed. "Art Historian Gets Five Years in Fraud." *Washington Post* (March 31, 1989): A17.

Buchanan, Sally. "Disaster: Prevention, Preparedness and Action." *Library Trends* 30:2 (fall 1981): 241–52.

Building Security and Personal Safety. ARL SPEC Kit 150. Washington, D.C.: Association of Research Libraries, 1989.

Burnett, Claudine. "Analysis of Inventory Losses from Long Beach Public Library." *Library & Archival Security* 10:1 (1990): 3–27.

Butterfield, Fox. "State Borrows Trouble with New Library Law." *New York Times* (September 16, 1990): 20.

Buzzard, Marion. "Library Security." *Unabashed Librarian*, no. 44 (1982): 32.

Carparelli, Felicia. "Public Library or Psychiatric Ward? It's Time for Administrators to Deal Firmly with Problem Patrons." *American Libraries* (April 1984): 212–15.

"Cataloging Head Slain in Murder-Suicide at Library." *American Libraries* (October 1996): 14–15.

Chadbourne, Robert D. "Disorderly Conduct." *Wilson Library Bulletin* 68 (March 1994): 23–25.

———. "The Problem Patron: How Much Problem, How Much Patron?" *Wilson Library Bulletin* 64 (June 1990): 59–60.

Chaney, Michael, and Alan F. MacDougall, eds. *Security and Crime Prevention in Libraries.* Brookfield, Vt.: Ashgate, 1992.

"Chapter Relations Coordinates Library Flooding Assistance." *American Libraries* (November 1994): 965.

"Chicago Librarian Stabbed." *Wilson Library Bulletin* 59 (October 1984): 88–89.

Columbo, Claire. "LAMA BES Safety and Security of Library Buildings Preconference." *Library Administration & Management* (summer 1994): 185.

"Computer Theft on the Rise." *Chronicle of Higher Education* (June 20, 1997): 4.

Comstock-Gay, Stuart. "Disruptive Behavior: Protecting People, Protecting Rights." *Wilson Library Bulletin* 69:6 (February 1995): 33–35.

Conable, Gordon. "Access and Indigence: Lessons from Morristown." *Public Libraries* 31 (January/February 1992): 29–32.

"Congressional Hearing Examines LC Security Flaws." *American Libraries* (January 1995): 14.

Constantinou, Constantia. "Destruction of Knowledge: A Study of Journal Mutilation at a Large University Library." *College & Research Libraries* (November 1995): 497–507.

"Controlling Crime: A Security Checklist." *Library & Archival Security* 8:1 (spring/summer 1986): 145–52.

"Conviction in Computer 'Virus' Case May Be U.S. First." *Detroit News* (September 21, 1988): 2.

Cooper, Frederic C., and others. *Implementing Internet Security: Survey Your Own Security Requirements, Risks, and Advantages.* Indianapolis: New Riders Press, 1995.

Corbus, Lawrence J. "Is the Trouble with Larry?" *Library Journal* 111 (June 15, 1986): 46–47.

Cory, Kenneth A., and David W. Hessler. "Imaging the Archives: Now Is the Time." *Library & Archival Security* 12:1 (1993): 7–16.

Cote, William C. "Attacking the Problem—Self-Assessment." *Library & Archival Security* 11:1 (1991): 125–56.

"Courts Sentence Book Thieves While LC Boosts Security." *American Libraries* (May 1992): 352–53.

Cox, Richard J. "Selecting Historical Records for Microfilming: Some Suggested Procedures for Repositories." *Library & Archival Security* 9:2 (1989): 21–42.

Crocker, Jane L. "Security at the Smaller Academic Library." *New Jersey Libraries* (fall 1994): 6–11.

Curran, Charles, and Laura Kelley. "You Never Told Us What to Do When the Roof Leaks." *American Libraries* (September 1996): 62, 64.

"Customer Sentenced for Assaulting MA Librarian." *School Library Journal* 41 (July 1995): 14.

Danford, Robert, and Susan Cirillo. "Violence in the Library: Protecting Staff and Patrons." *Library Administration & Management* (spring 1997): 64–88.

Darling, Pamela W. "Beset by Foes on Every Side." In *Disasters, Prevention and Coping*. Palo Alto: Stanford University Libraries, 1980: 14–21.

Davis, Ann. "The Body as Password." *Wired* (October 1997): 34–38.

Davis, M. C. "Be Prepared! Planning for Disaster." *Show-Me Librarian* (spring 1991): 62–68.

Davis, Mary B., and others. "Preparing for Library Emergencies: A Cooperative Approach." *Wilson Library Bulletin* 66:3 (November 1991): 42–44, 128.

Davis, Patricia. "Libraries in Crisis: Safety and Security in Today's Library." *Texas Library Journal* (summer 1995): 21–30.

DeLong, Suzanne. "Don't Stick Your Neck Out, Librarian." *American Libraries* (November 1995): 694–95.

Delph, Edward W. "Preventing Public Sex in Library Settings." *Library & Archival Security* 3:2 (summer 1980): 17–26.

DeRosa, Frank J. "The Disruptive Patron." *Library & Archival Security* 3 (1980): 29–37.

Dishneau, David. "'Tis Season to Be Wary of Thieves." *Sarasota Herald-Tribune* (December 16, 1993): D1.

"Dogs Sniff for More Bombs after Explosion at Rutgers." *American Libraries* (May 1995): 386.

Dole, Wanda V. "The Effectiveness of Guards in Reducing Library Noise." *Library & Archival Security* 9:3/4 (1989): 23–36.

———. *The Literature of Library Violence, 1959–89*. Mansfield, Ohio: Vance Bibliographies, 1990.

Donnelly, H., and M. Heaney. "Disaster Planning—a Wider Approach." *Aslib Information* 21:2 (February 1993): 69–71.

"Don't Drop the Laptop." *Newsweek* (May 6, 1996): 12.

Dowding, Martin. "Problem Patrons: What Are They Doing in the Library?" *Quill & Quire* (November 1985): 51–53.

Duitman, P. "Perils and Pitfalls in the Library." *PNLA Quarterly* 60:2 (winter 1996): 11–12.

Easton, C. "Sex and Violence in the Library: Scream a Little Louder, Please." *American Libraries* (October 1977): 484–88.

Eder, Peter F. "Privacy on Parade: Your Secrets for Sale." *The Futurist* (July-August 1994): 38–42.

"$8 Million to Preserve and Protect Yale University Lib." *American Libraries* (January 1996): 32.

Eisler, Benita. "Safe Reading." *New York Times* (June 8, 1979): A31.

"Electronic Illness: Computer Viruses Destroy Disks and Data." *Detroit News* (May 26, 1988): A4.

"Electronic Security." *Library & Archival Security* 4:1/2 (1982): 55–61.

Elliott, Joyce. "Disturbed Clients." *Unabashed Librarian,* no. 44 (1982): 16–17.

"Fatal Shelving Collapse Kills Woman." *Library Journal* (October 15, 1983): 1905.

Faulkner-Brown, Harry. "The Role of Architecture and Design in a Security Strategy." In *Security and Crime Prevention in Libraries.* M. Chaney and A. F. MacDougall, eds. Brookfield, Vt.: Ashgate, 1992, 70–87.

"FBI Posts Reward for Library Bomber." *Library Journal* 120 (July 1985): 386.

"FBI Seeks Paroled Book Thief." *American Libraries* 24 (January 1993): 18.

Fennelly, Lawrence J. *Handbook of Loss Prevention and Crime Prevention,* 3rd ed. London: Butterworths, 1995.

———. *Museum, Archive and Library Security,* 3rd ed. London: Butterworths, 1983.

"Fighting Parasites." *The Futurist* (July-August 1988): 54.

"Fire Destroys Pratt Media Center." *American Libraries* (September 1996): 17–18.

"Fire Totals School Library; Internet Comes to Rescue." *American Libraries* (March 1996): 14.

Flagg, Gordon. "Gunman Opens Fire at Cleveland PL." *American Libraries* 25 (February 1994): 135.

———. "New Haven Librarian Charged with Embezzlement." *American Libraries* (July 1987): 542.

"Flood Toll at Colorado State Could Reach $100 Million." *American Libraries* (September 1997): 16.

"Florida Libraries Escape Serious Damage from Opal." *American Libraries* (November 1995): 989.

Ford, B. E., C. F. Cummings, and G. Fitzhugh. "Security at the Newark Public Library." *New Jersey Libraries* 27:4 (fall 1994): 17–18.

"Former Employee Gets Life for Shooting Gus Harrer." *American Libraries* 15 (January 1988): 10.

Forrester, Penny. "The Facts about Larry." *Library Journal* 111 (June 15, 1986): 47.

Fortin, David. *A Guide to Emergency Preparedness Planning: Hazard Assessment and Risk Evaluation; Emergency Preparedness, Response, and Recovery.* Hartford, Conn.: ITT Hartford Insurance Group, 1996.

Fortson-James, Judith. "Fire Protection for Libraries." *Catholic Library World* 53 (December 1981): 211–13.

Fortuin, L. "Keep Your Library Safe: A Practical Approach." *Cape Librarian* 39:6 (June-July, 1995): 12–14.

"$48 Million to Preserve and Protect." *American Libraries* (January 1996): 32.

Fouty, Kathleen G. "Online Patron Records and Privacy: Service vs. Security." *Journal of Academic Librarianship* 19:5 (November 1993): 289–93.

Franklet, Duane. *Bad Memory: A Novel of Suspense.* New York: Pocket Books, 1997.

Freedman, David H., and Charles C. Mann. *@ Large: The Strange Case of the World's Biggest Internet Invasion.* New York: Simon & Schuster, 1997.

Gandert, Slade Richard. "Fictional Theft and the World of Reality." *Library & Archival Security* 4:3 (1982): 47–53.

———. "Greeks Bearing Gifts and Other Sad Tales." *Library & Archival Security* 4:3 (1982): 39–46.

Gaughan, Thomas M. "Prison Librarian Freed Unharmed after Being Held Hostage." *American Libraries* 23 (1992): 431.

"Gay Books Defaced at Central Michigan University." *American Libraries* (January 1996): 32.

George, Susan. *Emergency Planning and Management in College Libraries.* Chicago: Association of College and Research Libraries, 1994.

"Georgia Librarian Murdered While Working Alone." *American Libraries* (November 1993): 902.

Gerhardt, Lillian N. "Safe at Work?" *School Library Journal* 39 (February 1993): 4.

Goldberg, Martin. "The Never Ending Saga of Library Theft." *Library & Archival Security* 12:1 (1993): 87–100.

Goldman, Henry. "Rare Book Thief Is Sentenced." *Philadelphia Inquirer* (November 29, 1990): B1.

Goodman, Danny. *Living at Light Speed: Your Survival Guide to Life on the Information Superhighway.* New York: Random, 1994.

Gore, Albert, Jr. "Information Superhighways: The Next Information Revolution." *The Futurist* (January-February 1991): 21–23.

Griffen, Agnes M. "Potential Roles of the Public Library in the Local Emergency Management Program: A Simulation." *Special Libraries* 78:2 (spring 1987): 122–30.

Griffith, J. W. "After the Disaster: Restoring Library Service." *Wilson Library Bulletin* 58:4 (December 1983): 258–65.

Grossfeld, Stan. "Christmas Week by the Library." *Library & Archival Security* 8:3/4 (1988): 59–62.

"Gunman Kills Staff Member at Cleveland Public." *American Libraries* (February 1985): 78–79.

"Hacker, Virus Shut Down Libraries' Online Services." *American Libraries* (April 1997): 16–17.

Haitch, Richard. "Library Crime." *New York Times* (July 14, 1985): D1.

Hamilton, John Maxwell, "Is There a Klepto in the Stacks?" *New York Times Book Review* (November 18, 1990), reprinted in *Library & Archival Security* 12:1 (1993): 47–54.

Hanson, Carolyn Z. "Electronic Security Has Put a Spotlight on Theft." *Library & Archival Security* 9:3/4 (1989): 63–68.

Harvey, Bruce. "Fire Hazards in Libraries: Property Protection." *Library Security Newsletter* 1:2 (March 1975): 1–3.

"Has Workplace Violence Become Part of Your Job?" *Library Personnel Newsletter* (September-October 1994): 3–4.

Heap, J. "Tackling Workplace Violence." *Public Library Journal* (May/June 1990): 81–82.

Hicks, Larry. "City Expected to Boost Security at Its Buildings." *Sacramento Bee* (October 16, 1993): B1.

"High-Tech Sleuths Buy, Sell Information Online." *New York Times* (September 15, 1997): 1–14.

"Homeless Man Caught after Living in Library Ceiling." *Sarasota Herald Tribune* (November 12, 1992): A7.

Honan, William H. "At the National Archives: Technology's Flip Side." *New York Times* (October 1, 1995): A17.

Houlgate, J., and M. Chaney. "Planning and Management of a Crime Prevention Strategy." In *Security and Crime Prevention in Libraries.* M. Chaney and A. F. MacDougall, eds. Brookfield, Vt.: Ashgate, 1992, 46–69.

"Hours Cut after Alleged Theft." *American Libraries* (February 1996): 15.

Hubbard, William J., and Kathleen W. Langston. "Rx for Library Materials: The Holistic Approach." *Library & Archival Security* 6:4 (1984): 17–27.

Huntsberry, J. Steven. "Forged Identification: A Key to Library Archives." *Library & Archival Security* 9:3/4 (1989): 69–74.

———. "Library Security: The Blumberg Legacy." *Journal of Information Ethics* (fall 1992): 46–50.

———. "Student Library Security Patrol: A Viable Alternative." *Conservation Administration News* 49 (1992): 24–27.

"Hurricane Marilyn Devastates Univ. of Virgin Islands Library." *American Libraries* (November 1995): 988.

"Hurricane-hit Libraries Clean Up, Assess Damage." *American Libraries* (October 1992): 726–31.

"I Know That Face." *Newsweek* (February 19, 1996): 12.

Ingram, Carl. "Gunman Slain after Killing Two at Library Opening." *Los Angeles Times* (April 19, 1993): A9.

"Is Broward Co. Library Sick?" *American Libraries* (September 1996): 18.

Jackanicz, Donald W. "Theft in the National Archives: The Murphy Case, 1962–1975." *Library & Archival Security* 10:2 (1990): 23–50.

Jackson, Marie. "Library Security: Facts and Figures." *Library Association Record* 93 (June 1, 1991): 384.

"Jazz Mementos Ruined; Owner Blames Library." *American Libraries* (June 1995): 496.

"'Jock the Ripper' Is Apprehended in South Dakota." *Library Journal* (September 1, 1972): 1456.

Kahn, Miriam. *Disaster Prevention and Response for Special Libraries: An Information Kit.* Washington, D.C.: Special Libraries Association, 1995.

———. *Disaster Response and Planning for Libraries.* Chicago: American Library Association, 1997.

———. "Mastering Disaster: Emergency Planning for Libraries." *Library Journal* (December 1993): 73–75.

Kamm, Sue. "A Rose Is Not Necessarily a Rose: Issues in Public Library Security." *Library & Archival Security* 13:1 (1995): 41–47.

Karl, Gretchen. "LAPNet 2: Earthquake Preparedness Workshop." *Conservation Administration News* (July 1990): 12–14.

Kartman, J. "Guard Charged in Co-Worker's Shooting at Atlanta-Fulton PL." *American Libraries* 24 (January 1993): 14–15.

———. "Secretary Accused in $400K Library Embezzlement." *American Libraries* 23 (March 1992): 206–7.

Kehoe, Edward P. *The Security Officer's Handbook: Standard Operating Procedure.* London: Butterworths, 1994.

Kerns, Daniel M., Jr. "Out of the Ashes." *Momentum* 26:4 (October-November 1995): 56–58.

Kinney, John W. "Archival Security and Insecurity." *American Archivist* 38 (October 1975): 493–97.

Kinney, Joseph A., and Dennis L. Johnson. *Breaking Point: The Workplace Violence Epidemic and What to Do about It.* Chicago: National Safe Workplace Institute, 1993.

Kirkpatrick, John T. "Explaining Crime and Disorder in Libraries." *Library Trends* 33 (summer 1984): 13–28.

"KKK Vandal Sentenced." *American Libraries* (March 1996): 17.

"Knife-Wielding Youth Slays Public Library Staff Member." *American Libraries* (April 1983): 174.

Kristl, Carol. "Study Links Breast Cancer with Professional Occupations." *American Libraries* 24 (1993): 906.

Lane, Carol A. *Naked in Cyberspace: How to Find Personal Information Online.* Somerville, Mass.: Pemberton Press, 1997.

LaRue, James. "Hacked!" *American Libraries* (August 1996): 35.

Lattin, Don. "Layoffs Called One of the Biggest Causes of Violent Behavior." *San Francisco Chronicle* (August 16, 1994): A3.

"LC Security Flaws Prompt Federal Probes." *American Libraries* (October 1995): 868–69.

Leighton, Philip D. "Reducing Preservation Hazards within Library Facilities." In *Disasters, Prevention and Coping.* Palo Alto: Stanford University Libraries, 1980, 161–74.

Lewis, Janice S. "Workplace Violence." *RQ* (spring 1995): 287–95.

"Librarian Battles over E-mail Privacy." *American Libraries* (March 1996): 16.

"Librarian Doesn't Regret His Actions in Student Brawl." *American Libraries* (March 1995): 289–90.

"Librarian Grapples with Killer as Seven Are Slain in Library." *American Libraries* (July 1976): 428.

"Librarian Stabbed at Desk." *American Libraries* (April 1975): 213–14.

"Libraries Jolted by L.A. Earthquake." *American Libraries* (March 1994): 214–16.

"Libraries Questioned in Search for Unabomber." *American Libraries* (January 1996): 28.

"Library Card Required for Admission to Library." *Library Journal* (June 1, 1985): 22.

"Library Clerk Slain in Hahnville, Louisiana." *American Libraries* (December 1978): 642.

"Library Clerk Slain in West Virginia Library." *Library Journal* (May 15, 1997): 11.

"Library Crime." *New York Times* (July 14, 1985): A33.

"Library Embezzler Sentenced to Prison." *American Libraries* (July/August 1992): 550.

"Library Files Checked in Zodiac Investigation." *New York Times* (July 18, 1990): B4.

"Library Seeks Clientele Upgrade." *West Palm Beach Sun-Sentinel* (February 22, 1996): 1:1.

"Library Thieves Take All but the Covers." *New York Times* (April 7, 1992): A8.

Lilly, Roy S., Barbara F. Schloman, and Wendy Hu. "Ripoffs Revisited: Periodical Mutilation in a University Research Library." *Library & Archival Security* 11:1 (1991): 43–70.

Lincoln, Alan Jay. "Background Checks." *Library & Archival Security* 9:3–4 (1991): 107.

———. "Community Crime Protection." *Library & Archival Security* 9:1 (1989): 49–58.

———. "Computer Security." *Library & Archival Security* 11:1 (1991): 157–71.

———. *Crime in the Library: A Study of Patterns, Impact, and Security.* New York: Bowker, 1984.

———. "Key Control." *Library & Archival Security* 9:2 (1989): 59–65.

———. "Library Legislation Related to Crime and Security." *Library & Archival Security* 10:2 (1990): 77–102; 11:1 (1991): 71–102.

———. "Patterns and Costs of Crime." *Library Trends* (summer 1984): 69–76.

———. "Vandalism: Causes, Consequences and Prevention." *Library & Archival Security* 9:3/4 (1989): 37–61.

———. "Visibility Enhancement." *Library & Archival Security* 8:3/4 (1988): 68–70.

Lipinski, B. V. "A Practical Approach to Library Security." *New Jersey Librarian* (fall 1994): 19–20.

"Local Press Defends Ann Arbor PL Behavior Rules Banning Problem Patrons." *American Libraries* 16 (January 1985): 7.

Lowry, Maynard, and Philip M. O'Brien. "Rubble with a Cause: Earthquake Preparedness in California." *College & Research Library News* (March 1990): 192–97.

Ludlow, Peter. *High Noon on the Electronic Frontier: Conceptual Issues in Cyberspace.* Cambridge, Mass.: MIT Press, 1996.

Lund, R. "Library Security." *Cape Librarian* 37:6 (June-July 1993): 4–6.

Lynskey, Thomas A. "Safety Hazards in Libraries: Causes and Prevention." *Library & Archival Security* 2:2 (1978): 1, 7–8.

"Man Arrested after Shooting into Library." *American Libraries* 25 (October 1994): 815.

"Man Jailed for Failing to Pay Library Fines." *New York Times* (March 31, 1989): A11.

Mantell, Michael, and Steve Albrecht. *Ticking Bombs: Defusing Violence in the Workplace.* Burr Ridge, Ill.: Irwin, 1994.

Markoff, John. "FBI Defends Wiretap Proposal, Says Public Will Accept Trade-off." *New York Times* (February 28, 1994): 1:1.

Mason, Philip. "Archival Security: New Solutions to an Old Problem." *American Archivist* 38 (October 1975): 477–92.

"Massacre at California State: Seven Staffers Killed." *Library Journal* (September 15, 1976).

"Massive Mutilation at Case." *Library Journal* (September 15, 1982): 1678.

Mast, Sharon. "Ripping Off and Ripping Out: Book Theft and Mutilation from Academic Libraries." *Library & Archival Security* 5:4 (1983): 31–51.

Matthews, Fred W. "Dalhousie Fire." *Canadian Library Journal* (August 1986): 221–26.

McCann, Janice, and Betsy Shand. *Surviving Natural Disasters: How to Prepare for Earthquakes, Hurricanes, Tornadoes, Floods, Wildfires, Thunderstorms, Blizzards, Tsunamis, Volcanic Eruptions, and Other Calamities.* Atlanta, Ga.: Gallery Pubs., 1995.

McCarthy, J., and E. Perica. "Burglary: A Rising Problem in Library Security." *Unabashed Librarian,* no. 37 (1980): 19–20.

McKimmie, Tim, and Jeanette Smith. "The ELF in Your Library." *Computers in Libraries* 14:8 (1994): 16–20.

McNeil, Beth, and Denise Johnson, eds. *Patron Behavior in Libraries.* Chicago: American Library Association, 1995.

McWilliams, Peter. "Viruses Can Be Downloaded, Shared." *Sarasota Herald-Tribune* (January 18, 1996): D1.

Mika, Joseph J., and Bruce A. Shuman. "Legal Issues Affecting Libraries and Librarians." *American Libraries* 19 (April 1988): 314–16.

Miller, Bruce. "Contingency Planning Resources." *Information Technology & Libraries* (June 1990): 179–80.

——. "Libraries and Computers: Disaster Prevention and Recovery." *Information Technology & Libraries* (December 1988): 349–58.

Minor, Marianne. *Preventing Workplace Violence: Positive Management Strategies*. Menlo Park, Calif.: Crisp Publications, 1995.

"Missing $50,000 Traced to Former Library Director." *Library Journal* (September 15, 1985): 611.

Moffett, William. "Guidelines Regarding Thefts in Libraries." *College & Research Libraries News* (March 1988): 159–62.

Morris, John. "Is Your Library Safe from Fire?" *Library & Archival Security* 3 (1980): 139–45.

——. *The Library Disaster Preparedness Handbook*. Chicago: American Library Association, 1986.

——. "The Los Angeles Library Fire—Learning the Hard Way." *Canadian Library Journal* 44:4 (August 1987): 217–21.

——. "Protecting the Library from Fire." *Library Trends* 33 (1984): 35–39.

Morrison, Perry R. "Computer Parasites: Software Diseases May Cripple Our Computers." *The Futurist* (March-April 1986): 36–38.

Morrissett, Linda A. "Developing and Implementing a Behavior Policy for an Academic Library." *College and Undergraduate Libraries* 1:2 (1994): 71–91.

"Morristown Ruling Reversed." *Newsletter on Intellectual Freedom* 41 (May 1992): 73ff.

"Most Libraries Spared in Oregon Floods." *American Libraries* (March 1996): 11.

Munn, Ralph. "The Problems of Theft and Mutilation." *Library Journal* (August 1935): 589.

"Mutilated Books Prompt LC Security Crackdown." *American Libraries* (September 1995): 749.

"My Info Is NOT Your Info: Publishers and Government Call for Protection against Online Data Snatchers." *Newsweek* (July 18, 1994): 54.

"Nation's Librarians Attempt to Shush Snoopers." *Sarasota Herald-Tribune* (December 8, 1988): A6.

Nelson, James B. "Safety in the Public Library." *Show-Me Libraries* 44:2 (winter/spring 1993): 368.

"A New Leaf: Man Jailed for Overdue Library Books." *New York Times* (February 6, 1979): C6.

"A New Strain of Electronic Vandalism." *Newsweek* (December 25, 1989): 82.

Nicewarner, Metta, and Shelley Heaton. "Providing Security in an Urban Academic Library." *Library & Archival Security* 13:1 (1995): 9–20.

"No Hard Feelings from Patron Jailed over Overdue." *American Libraries* (November 1995): 990.

"Norfolk, Va. Library Stunned by Stabbing Murder." *Library Journal* 108 (April 15, 1983): 785.

O'Connell, Mildred. "Disaster Planning: Writing and Implementing Plans for Collections-Holding Institutions." *Technology and Conservation* 8 (summer 1983): 18–24.

"Officer Wounded; Shootout Leaves Elderly Man Dead." *Chicago Sun-Times* (June 26, 1996): Metro 20.

"Oklahoma City Bomb Explosion Closes Downtown Library." *American Libraries* (June 1995): 490–92.

O'Neil, James W. "Strengthen Your Security Posture." *Library & Archival Security* 1:2 (1975): 1–3.

"Outstanding Librarian Sentenced in Library Theft." *American Libraries* 16 (April 1985): 206–7.

Owens, Sheryl. "Proactive Problem Patron Preparedness." *Library & Archival Security* 12:2 (1994): 11–24.

Pacey, Anthony. "Halon Gas and Library Fire Protection." *Canadian Library Journal* 48:1 (February 1991): 33–36.

"Patron Kills Two Reference Librarians in Sacramento PL." *Library Journal* (May 15, 1993): 14–15.

Pease, B. G. "Workplace Violence in Libraries." *Library Management* 16:7 (1995): 30–39.

Pederson, Terri L. "Theft and Mutilation of Library Materials." *College & Research Libraries* 51:2 (March 1991): 120–28.

Person, R. C., and N. A. Ferry. "Cutting Down on Crime in the Library." *College & Research Libraries News* 55 (1994): 428–29.

Pia, J. Joseph. "Information Security." *Bulletin of the American Society for Information Science* (April-May 1987): 16–18.

Pinzelik, Barbara P. "Monitoring Book Losses in an Academic Library." *Library & Archival Security* 6:4 (1984): 1–12.

"PL Book Drop Fire Prank Destroys Carnegie Building." *Library Hotline* (July 29, 1996): 1.

Platz, Valerie A., and Charles E. Kratz. *The Personnel Manual: An Outline for Libraries*. Chicago: American Library Association, 1993.

Plotnik, Arthur. "Better On-the-Job Embezzlement." *American Libraries* (October 1987): 808.

"Priceless Manuscripts Are Stolen from Columbia University." *New York Times* (October 9, 1994): A5.

"The Problem Patron: Sioux City Briefings." *Library Journal* (December 1, 1980): 2536.

"Proceedings of the ALA Conference Program on Collection Security and Life Safety." *Library & Archival Security* 4:3 (1981): 9–21.

"Public Libraries Are Cracking Down on People Who Borrow Items and Fail to Return Them." *Bottom Line Personal* (July 15, 1995): 2.

"Rape of Teenager Raises Security Issues." *American Libraries* (September 1996): 15–16.

Reed, Christopher. "Biblioklepts." *Harvard Magazine* (March-April 1997): 38–55.

"Restoration Continues Three Years after Uffizi Bombing." *American Libraries* (March 1996): 19.

Riley, Gordon. "Managing Microcomputer Security: Policy and Practice Considerations for CD-ROM and Public Access Workstations." *Library & Archival Security* 11:2 (1992): 1–22.

Roberts, Matt. "Guards, Turnstiles, Electronic Devices, and the Illusion of Security." *College & Research Libraries* 29 (July 1968): 259–75.

Robinson, C. L., J. D. Marshall Jr., and P. J. Cravey. "Legal and Practical Aspects of Securing the General Collection in Academic Libraries." In *Academic Libraries in Urban and Metropolitan Areas: A Management Handbook*. G. B. McCabe, ed. New York: Greenwood Press, 1991, 159–72.

Rockman, Ilene F. "Coping with Library Incidents." *College & Research Libraries News* 56:7 (July-August 1995): 456–57.

Roth, Harold. "A Case Study in Library-Police Relations." *Library & Archival Security* 1:2 (1975): 2–5.

Ruane, Michael. "Book Theft Suspect Ruled Insane in '77." *Philadelphia Inquirer* (January 20, 1990): B1.

———. "Suspect in Theft at Penn Is Arrested." *Philadelphia Inquirer* (January 18, 1990): B8.

Rubin, Rhea. "Anger in the Library." *The Reference Librarian*, no. 31 (1990): 39–50.

Rude, Reneé, and Robert Hauptman. "Theft, Dissimulation, and Trespass: Some Observations on Security." *Library & Archival Security* 12:1 (1993): 17–22.

Rundell, Walter. "Relations between Historical Researchers and Custodians of Source Materials." *College & Research Libraries News* 29 (July 1968): 466–76.

"Rural Library Damaged during Arson Spree." *American Libraries* (November 1995): 992.

Rutherford, Christine. "Disaster: Planning, Preparation, Prevention." *Public Libraries* 29:5 (September-October 1990): 271–76.

Sable, Martin H. "Problem Patrons in Public and University Libraries." *Encyclopedia of Library and Information Science* 43, Supplement 8 (1985): 180–91.

———. "Protection of the Librarian." *International Library Review* 16 (April 1984): 103–23.

Sager, Donald. "Vandalism in Libraries: How Senseless Is It?" *Library Security Newsletter* 1:1 (January 1975): 5.

St. Lifer, Evan. "How Safe Are Our Libraries?" *Library Journal* (August 1994): 35–39.

Salter, Charles, and Jeffrey L. Salter. *On the Frontlines: Coping with the Library's Problem Patrons*. Englewood, Colo.: Libraries Unlimited, 1988.

Samet, Norman T. "Why Does That Man Stare at Me?" *Library Journal* 94 (January 15, 1969): 156–57.

"San Diego Branch Library Torched by Arsonists." *Library Journal* (December 1, 1980): 2536.

Saulmon, Sharon A. "Book Security Systems' Use and Cost in Southwest Public Libraries." *Library & Archival Security* 8:3/4 (1988): 25–36.

"Scandal at University of Georgia over Theft of Rare Items." *Library Journal* (April 1, 1987): 15.

Schindler, Pat. "The Use of Security Guards in Libraries." *Library & Archival Security* 2:2 (1978): 1–6.

Schwartau, Winn. *Information Warfare: Cyberterrorism: Protecting Your Personal Security in the Electronic Age,* 2nd ed. New York: Thunder's Mouth Press, 1996.

Scilken, Marvin. "Child Safety in the Library." *Unabashed Librarian,* no. 59 (1986): 11–12.

Scott, Betty Ann. "Waging the War against Crimes in Florida's Public Libraries." *Library & Archival Security* 3:2 (1980): 27–30.

Scott, Janny. "Public Library No Longer a Refuge for Readers." *Los Angeles Times* (August 10, 1993): C1.

Scott, Marianne. "Mass Deacidification at the National Library of Canada." *Library & Archival Security* 8:3/4 (1987): 49–61.

"Screening: Lawsuits against Companies Whose Employees Commit Crimes against Co-Workers or Customers Have Fueled Demand for Employment Screening Services." *New York Times* (March 21, 1994): A10–11.

Seeman, Scott, and Ann Miller. "State Statutes." *Library & Archival Security* 13:2 (1996): 66–89.

Seith, Jeff. "The Objects of His Devotion." *College & Research Libraries News* (December 1991): 712–15.

"'Seven' and Patron Confidentiality: Serial Killer Has Been Checking Out Such Classics as *The Canterbury Tales, The Divine Comedy,* and *The City of God.* FBI Connection with Library Regarding Who Borrows What?" *American Libraries* (January 1996): 46.

"Sex Offenses." In *The Guide to the Law: Everyone's Legal Encyclopedia,* vol. 9. St. Paul, Minn.: West, 1995, 227–28.

Shuman, Bruce A. "Down and Out in the Reading Room: The Homeless in the Public Library." In *Patron Behavior in Libraries.* Beth McNeil and Denise Johnson, eds. Chicago: American Library Association, 1995.

———. "Problem Patrons in Libraries—A Review Article." *Library & Archival Security* 9:2 (1989): 3–11.

———. *River Bend Revisited: The Problem Patron in the Library.* Phoenix: Oryx Press, 1984.

———, and J. J. Mika. "Copyright Issues: The Law and Library Interests." *Library & Archival Security* 10:2 (1990): 103–15.

Smith, Frederick E. "Analytical Approaches Used in a Library Security Study." *Library & Archival Security* 5:4 (1983): 53–68.

———. "Door Checkers: An Unacceptable Security Alternative." *Library & Archival Security* 7:1 (1985): 7–13.

———. "Questionable Strategies in Library Security Studies." *Library & Archival Security* 6:4 (1984): 43–54.

Smith, Nancy M. "Staff Harassment by Patrons." *American Libraries* 25 (1994): 316.

"Standards for Central University Library Security Guards." La Jolla: University of California, San Diego, Central University Library, 1995. Unpublished manual.

Steinmetz, William H. "How a Campus Handles an Earthquake Disaster." In *Proceedings, 26th National Conference on Campus Safety.* Chicago: National Safety Council, 1979.

Sterling, Bruce. *The Hacker Crackdown: Law and Disorder on the Electronic Frontier.* New York: Bantam Books, 1992.

Stoll, Clifford. *The Cuckoo's Egg: Tracking a Spy through the Maze of Computer Espionage.* New York: Doubleday, 1989.

———. "Stalking the Wily Hacker." In *Computerization and Controversy: Value Conflicts and Social Choices.* Charles Dunlop and Rob Kling, eds. Boston: Academic Press, 1991, 533–53.

Streitfeld, David. "The Library of Congress Rip-off; Increased Security Measures Taken to Stem Massive Thefts." *Washington Post* (March 29, 1992): A9.

Strong, Gary E. "Rats? Oh No, Not Rats!" *Special Libraries* 78:2 (spring 1987): 105–11.

———. "Rats, Rain, Fire: Emergency Library Planning in California." *PNLA Quarterly* 52 (winter 1988): 14–16.

"Study Validates Integrity Testing." *Personnel Journal* 70 (May 1991): 17.

Sutcliffe, Charles. "A Model of the Financial Appraisal of Electronic Book Security Systems with an Application to Berkshire County Libraries." *Library & Archival Security* 6:4 (1984): 27–42.

Sweeney, Louise. "Vandals Pilfer Library of Congress Books, Art." *Christian Science Monitor* (May 4, 1992): A6.

Swisher, Kara. "Working under the Gun: Office Violence Is on the Rise, and Most Firms Aren't Ready to Deal with It." *Washington Post* (May 8, 1994): H1.

"Teens Threaten to Blow Away Librarian." *American Libraries* 24 (September 1993): 696.

"37-Year Employee Admits $70,000 Materials Theft." *American Libraries* 25 (November 1994): 905.

Thompson, Enid Thornton. "The Permanent Collection: Protecting the Esthetic and Intellectual Value of Resources." *Library & Archival Security* 3:2 (1980): 31–39.

Thompson, Lawrence S. "Biblioclasm in Norway." *Library & Archival Security* 6:4 (1984): 13–16.

———. "Library Pests." *Library & Archival Security* 7:1 (1985): 15–24.

———. "Mutalitis Mutilandis." *Library & Archival Security* 2:2 (1978): 15–16.

"Timely Rescue Saves Priceless Naval Collection." *American Libraries* (March 1996): 11.

Tomaiuolo, Nicholas. "Deterring Book Theft: Our Common Responsibility." *Wilson Library Bulletin* (January 1987): 58–60.

Tomer, Christinger. "Selecting Library Materials for Preservation." *Library & Archival Security* 7:1 (1985): 1–6.

"Torrential Rains Flood Libraries in Illinois, Pennsylvania." *American Libraries* (September 1996): 12.

Traister, Daniel. "Seduction and Betrayal: An Insider's View of Insider Theft of Rare Materials." *Wilson Library Bulletin* 69 (September 1994): 30–34.

Treadwell, Jane. "Determining a Fair Price for Lost Books: A Case Study." *Library & Archival Security* 9:1 (1989): 19–26.

Trinkaus-Randall, Gregor. "Preserving Special Collections through Internal Security." *College & Research Libraries* 50:4 (July 1989): 448–54.

"The Troublesome Patron: Approaches Eyed in NY." *Library Journal* (December 1, 1978): 33–34.

Tryon, Jonathan S. "Premises Liability for Librarians." *Library & Archival Security* 10:2 (1990): 3–21.

Turner, Anne M. *It Comes with the Territory: Handling Problem Situations in Libraries.* Jefferson, N.C.: McFarland, 1993.

"Two Teens Face Bomb-making Charge." *Sarasota Herald-Tribune* (February 28, 1996): B1.

Ungarelli, Donald L. "Are Our Libraries Safe from Losses?" *Library & Archival Security* 9:1 (1988): 45–47.

———. "Attacking the Problem: Self-Assessment." *Library & Archival Security* 11:1 (1991): 125.

———. "Insurance and Prevention: Why and How?" *Library Trends* 33:1 (summer 1984): 57–67.

"University of Florida Library Director Shot by Former Employee." *American Libraries* (June 1983): 334.

"Vandals Wreck Baltimore Branch." *American Libraries* (September 1997): 26.

Varlejs, Jana, ed. *Safeguarding Electronic Information: Proceedings of the Thirty-second Symposium of the Graduate Alumni and Faculty of the Rutgers School of Communication, Information and Library Studies, 21 April 1995.* Jefferson, N.C.: McFarland, 1995.

Varner, Carroll. "Journal Mutilation in Academic Libraries." *Library & Archival Security* 5:4 (1983): 19–29.

"Vigilant Eyes, Bugs and Firewalls, the Costs of Library Security." *The Bottom Line* 8:4 (1995): 35–46.

Vitale, Cammie. "The Blumberg Case and Its Implications for Library Security at the Central University Libraries, Southern Methodist University." *Library & Archival Security* 12:1 (1993): 79–85.

Waters, Peter. "Disasters Revisited." In *Disasters, Prevention and Coping.* Palo Alto: Stanford University Libraries, 1980, 61–69.

Watkins, Christine. "Chapter Report: Disaster Planning Makes (Dollars and) Sense." *American Libraries* (September 1996): 9.

Waugh, W. L., Jr., and R. J. Hy. *Handbook of Emergency Management.* New York: Greenwood Press, 1990, 61.

Webb, Ellen L. "Management by Inaction." *Library Journal* 111 (June 15, 1986): 48.

Weight, Glenn S. "America's First Librarian Kept Patrons Awake." *Wilson Library Bulletin* 32 (May 1958): 649.

Weiss, Dana. "Book Theft and Book Mutilation in a Large Urban University Library." *College & Research Libraries* 42 (1981): 341–47.

Welch, Timothy. "Improvement of Library Security." *College & Research Libraries* 38 (March 1987): 100–103.

Welsh, William J. "The Perils of Paper: Attempts for Survival." *Library & Archival Security* 5:4 (1983): 1–8.

Whiting, Brent. "Buckeye Man Found Guilty in '92 Slaying of Librarian." *Arizona Republic* (April 16, 1994): B6.

Wilkinson, M. A. "Larceny in the Library." *Public Library Quarterly* 12:4 (1992): 43–55.

Wiltz, Teresa. "Libraries Are No Longer Just for Readers." *Chicago Tribune* (October 14, 1993): Chicagoland section, 1.

Winters, Sharon. "A Proactive Approach to Building Security." *Public Libraries* 33:5 (September-October 1994): 151–56.

Yarnall, Louise. "Computer Theft at UCLA." *Los Angeles Times* (November 5, 1997): B8.

Zeidberg, David S. *Collection Security in ARL Libraries.* ARL SPEC Kit 100. Washington, D.C.: Association of Research Libraries, 1984.

———. "The Crime of Stealing Historical Documents." *Sacramento Bee* (April 20, 1988): B7.

———. "Library Theft Isn't Petty; Make This Crime a Felony, with Prison the Penalty." *Los Angeles Times* (April 16, 1988): D1.

Index

S